THE SIXTH GUN

BOOK 3: BOUND

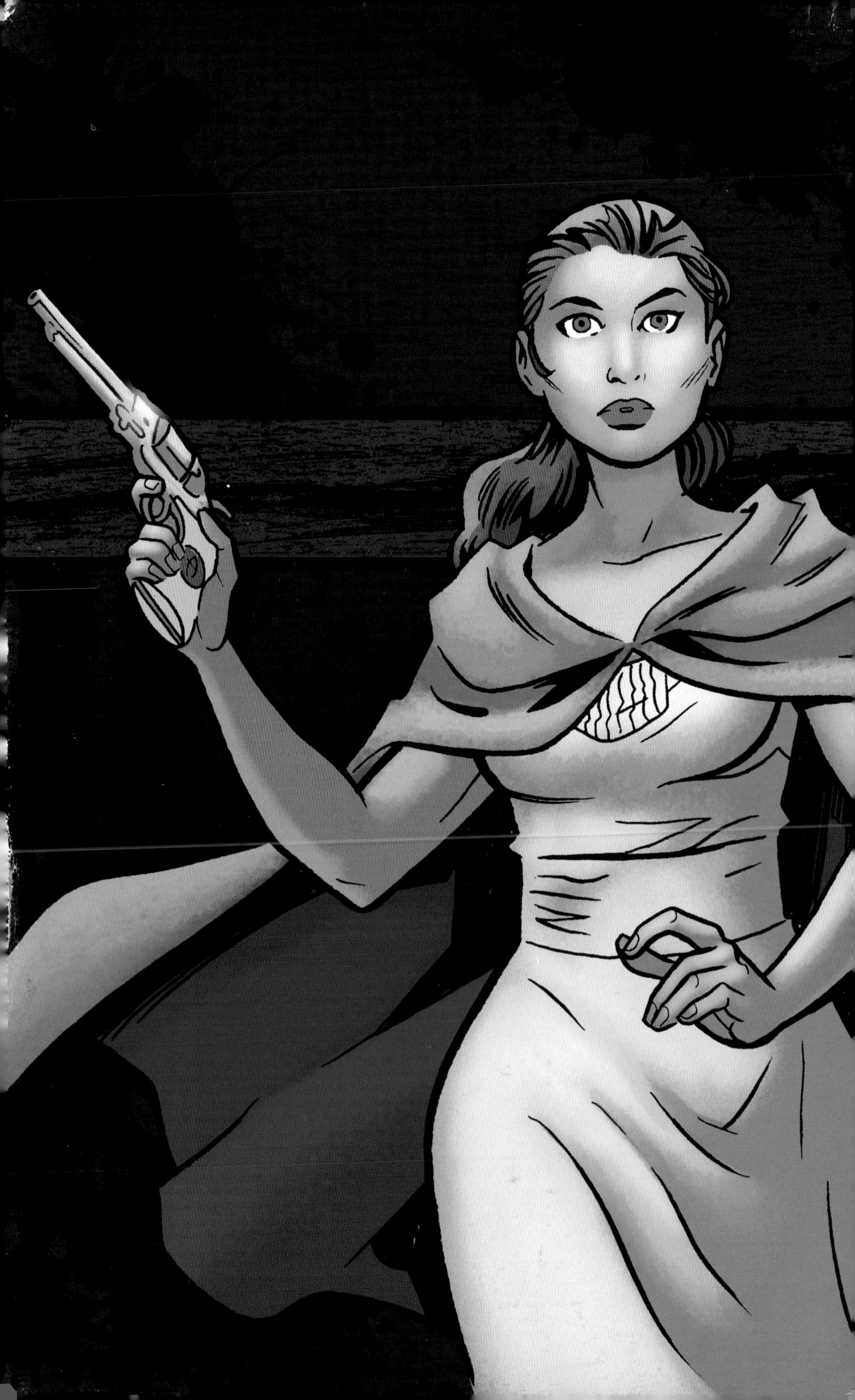

THE SIXTH GUN

BOOK 3: BOUND

WRITTEN BY
CULLEN BUNN

ILLUSTRATED BY
BRIAN HURTT

CHAPTER 3 ILLUSTRATED BY
TYLER CROOK

COLORS BY
BILL CRABTREE

LETTERED BY
DOUGLAS E. SHERWOOD

EDITED BY
CHARLIE CHU

DESIGN BY
KEITH WOOD

ONI PRESS

AN ONI PRESS PUBLICATION

THE SIXTH GUN™

BY CULLEN BUNN & BRIAN HURTT

PUBLISHED BY ONI PRESS, INC.

JOE NOZEMACK *publisher*

JAMES LUCAS JONES *editor in chief*

CORY CASONI *marketing director*

KEITH WOOD *art director*

GEORGE ROHAC *operations director*

JILL BEATON *editor*

CHARLIE CHU *editor*

TROY LOOK *digital prepress lead*

This volume collects issues #12–17 of the Oni Press series
The Sixth Gun.

ONI PRESS, INC.
1305 SE MARTIN LUTHER KING JR. BLVD.
SUITE A
PORTLAND, OR 97214
USA

onipress.com
cullenbunn.com
thehurttlocker.blogspot.com
onegok.com

First edition: March 2012
ISBN: 978-1-934964-78-1
eISBN: 978-1-62010-021-9

Library of Congress Control Number: 2011933169

10 9 8 7 6 5 4 3 2

Printed in China

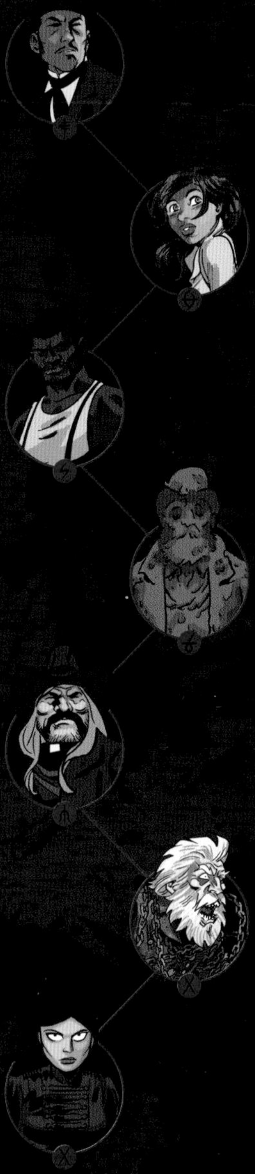

Drake Sinclair - A treasure hunter with a bleak past. He now holds four of the Six.

Becky Montcrief - A brave young woman who holds the Sixth Gun, a weapon that can divine the future.

Gord Cantrell - Drake and Becky's ally. He knows some small measure of the dark arts, and his past is bound to the history of the Six in a terrible way.

Billjohn O'Henry - Drake's friend. Killed at the battle of the Maw and raised as a golem-like creature by the power of the guns.

Brother Roberto - A monk in the service of the Sword of Abraham, a religious order dedicated to preventing Armageddon.

General Oliander Bedford Hume - A murderer and a fiend, killed at the battle of the Maw. But he's been killed before.

Missy Hume - The General's widow, whose powers of regeneration stem from one of the Six. She will stop at nothing to retrieve her husband's body and the remaining guns.

CHAPTER ONE

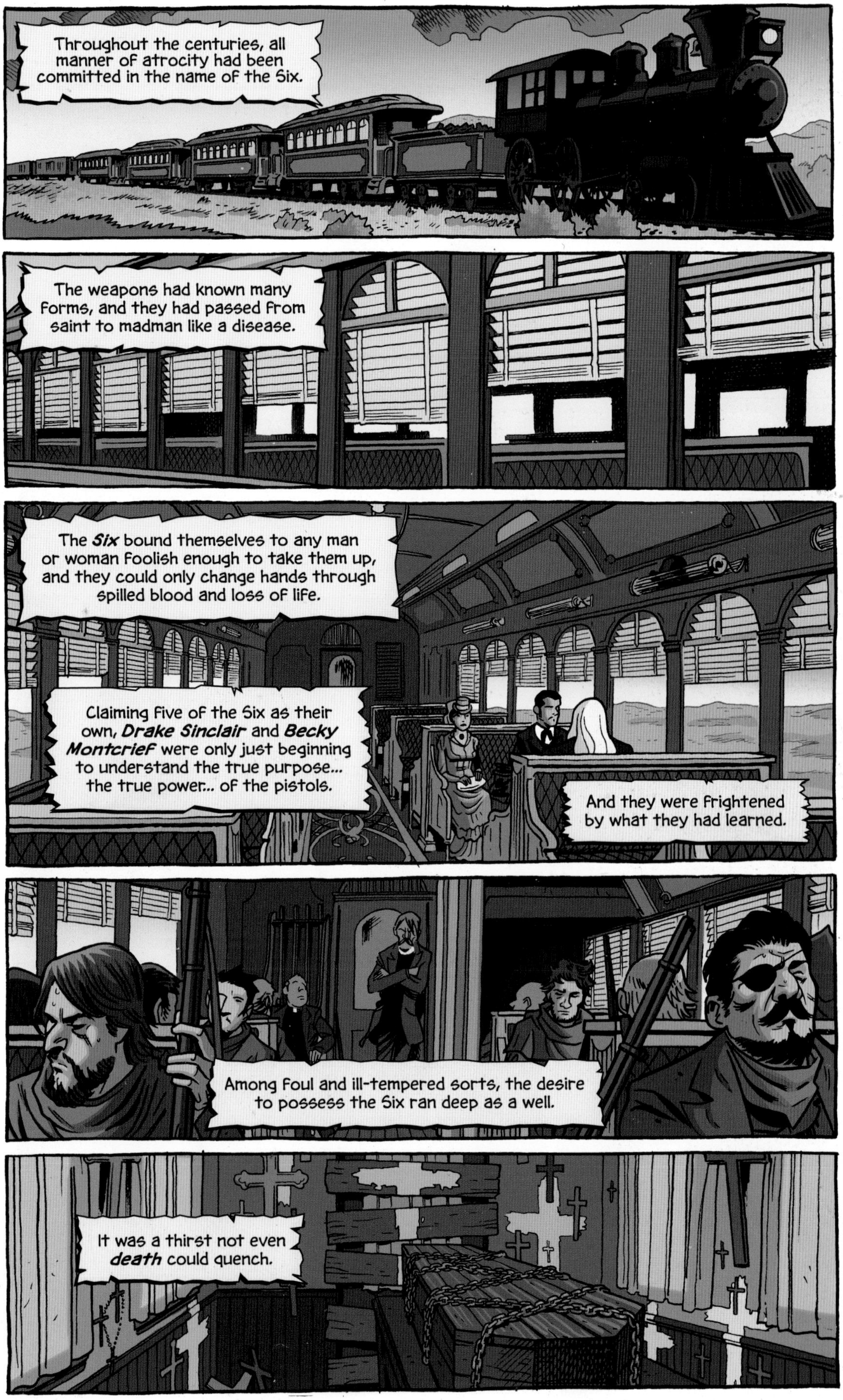
Throughout the centuries, all manner of atrocity had been committed in the name of the Six.
The weapons had known many forms, and they had passed from saint to madman like a disease.
The *Six* bound themselves to any man or woman foolish enough to take them up, and they could only change hands through spilled blood and loss of life.
Claiming five of the Six as their own, ***Drake Sinclair*** and ***Becky Montcrief*** were only just beginning to understand the true purpose... the true power... of the pistols.
And they were frightened by what they had learned.
Among foul and ill-tempered sorts, the desire to possess the Six ran deep as a well.
It was a thirst not even *death* could quench.

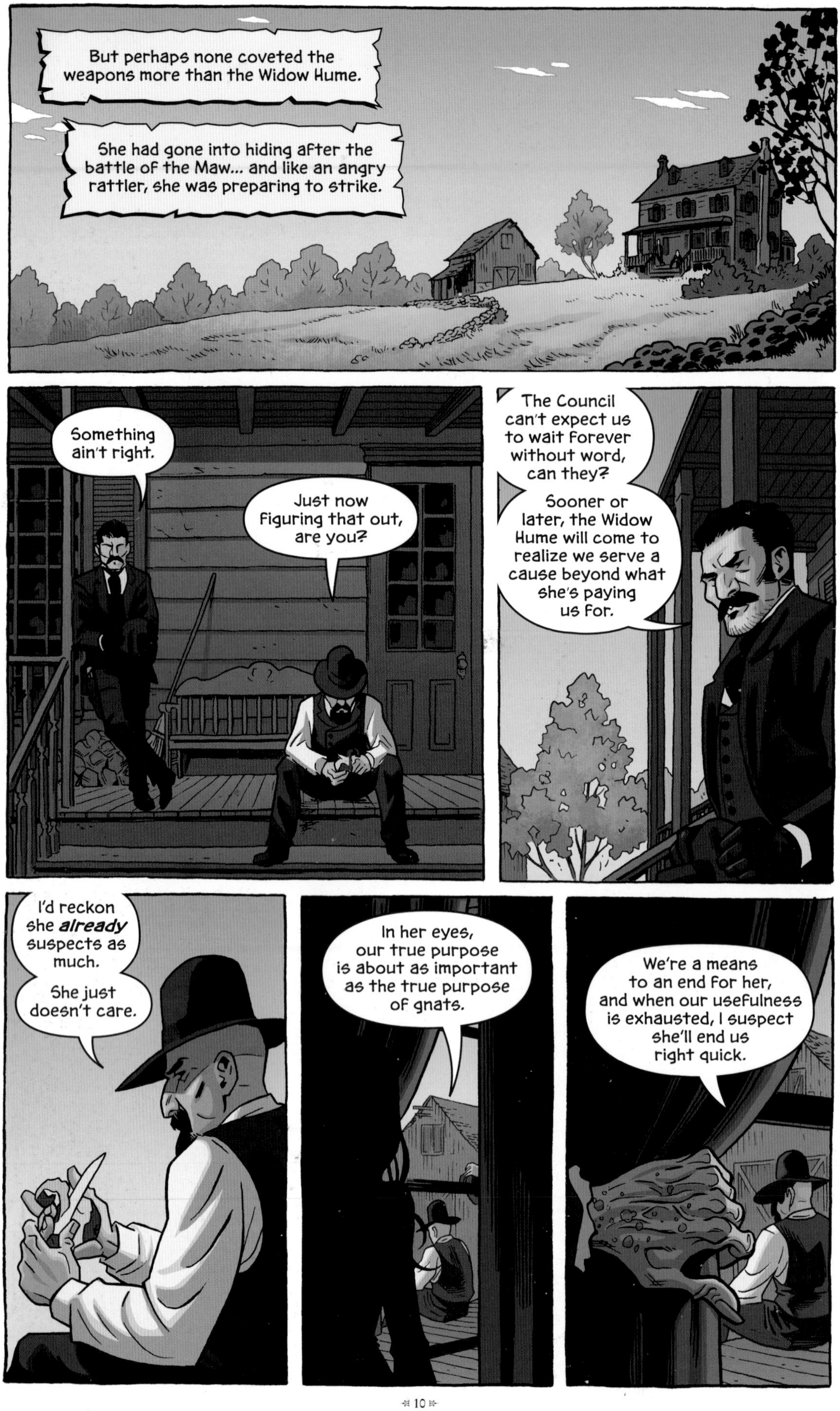

But perhaps none coveted the weapons more than the Widow Hume.
She had gone into hiding after the battle of the Maw... and like an angry rattler, she was preparing to strike.
Something ain't right.
Just now figuring that out, are you?
The Council can't expect us to wait forever without word, can they?
Sooner or later, the Widow Hume will come to realize we serve a cause beyond what she's paying us for.
I'd reckon she *already* suspects as much.
She just doesn't care.
In her eyes, our true purpose is about as important as the true purpose of gnats.
We're a means to an end for her, and when our usefulness is exhausted, I suspect she'll end us right quick.

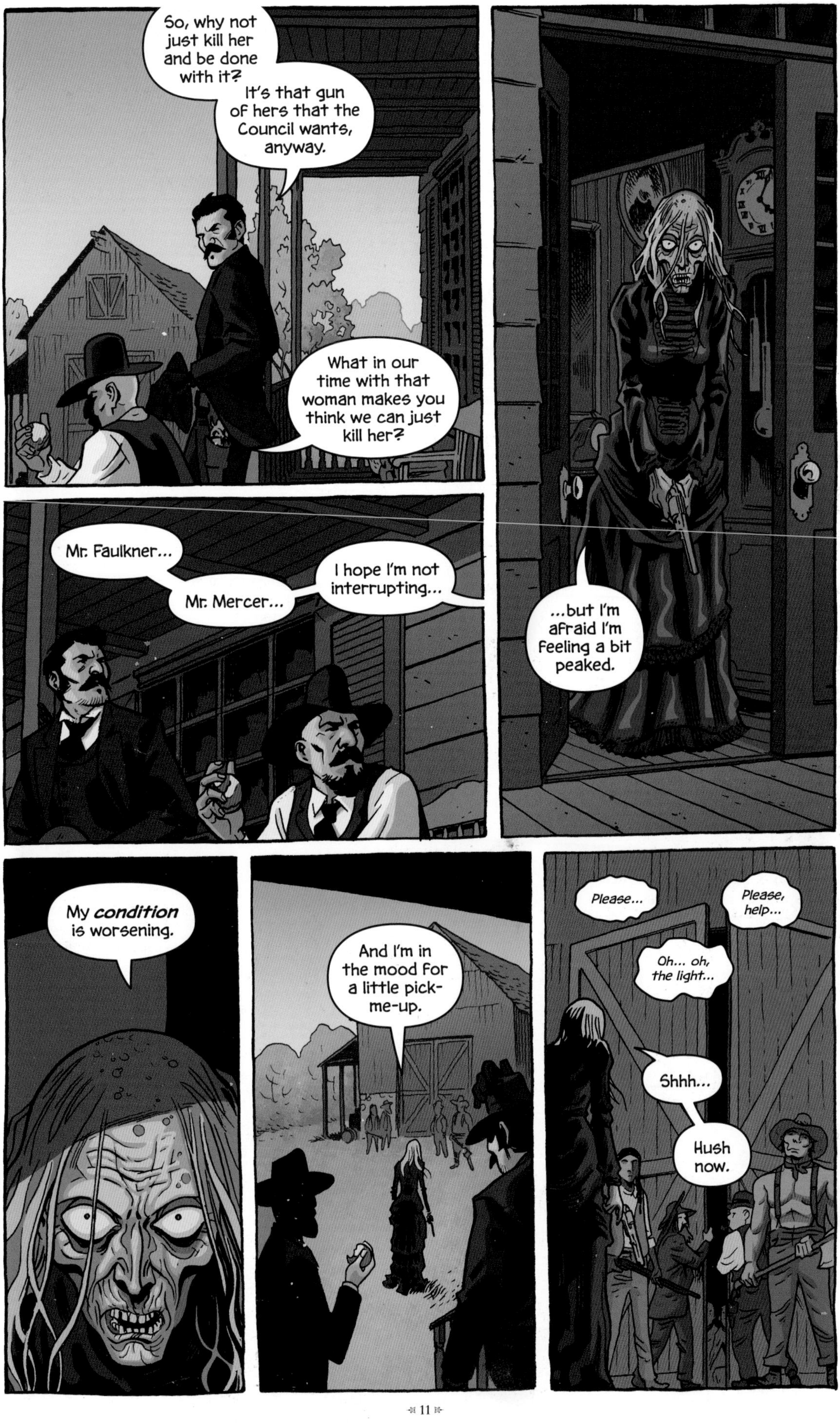
So, why not just kill her and be done with it?
It's that gun of hers that the Council wants, anyway.
What in our time with that woman makes you think we can just kill her?
Mr. Faulkner...
Mr. Mercer...
I hope I'm not interrupting...
...but I'm afraid I'm feeling a bit peaked.
My *condition* is worsening.
And I'm in the mood for a little pick-me-up.
Please...
Please, help...
Oh... oh, the light...
Shhh...
Hush now.

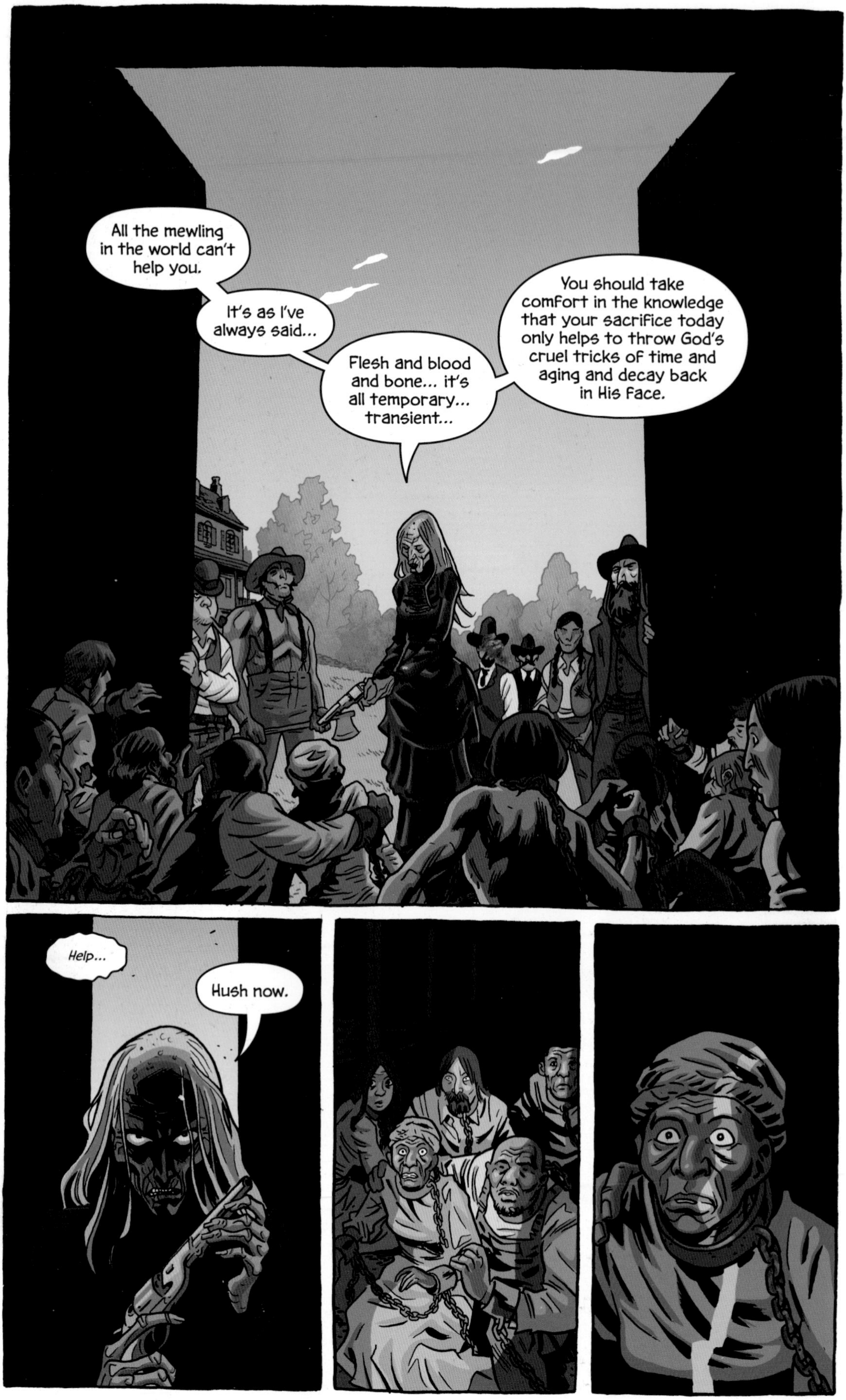
All the mewling in the world can't help you.
It's as I've always said...
Flesh and blood and bone... it's all temporary... transient...
You should take comfort in the knowledge that your sacrifice today only helps to throw God's cruel tricks of time and aging and decay back in His face.
Help...
Hush now.

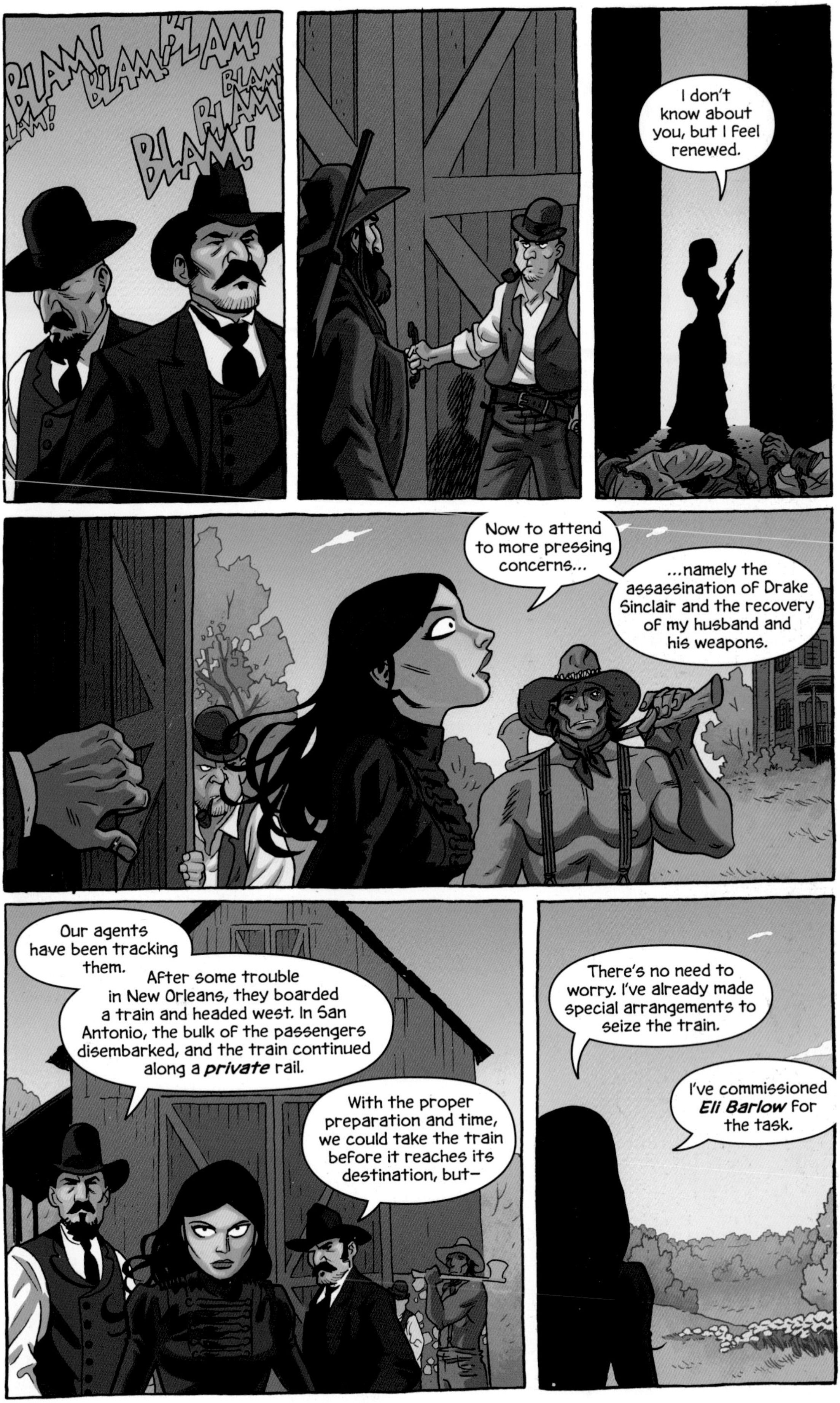
BLAM! BLAM! BLAM! BLAM! BLAM! BLAM!
I don't know about you, but I feel renewed.
Now to attend to more pressing concerns...
...namely the assassination of Drake Sinclair and the recovery of my husband and his weapons.
Our agents have been tracking them.
After some trouble in New Orleans, they boarded a train and headed west. In San Antonio, the bulk of the passengers disembarked, and the train continued along a *private* rail.
With the proper preparation and time, we could take the train before it reaches its destination, but—
There's no need to worry. I've already made special arrangements to seize the train.
I've commissioned **Eli Barlow** for the task.

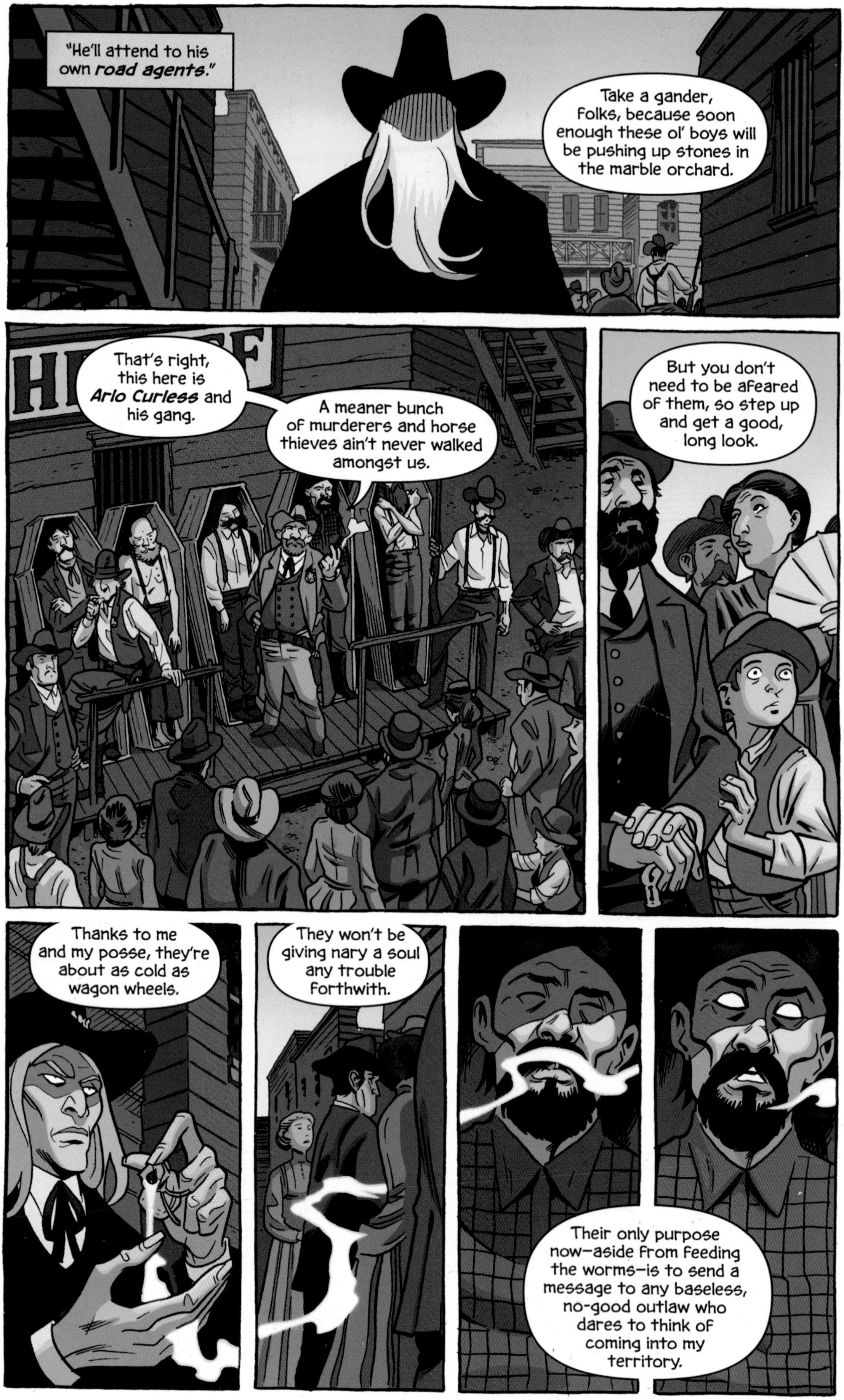
"He'll attend to his own *road agents.*"
Take a gander, folks, because soon enough these ol' boys will be pushing up stones in the marble orchard.
That's right, this here is *Arlo Curless* and his gang.
A meaner bunch of murderers and horse thieves ain't never walked amongst us.
But you don't need to be afeared of them, so step up and get a good, long look.
Thanks to me and my posse, they're about as cold as wagon wheels.
They won't be giving nary a soul any trouble forthwith.
Their only purpose now—aside from feeding the worms—is to send a message to any baseless, no-good outlaw who dares to think of coming into my territory.

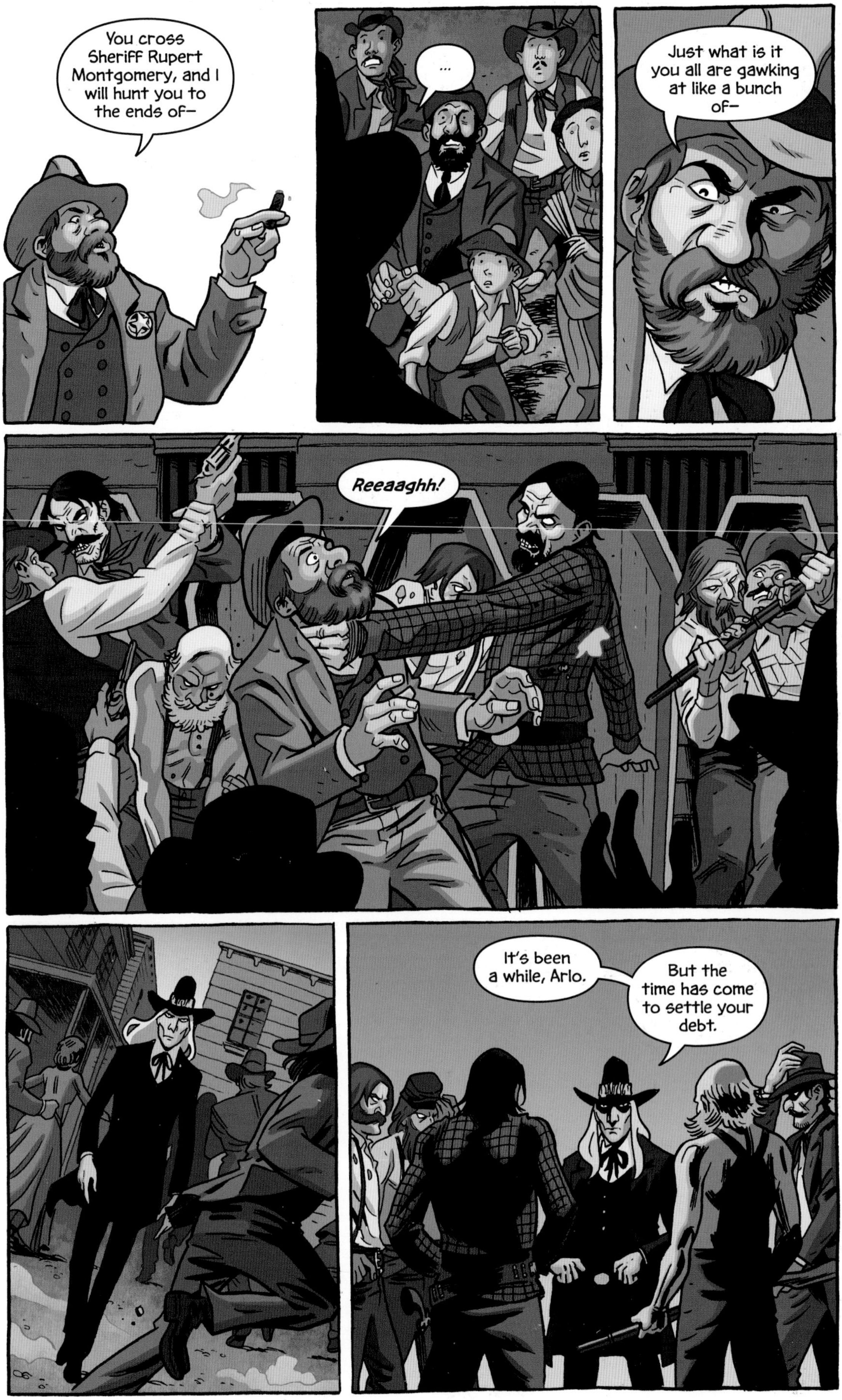
You cross Sheriff Rupert Montgomery, and I will hunt you to the ends of—
...
Just what is it you all are gawking at like a bunch of—
Reeeaaghh!
It's been a while, Arlo.
But the time has come to settle your debt.

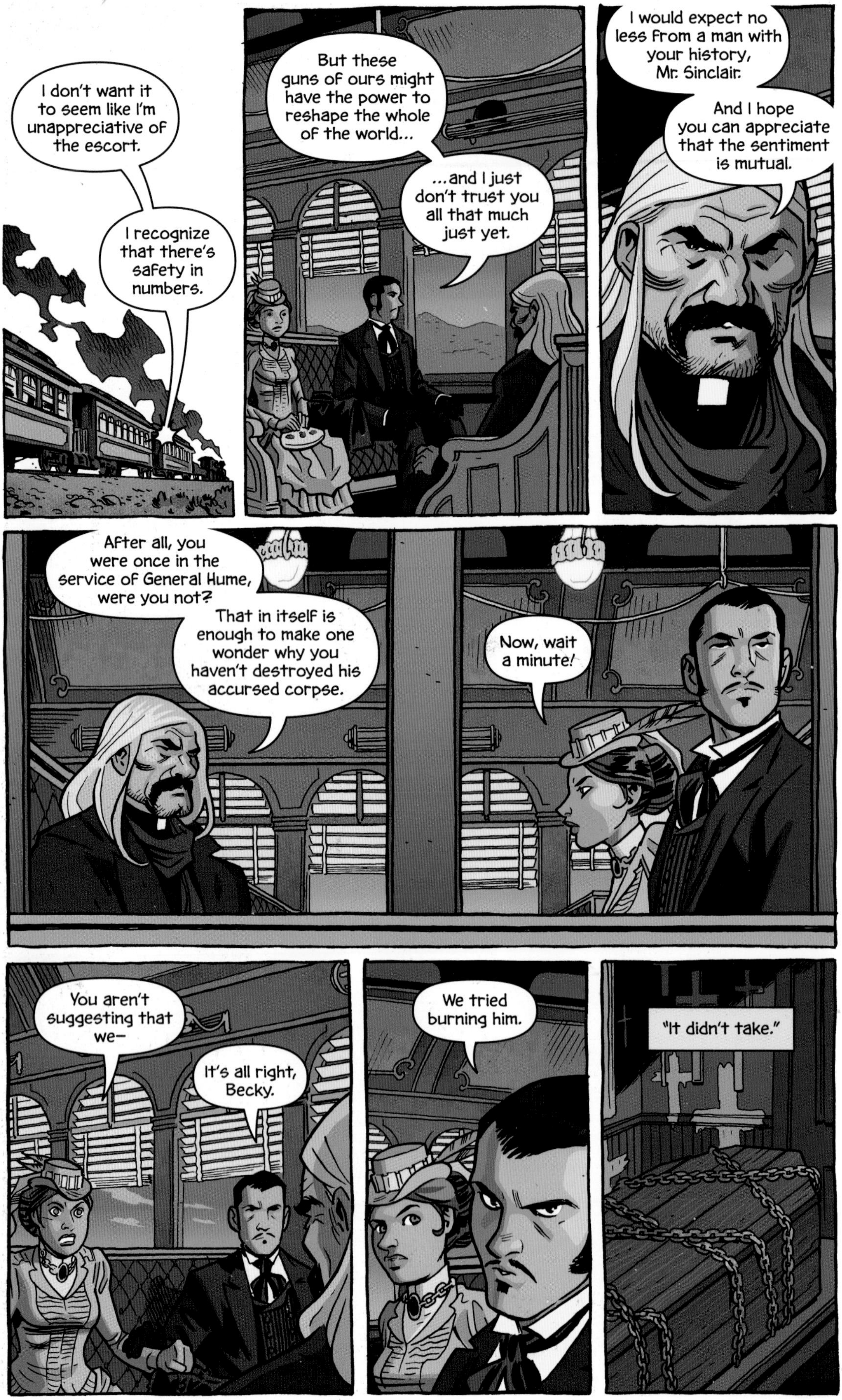
I don't want it to seem like I'm unappreciative of the escort.
I recognize that there's safety in numbers.
But these guns of ours might have the power to reshape the whole of the world...
...and I just don't trust you all that much just yet.
I would expect no less from a man with your history, Mr. Sinclair.
And I hope you can appreciate that the sentiment is mutual.
After all, you were once in the service of General Hume, were you not?
That in itself is enough to make one wonder why you haven't destroyed his accursed corpse.
Now, wait a minute!
You aren't suggesting that we–
It's all right, Becky.
We tried burning him.
"It didn't take."

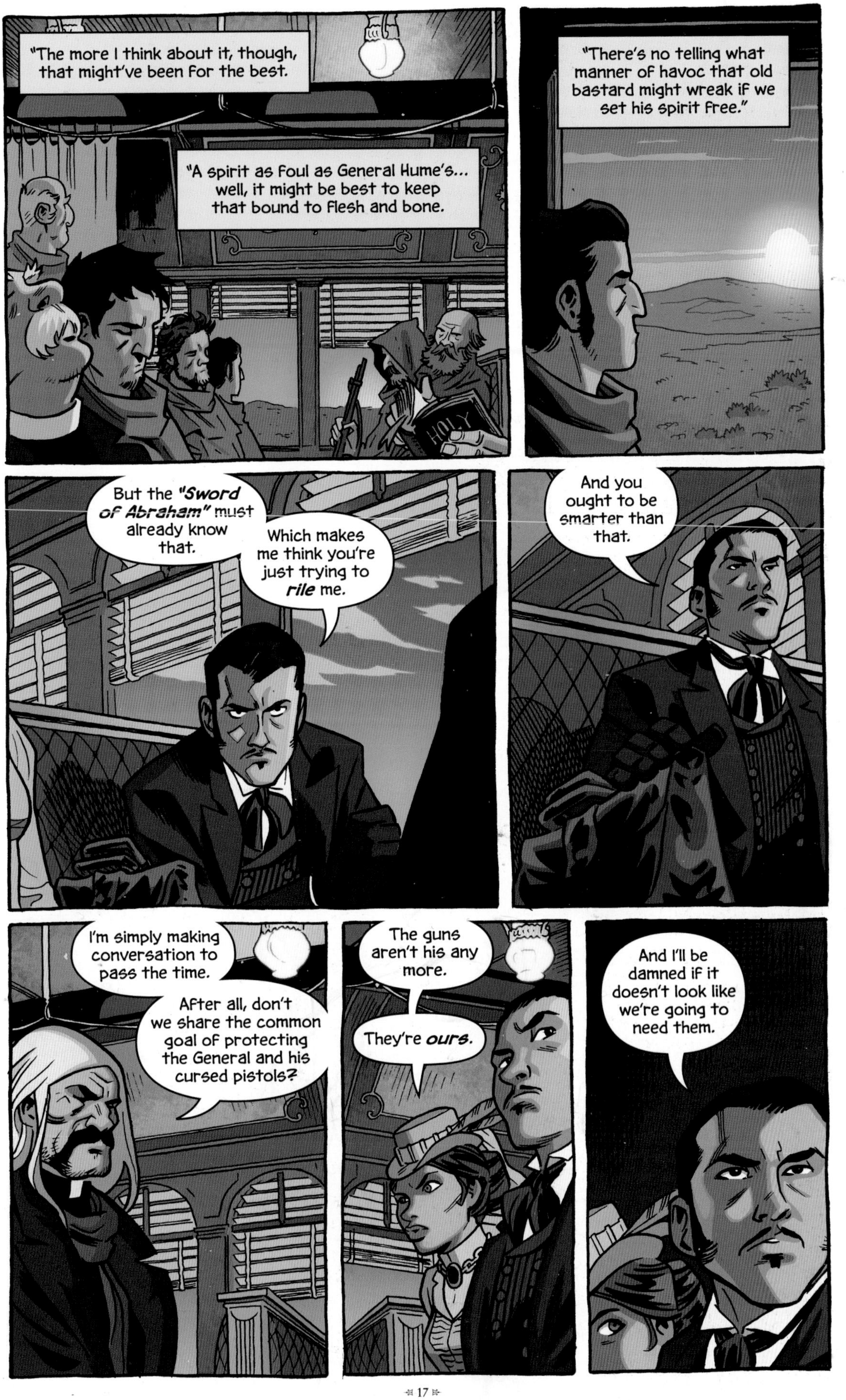
"The more I think about it, though, that might've been for the best.
"A spirit as foul as General Hume's... well, it might be best to keep that bound to flesh and bone.
"There's no telling what manner of havoc that old bastard might wreak if we set his spirit free."
But the "Sword of Abraham" must already know that.
Which makes me think you're just trying to rile me.
And you ought to be smarter than that.
I'm simply making conversation to pass the time.
After all, don't we share the common goal of protecting the General and his cursed pistols?
The guns aren't his any more.
They're ours.
And I'll be damned if it doesn't look like we're going to need them.

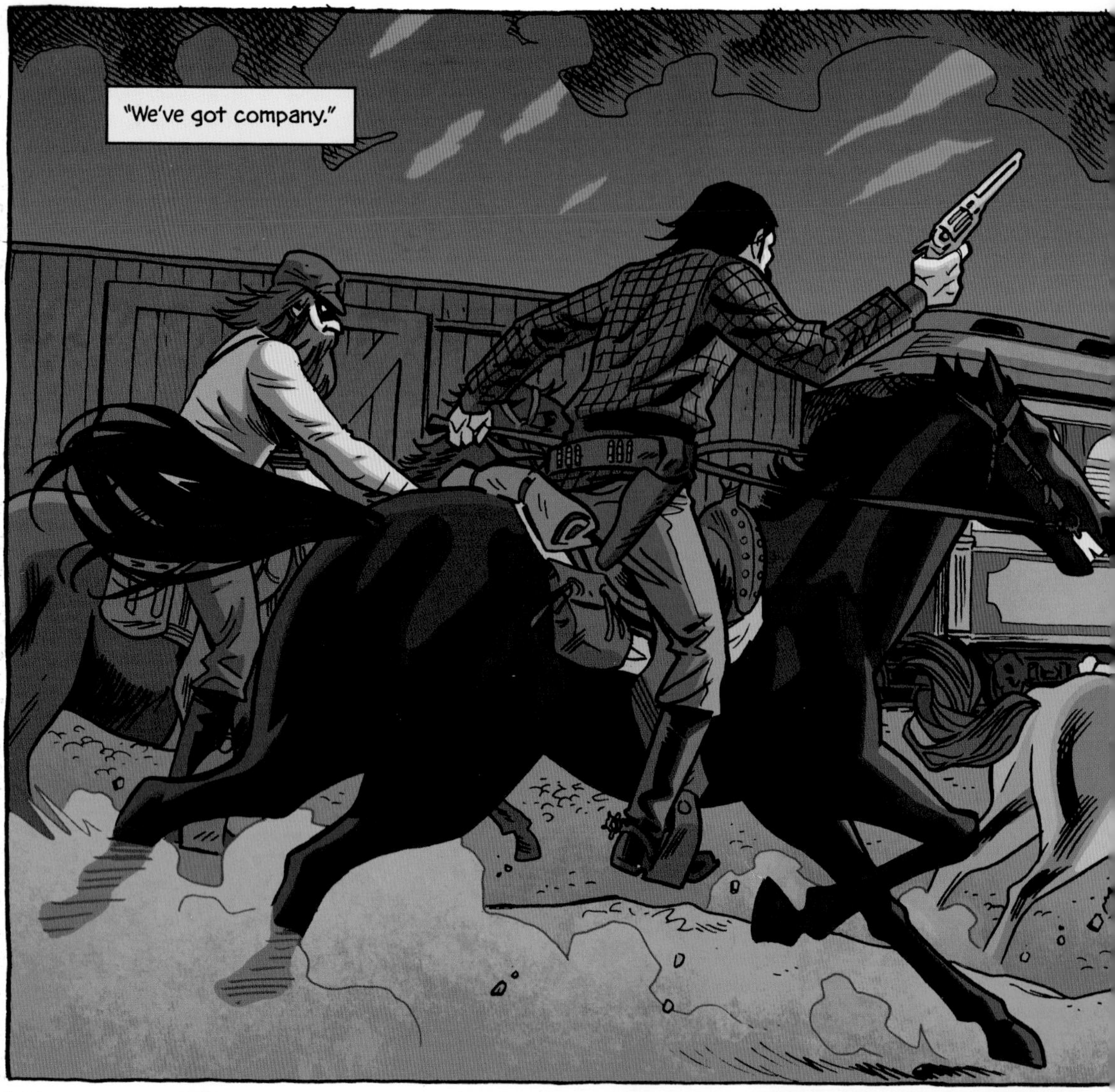
"We've got company."

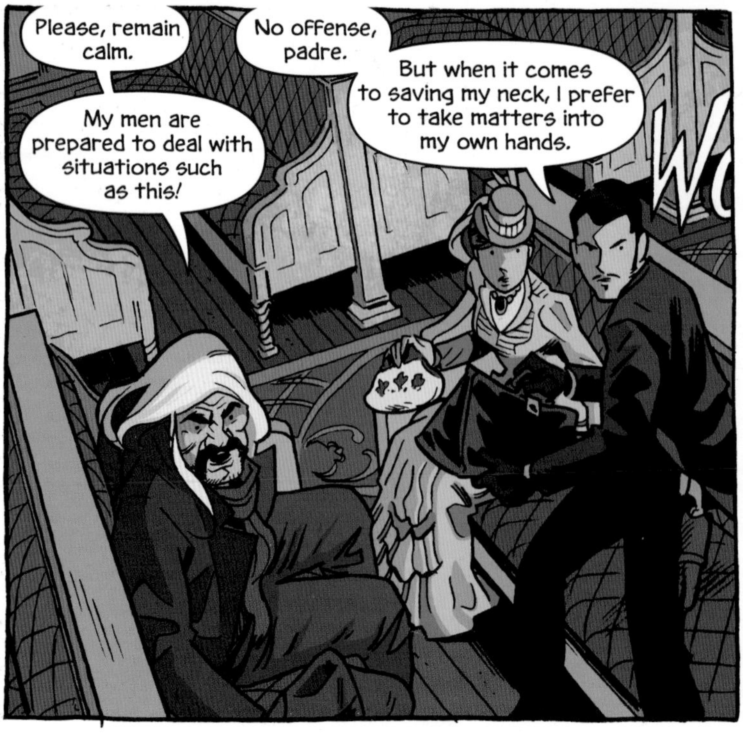
Please, remain calm.
My men are prepared to deal with situations such as this!
No offense, padre.
But when it comes to saving my neck, I prefer to take matters into my own hands.

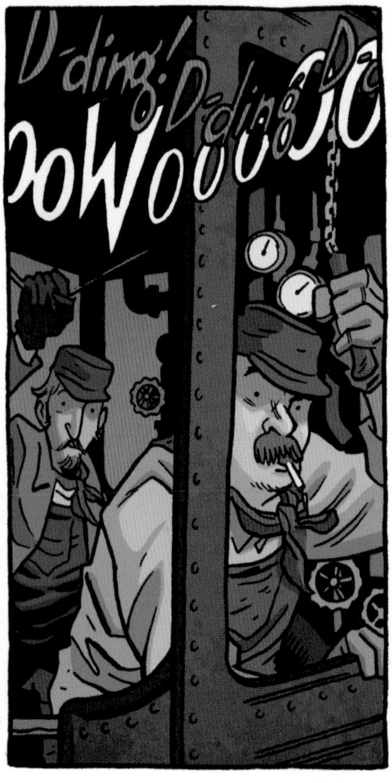
D-ding! D-ding!
WooWoooo

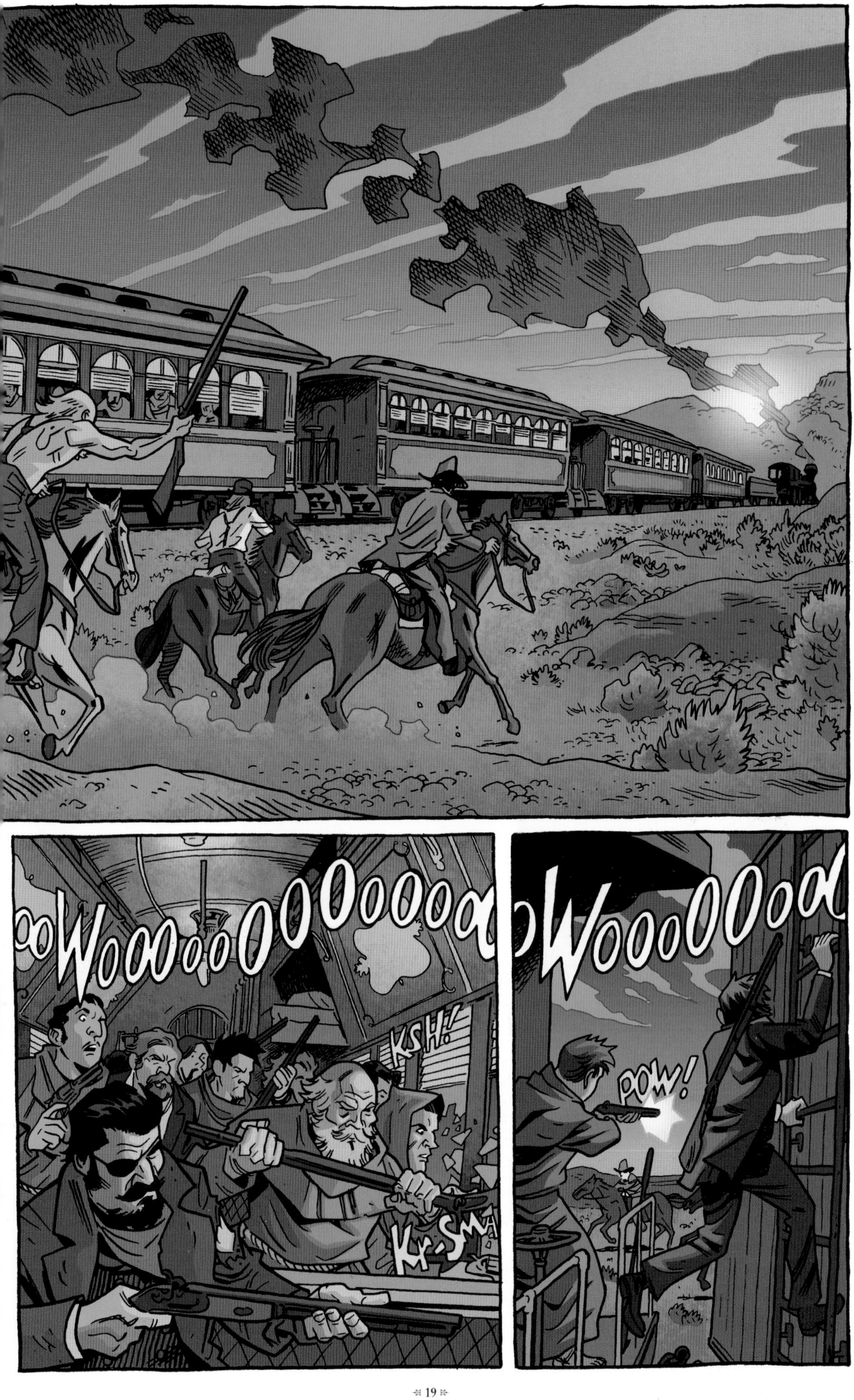
ooWoooooOOOOoooo
KSH!
Kr-SMA
oWoooOOooo
POW!

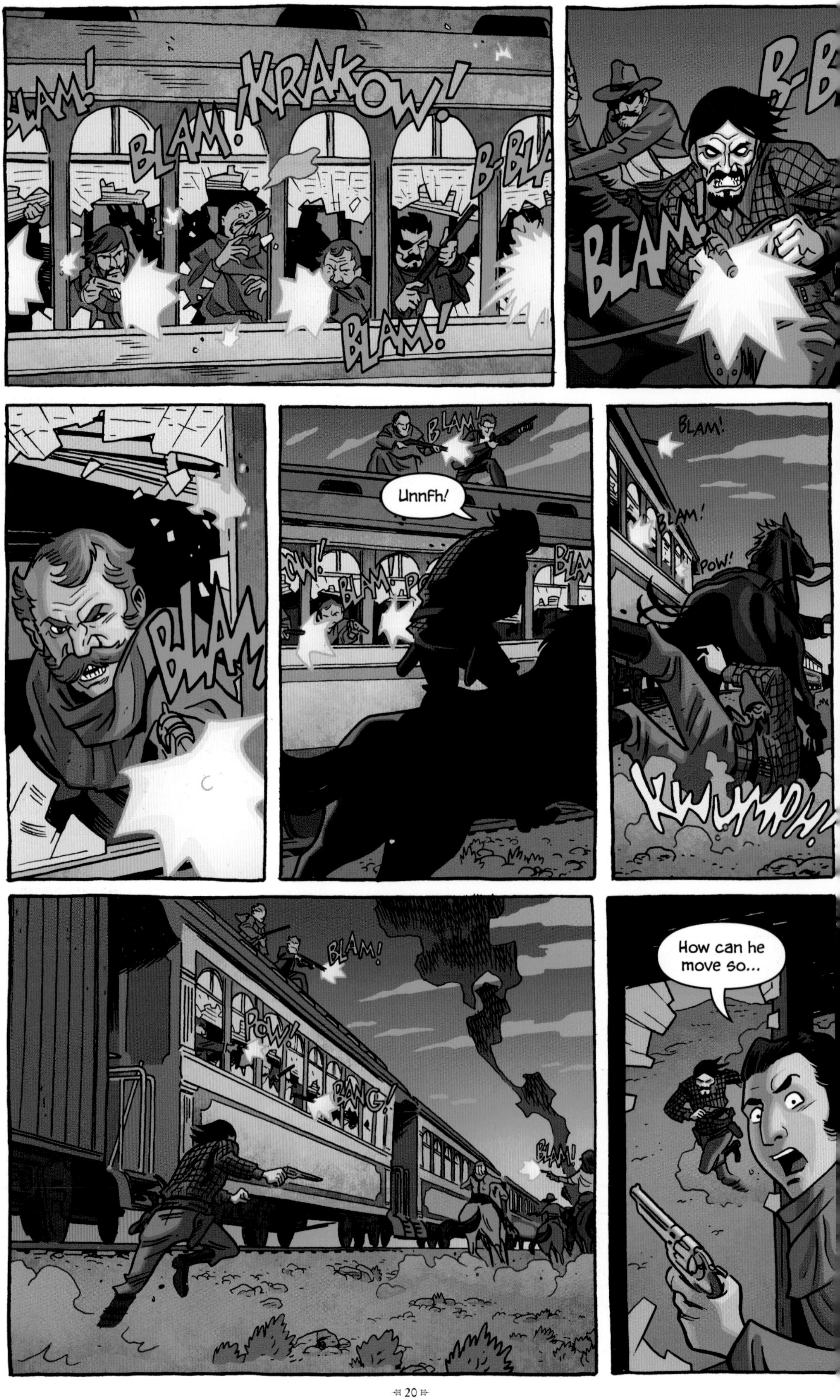
BLAM!
KRAKOW!
BLAM!
B-BLAM
BLAM!
B-B
BLAM!
BLAM
BLAM!
Unnfh!
POW!
BLAM!
BLAM!
BLAM!
BLAM!
POW!
KWUMPH!
BLAM!
POW!
BANG!
BLAM!
How can he move so...

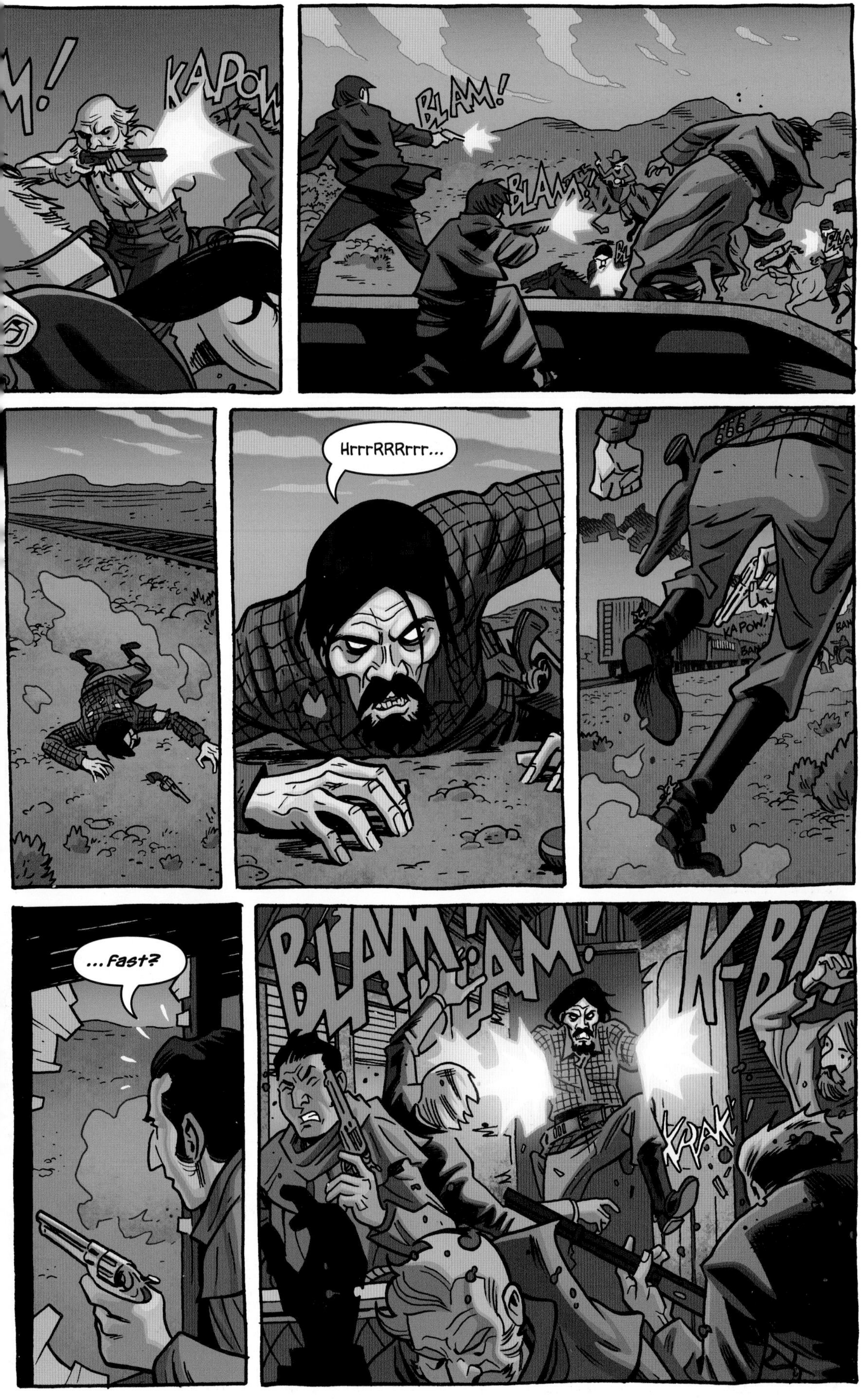
BLAM!
HrrrRRRrrr...
KAPOW!
...fast?
KRAK!

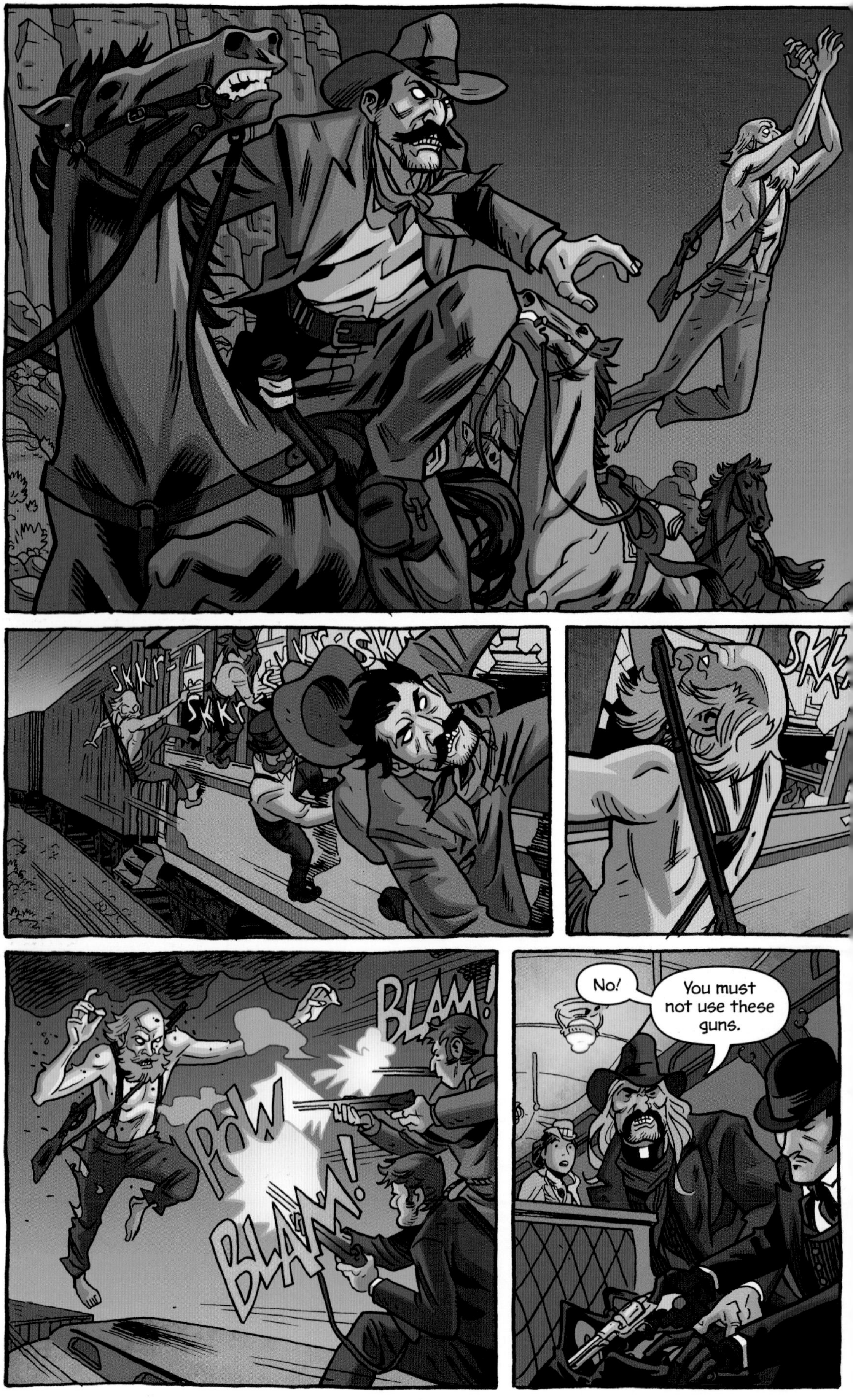
Skkr-
Skkr-
SKKR-SKKR
SKK
BLAM!
POW
BLAM!
No!
You must not use these guns.

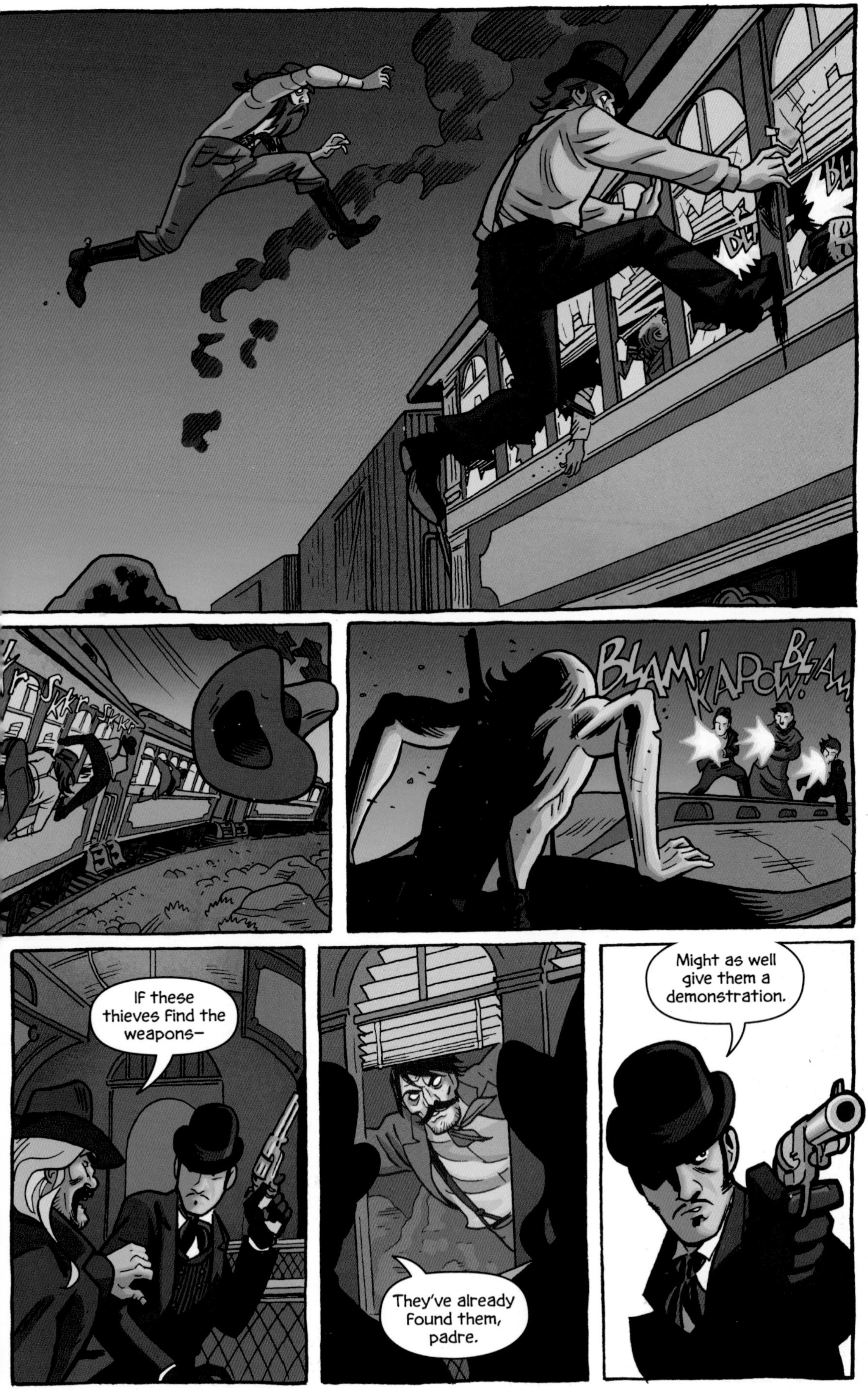
BLAM! KAPOW!
If these thieves find the weapons–
They've already found them, padre.
Might as well give them a demonstration.

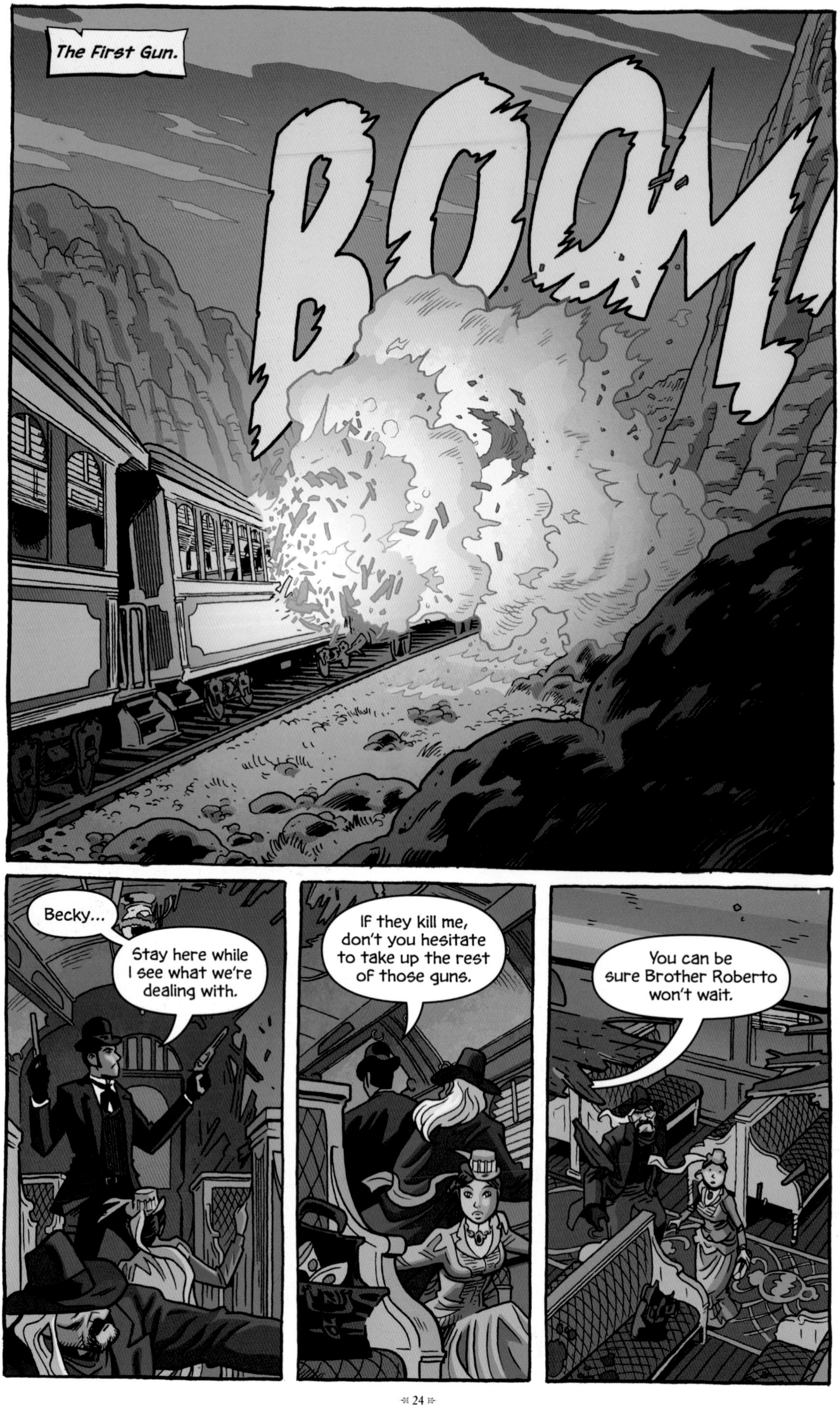

The First Gun.
BOOM
Becky...
Stay here while I see what we're dealing with.
If they kill me, don't you hesitate to take up the rest of those guns.
You can be sure Brother Roberto won't wait.

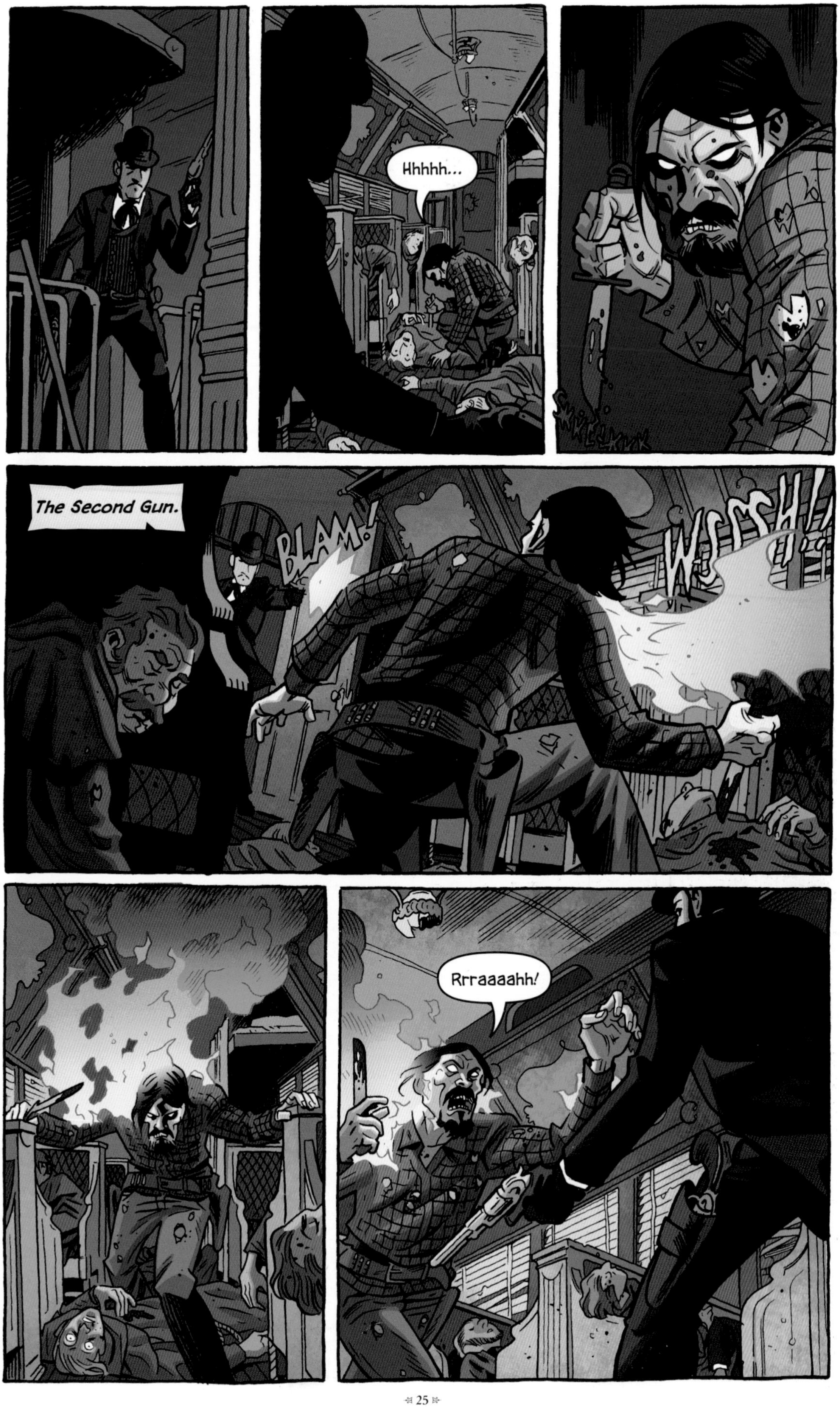
Hhhhh...
The Second Gun.
BLAM!
Rrraaaahh!

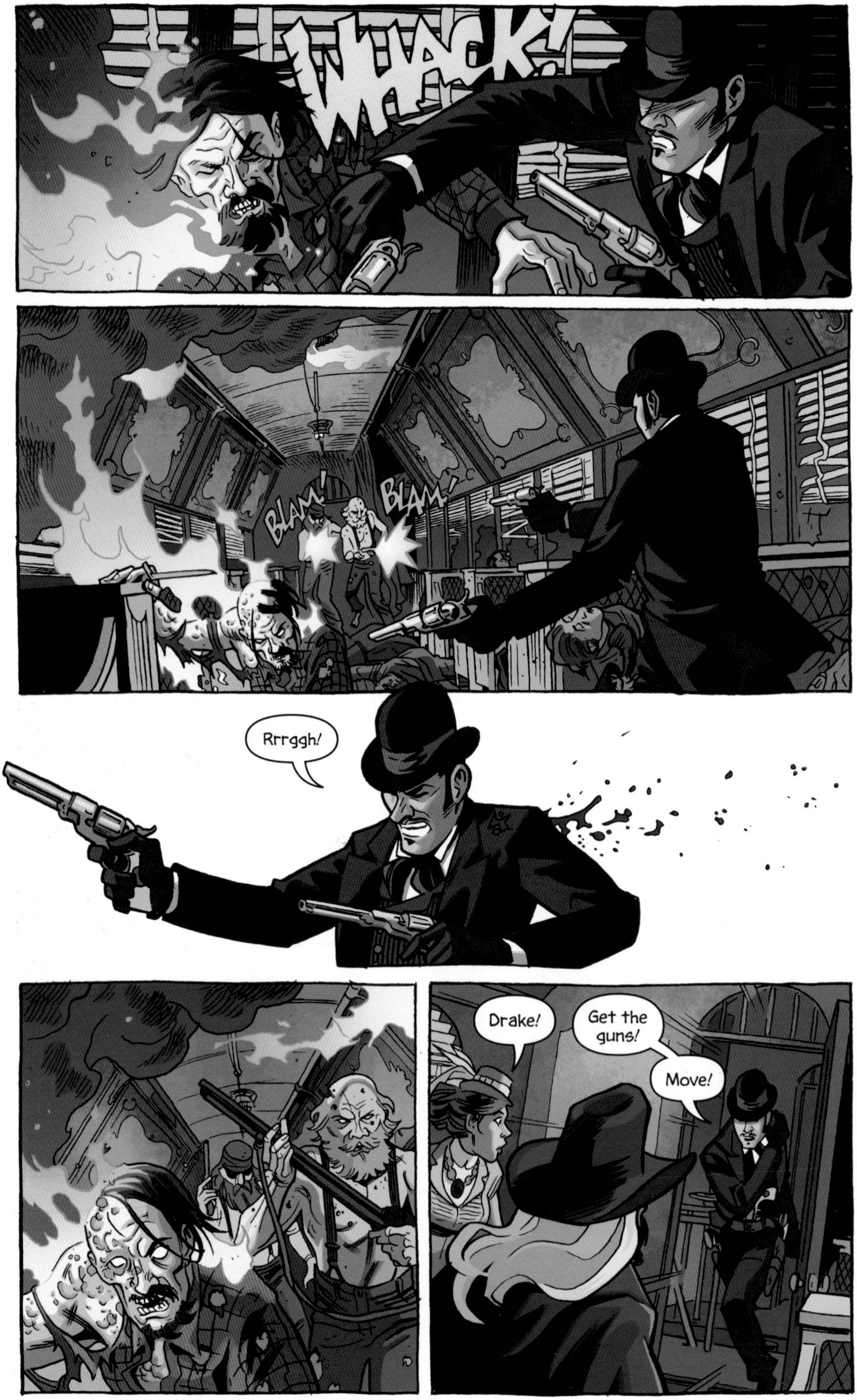
WHACK!
BLAM!
BLAM!
Rrrggh!
Drake!
Get the guns!
Move!

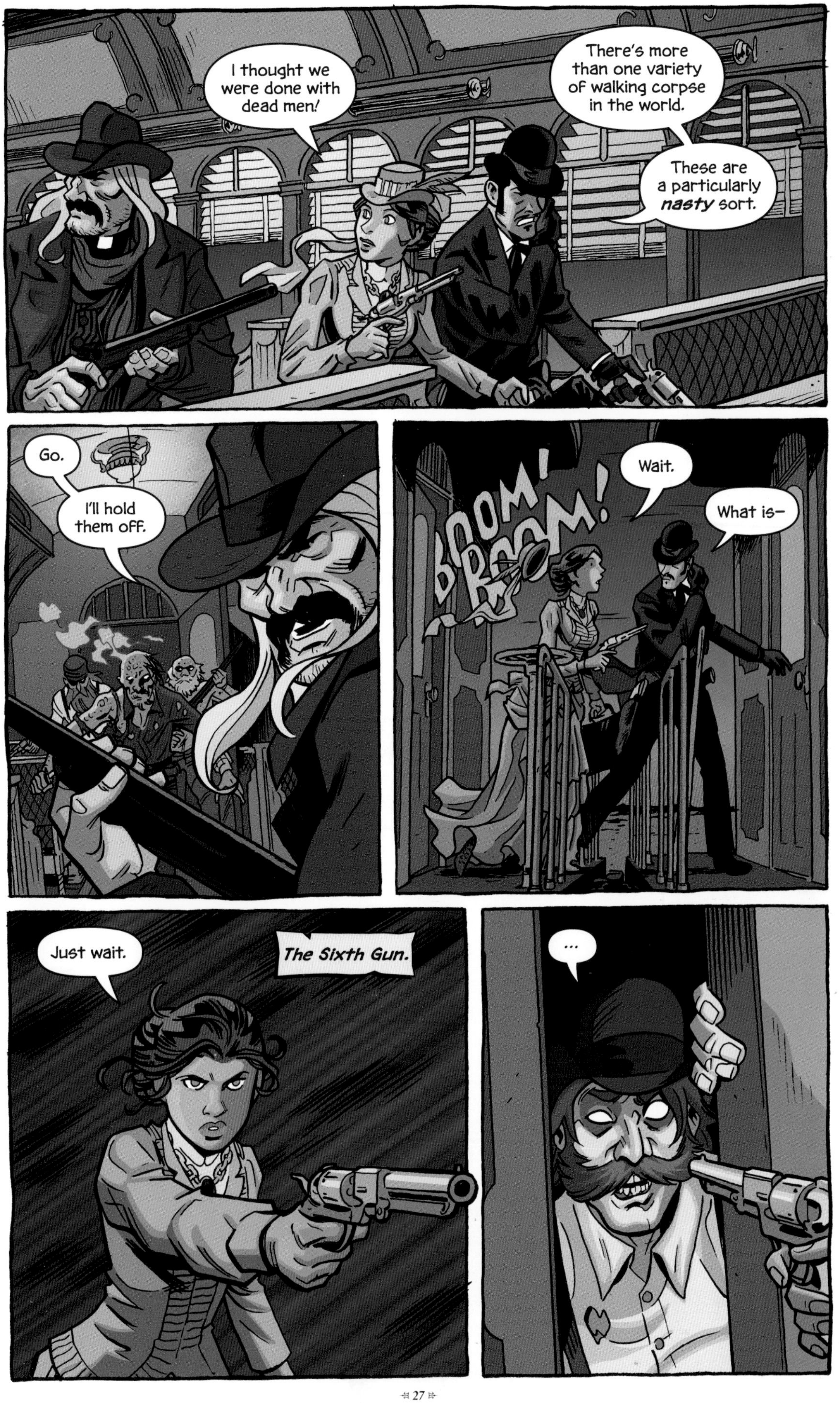
I thought we were done with dead men!
There's more than one variety of walking corpse in the world.
These are a particularly *nasty* sort.
Go.
I'll hold them off.
BOOM! BOOM!
Wait.
What is–
Just wait.
The Sixth Gun.
...

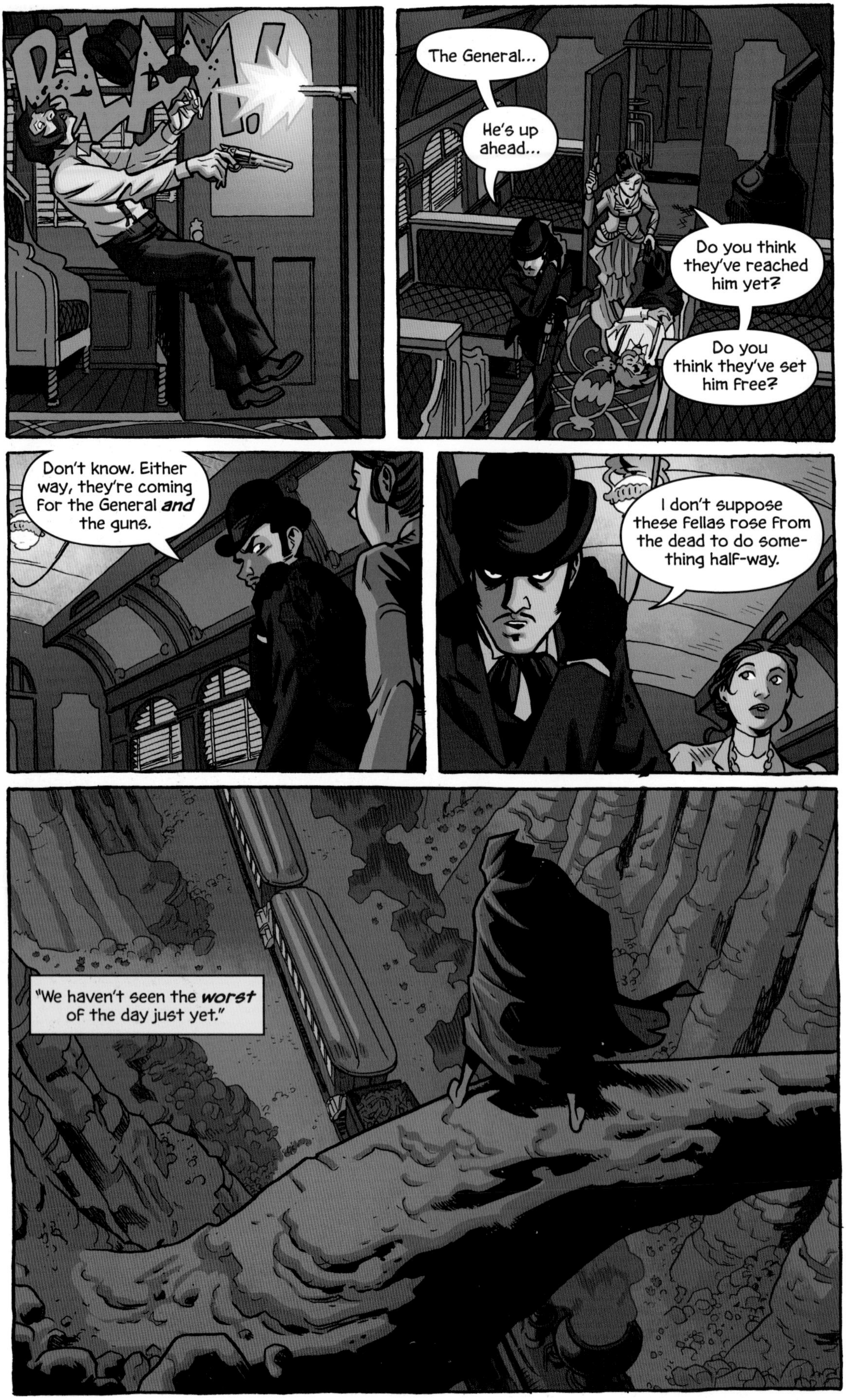
BLAM!
The General...
He's up ahead...
Do you think they've reached him yet?
Do you think they've set him free?
Don't know. Either way, they're coming for the General *and* the guns.
I don't suppose these fellas rose from the dead to do some-thing half-way.
"We haven't seen the *worst* of the day just yet."

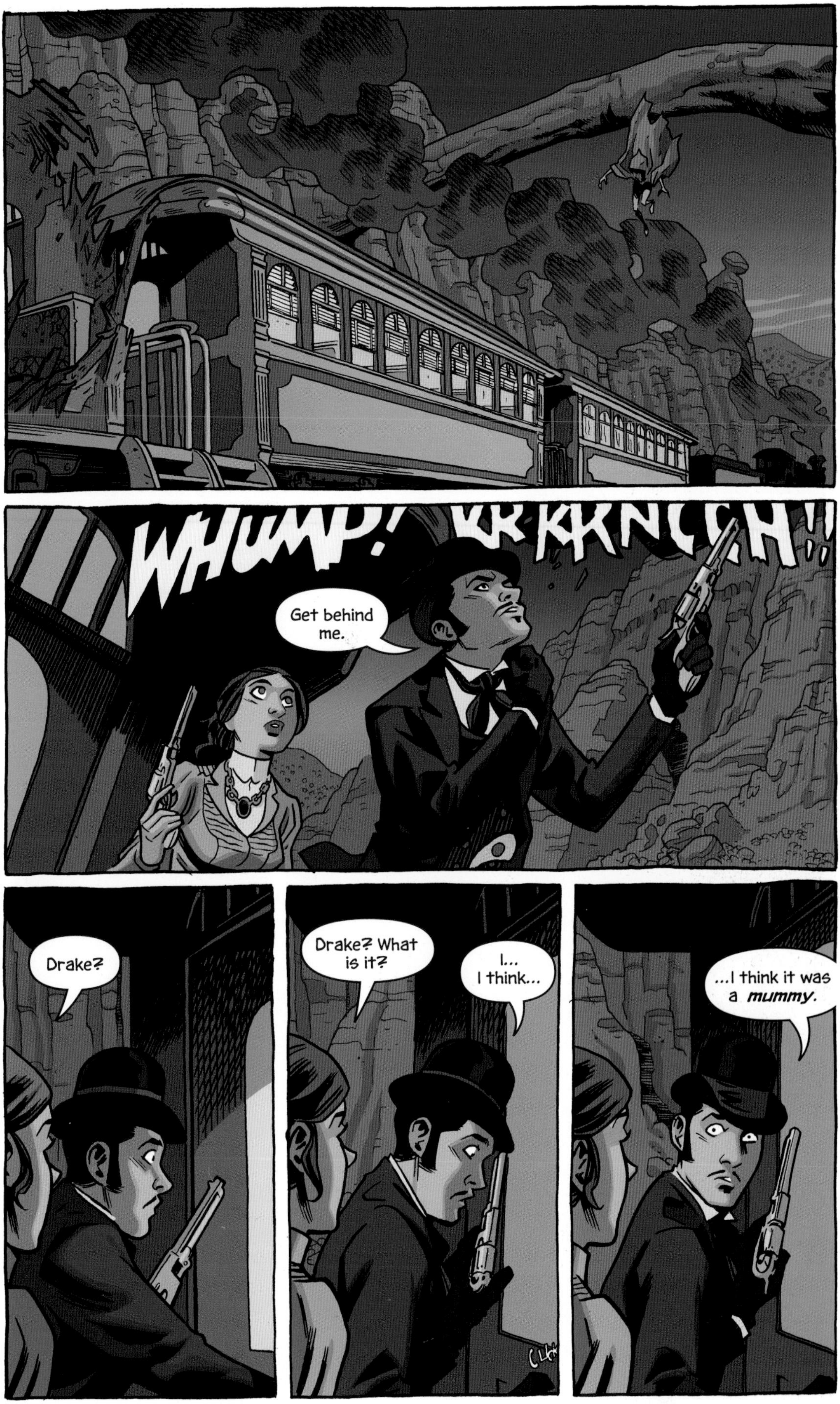

WHUMP!
Get behind me.
Drake?
Drake? What is it?
I... I think...
...I think it was a *mummy*.

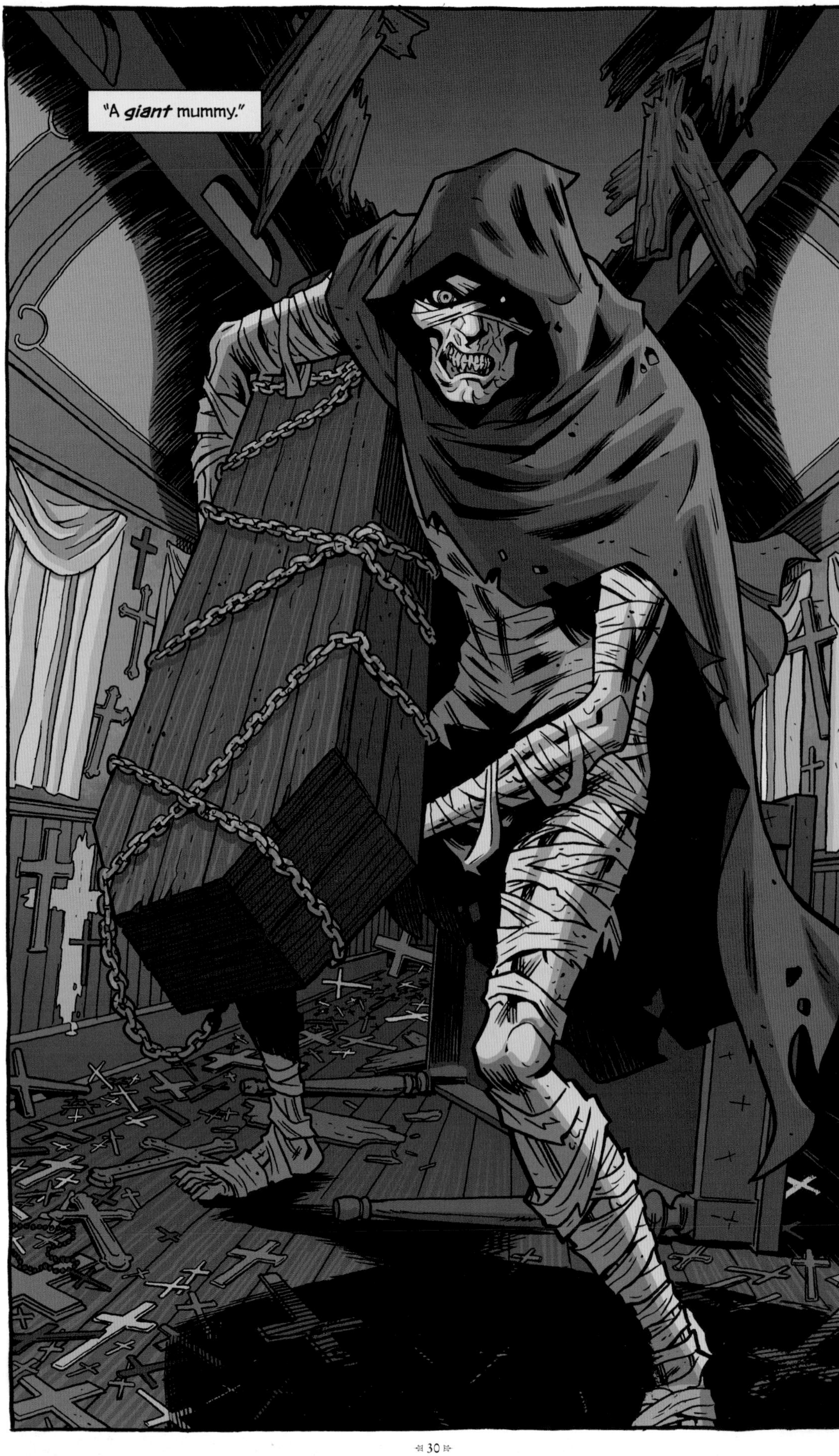
"A *giant* mummy."

CHAPTER TWO

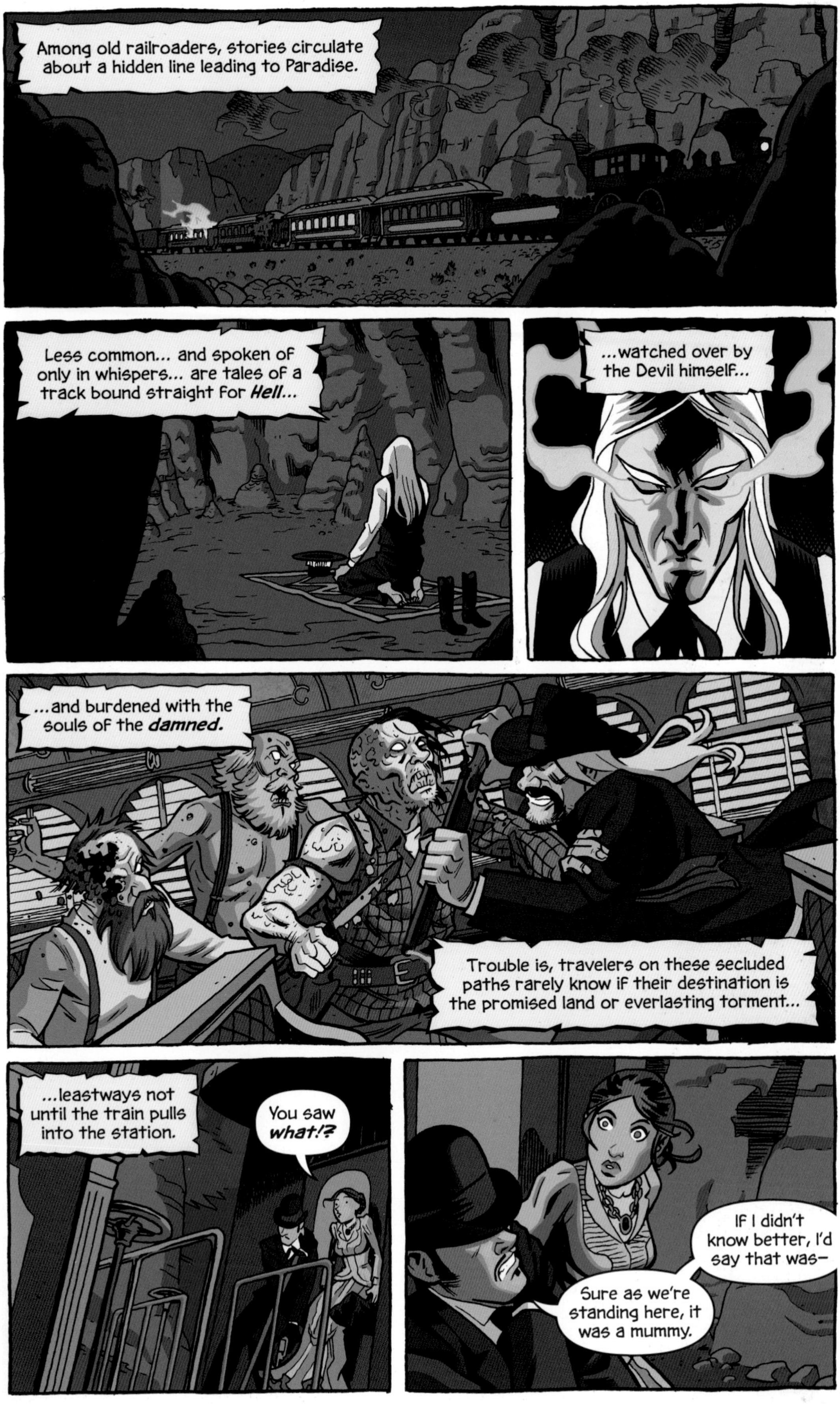
Among old railroaders, stories circulate about a hidden line leading to Paradise.
Less common... and spoken of only in whispers... are tales of a track bound straight for *Hell*...
...watched over by the Devil himself...
...and burdened with the souls of the *damned.*
Trouble is, travelers on these secluded paths rarely know if their destination is the promised land or everlasting torment...
...leastways not until the train pulls into the station.
You saw *what!?*
If I didn't know better, I'd say that was—
Sure as we're standing here, it was a mummy.

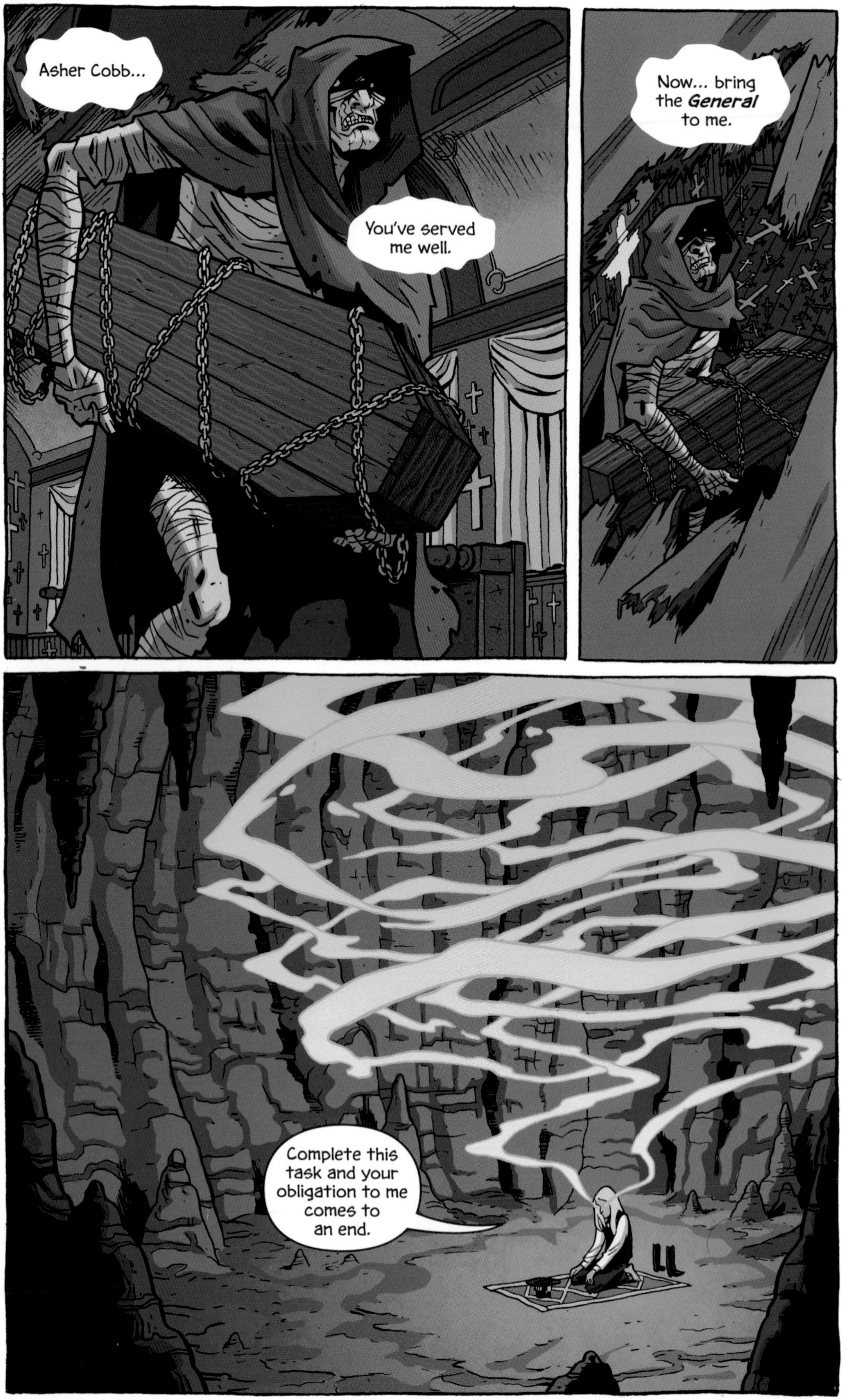
Asher Cobb...
You've served me well.
Now... bring the *General* to me.
Complete this task and your obligation to me comes to an end.

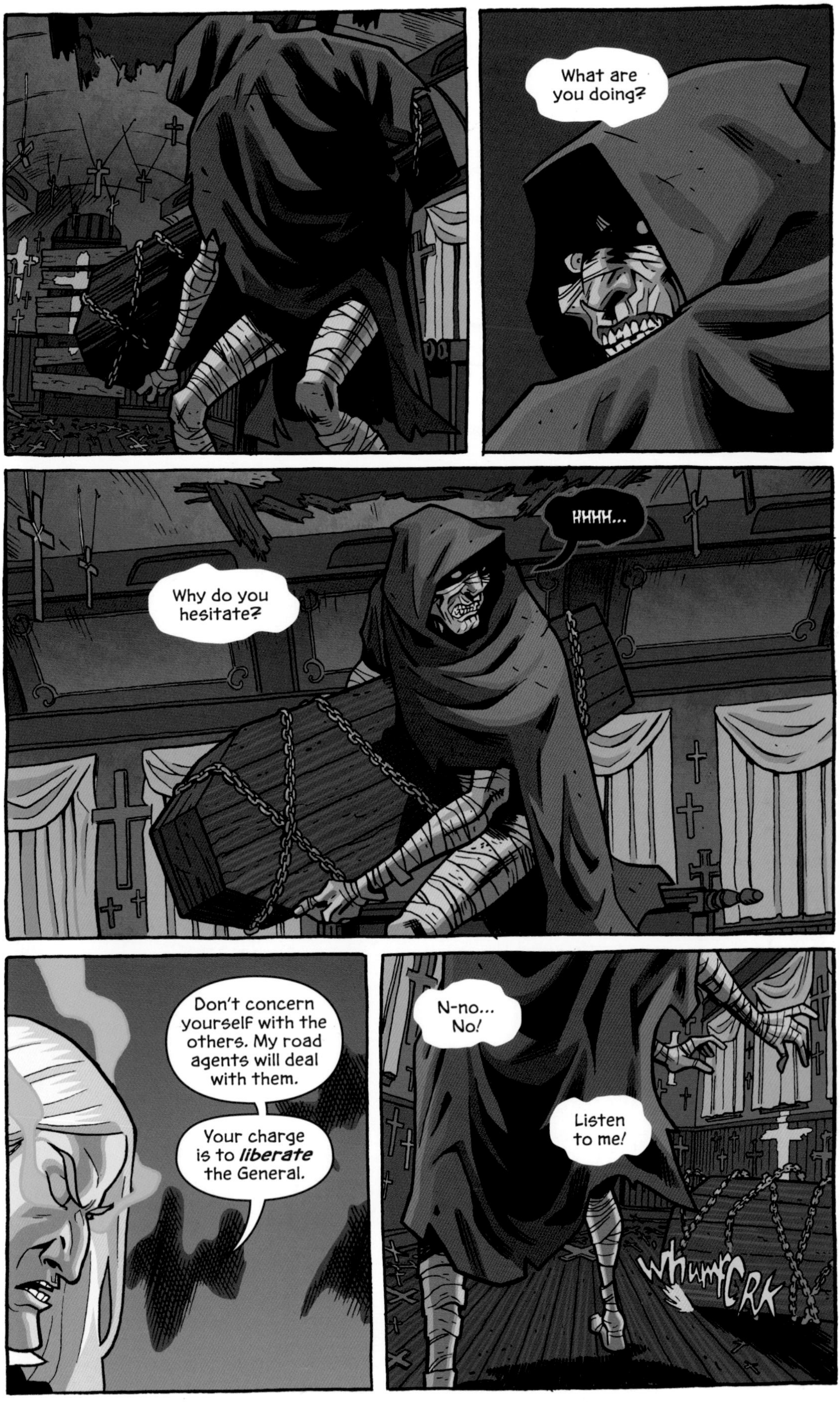
What are you doing?
HHHH...
Why do you hesitate?
Don't concern yourself with the others. My road agents will deal with them.
Your charge is to *liberate* the General.
N-no... No!
Listen to me!
WHUMFCRK

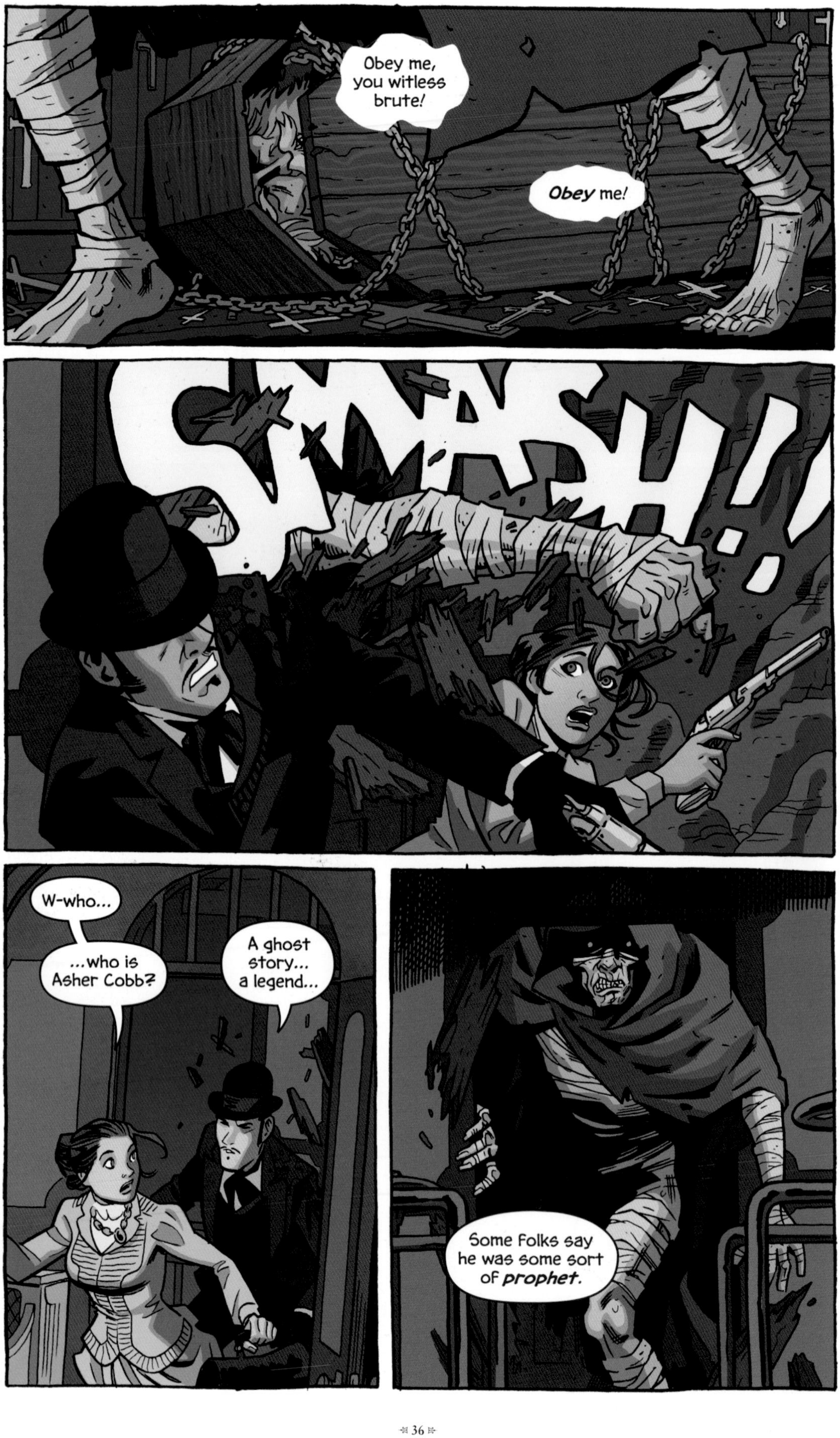

Obey me, you witless brute!
Obey me!
SMASH!!!
W-who...
...who is Asher Cobb?
A ghost story... a legend...
Some folks say he was some sort of ***prophet***.

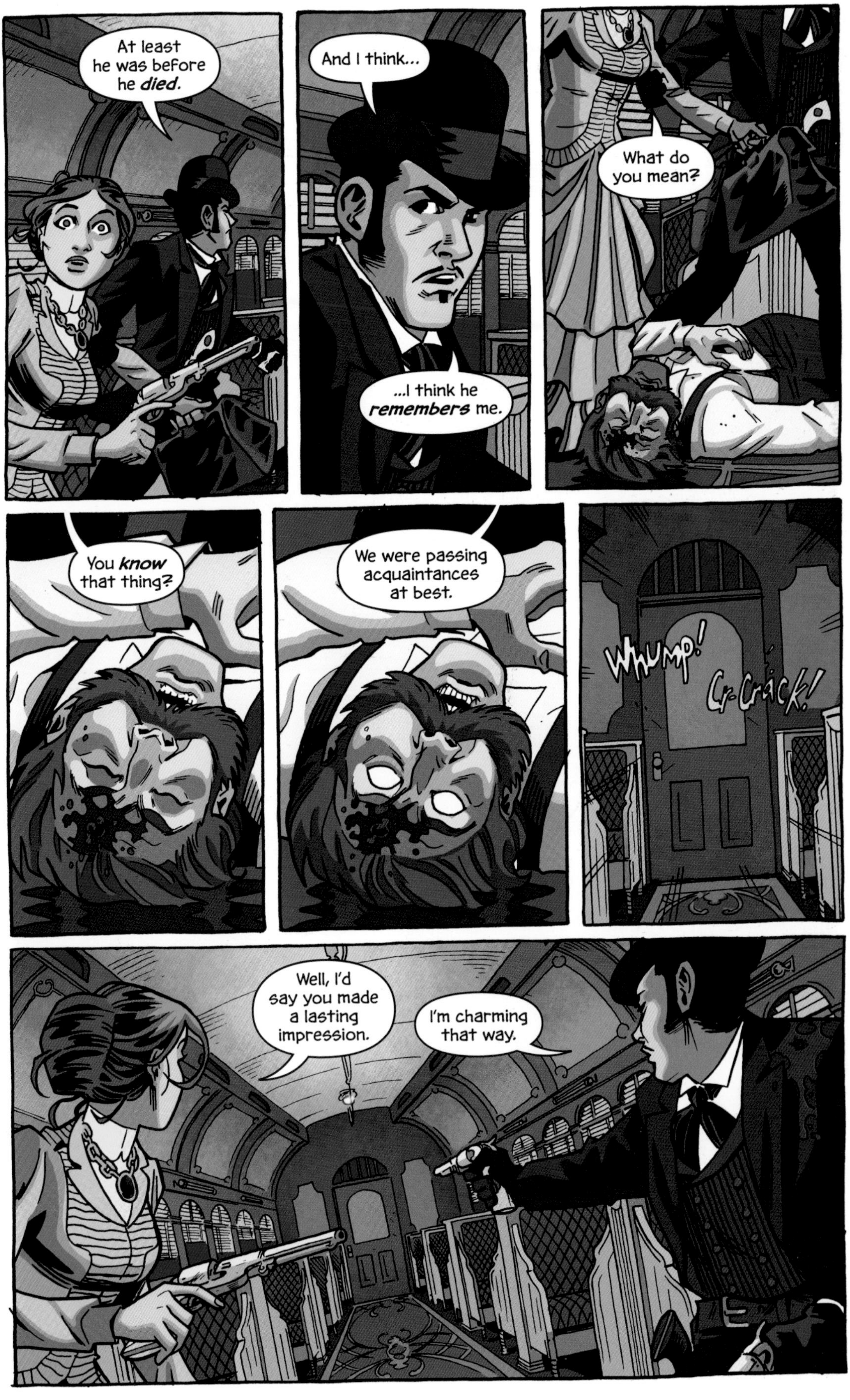
At least he was before he *died*.
And I think...
...I think he *remembers* me.
What do you mean?
You *know* that thing?
We were passing acquaintances at best.
WHUMP!
Cr-CRACK!
Well, I'd say you made a lasting impression.
I'm charming that way.

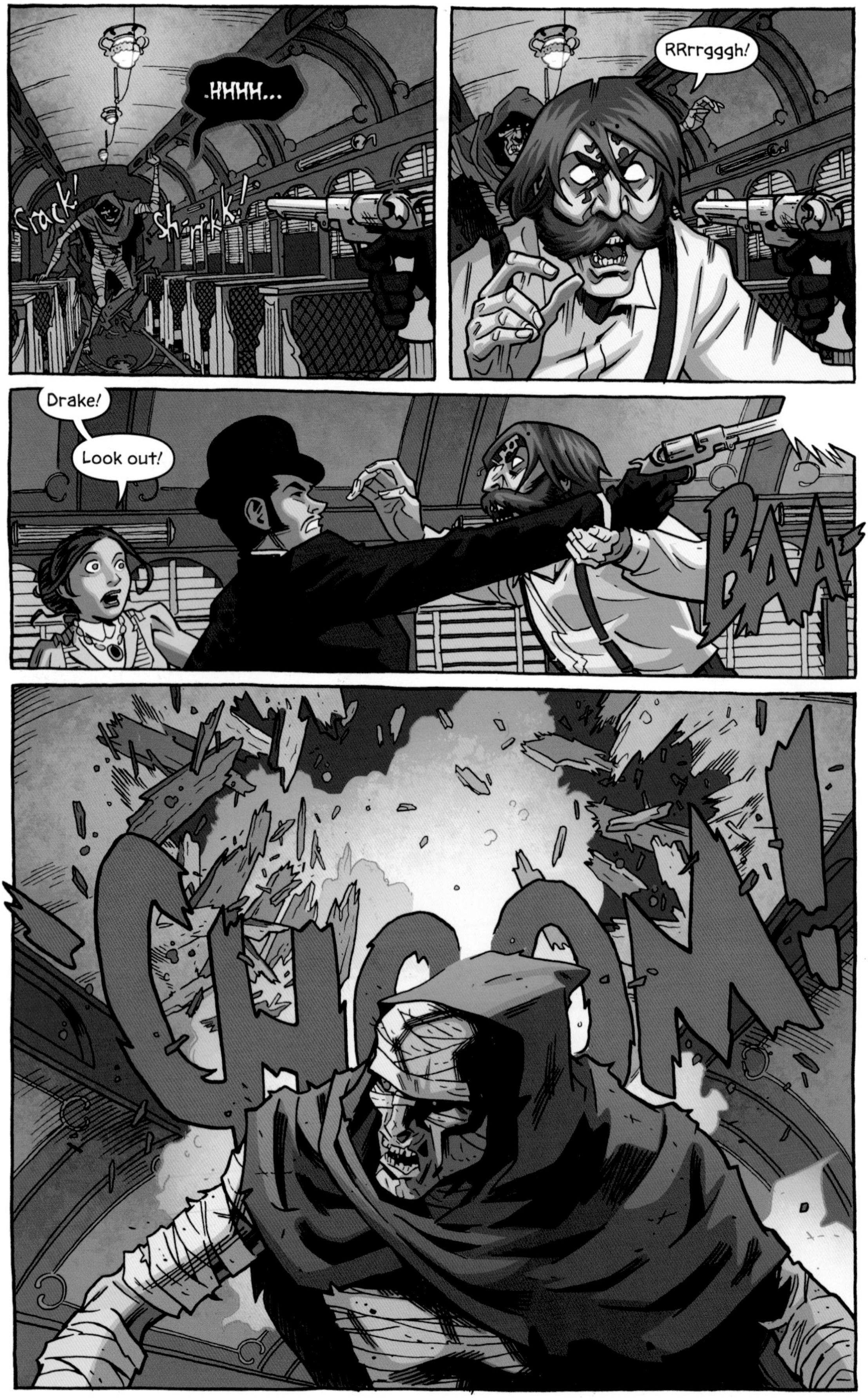

Crack!
Shi-rrkk!
.HHHH...
RRrrgggh!
Drake!
Look out!
BAA
CHOOM!

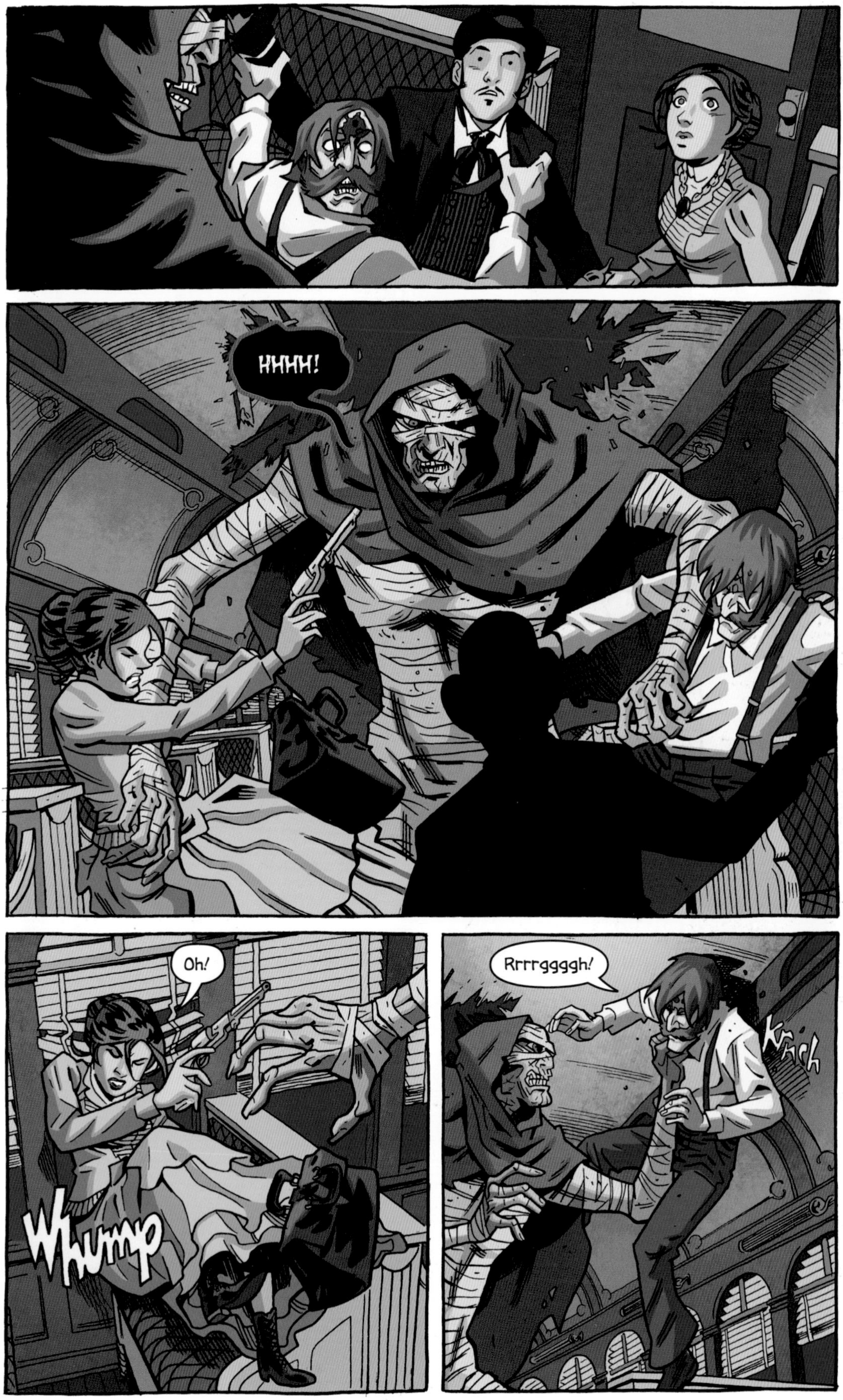
HHHH!
Oh!
Whump
Rrrrggggh!
Krrch

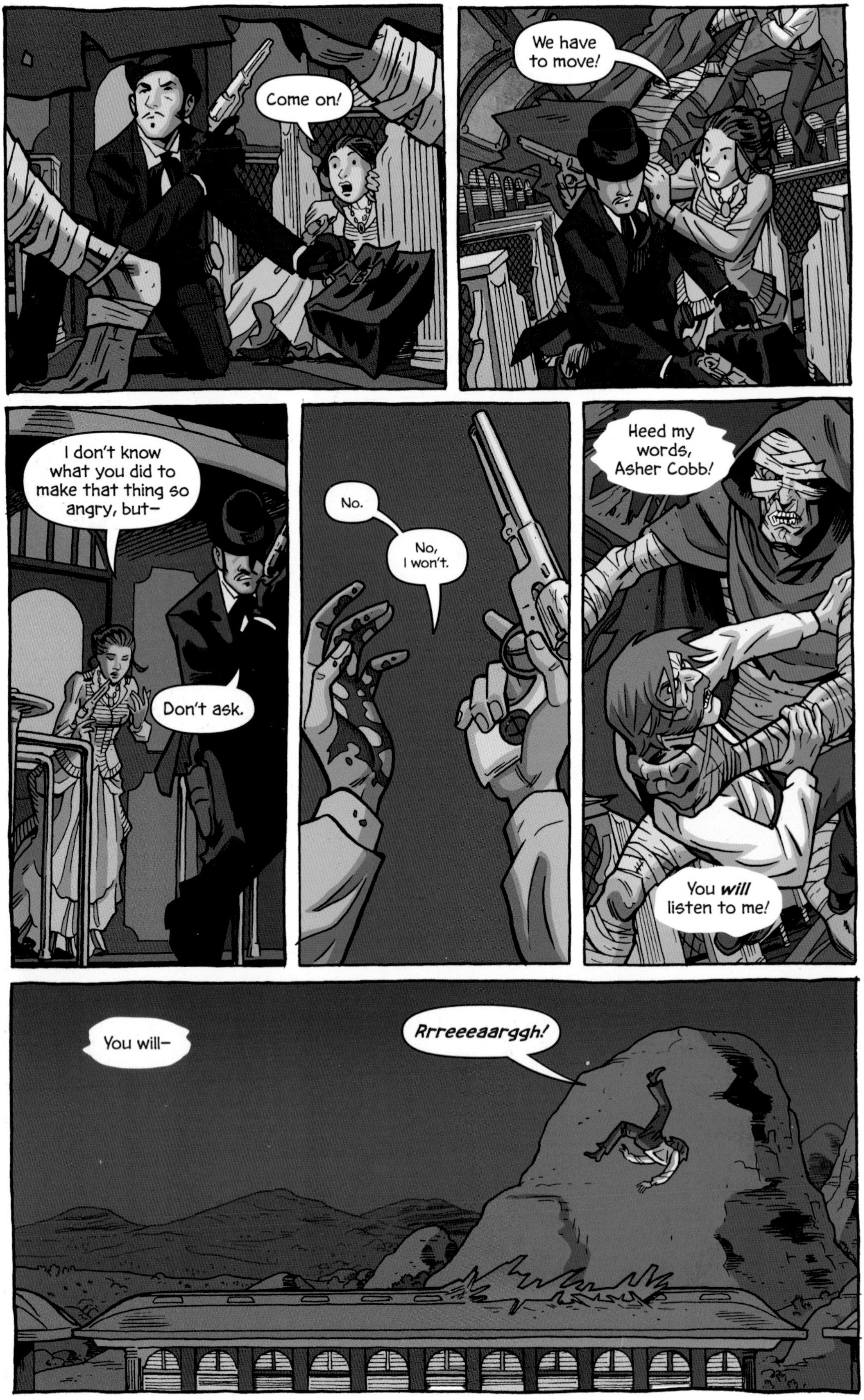
Come on!
We have to move!
I don't know what you did to make that thing so angry, but–
Don't ask.
No.
No, I won't.
Heed my words, Asher Cobb!
You *will* listen to me!
You will–
Rrreeeaarggh!

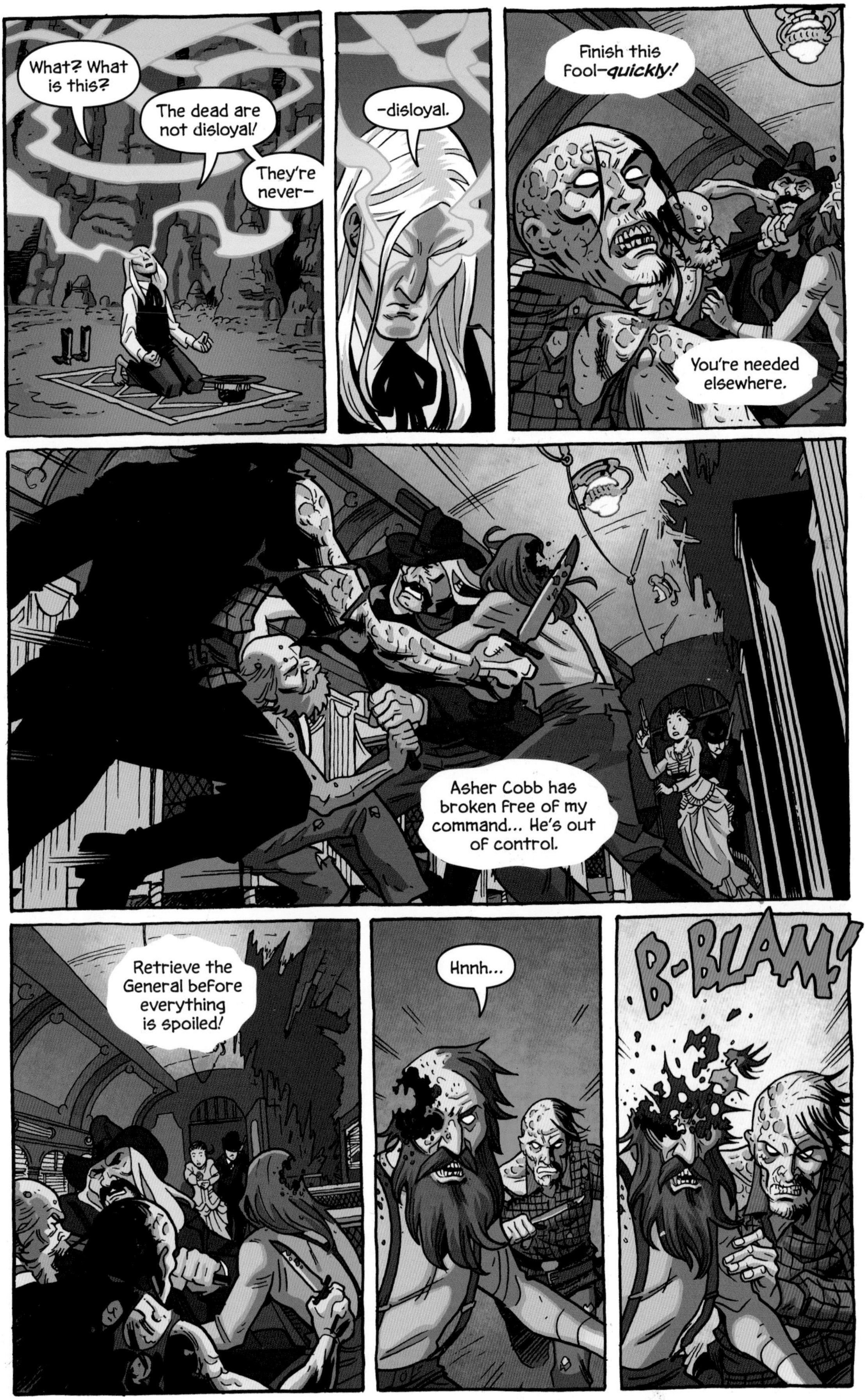
What? What is this?
The dead are not disloyal!
They're never-
-disloyal.
Finish this fool-*quickly!*
You're needed elsewhere.
Asher Cobb has broken free of my command... He's out of control.
Retrieve the General before everything is spoiled!
Hnnh...
B-BLAM!

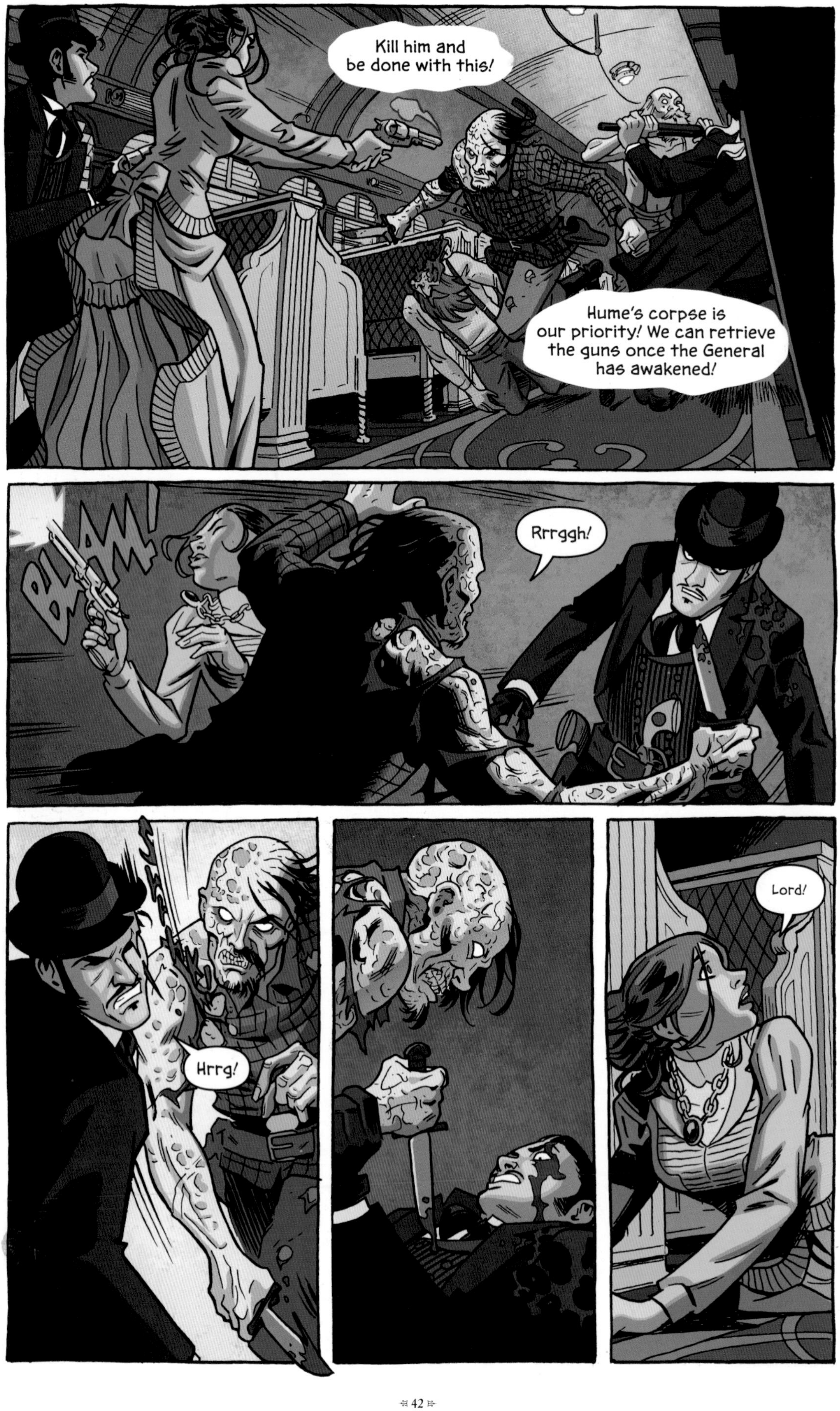
Kill him and
be done with this!
Hume's corpse is
our priority! We can retrieve
the guns once the General
has awakened!
BLAM!
Rrrggh!
Hrrg!
Lord!

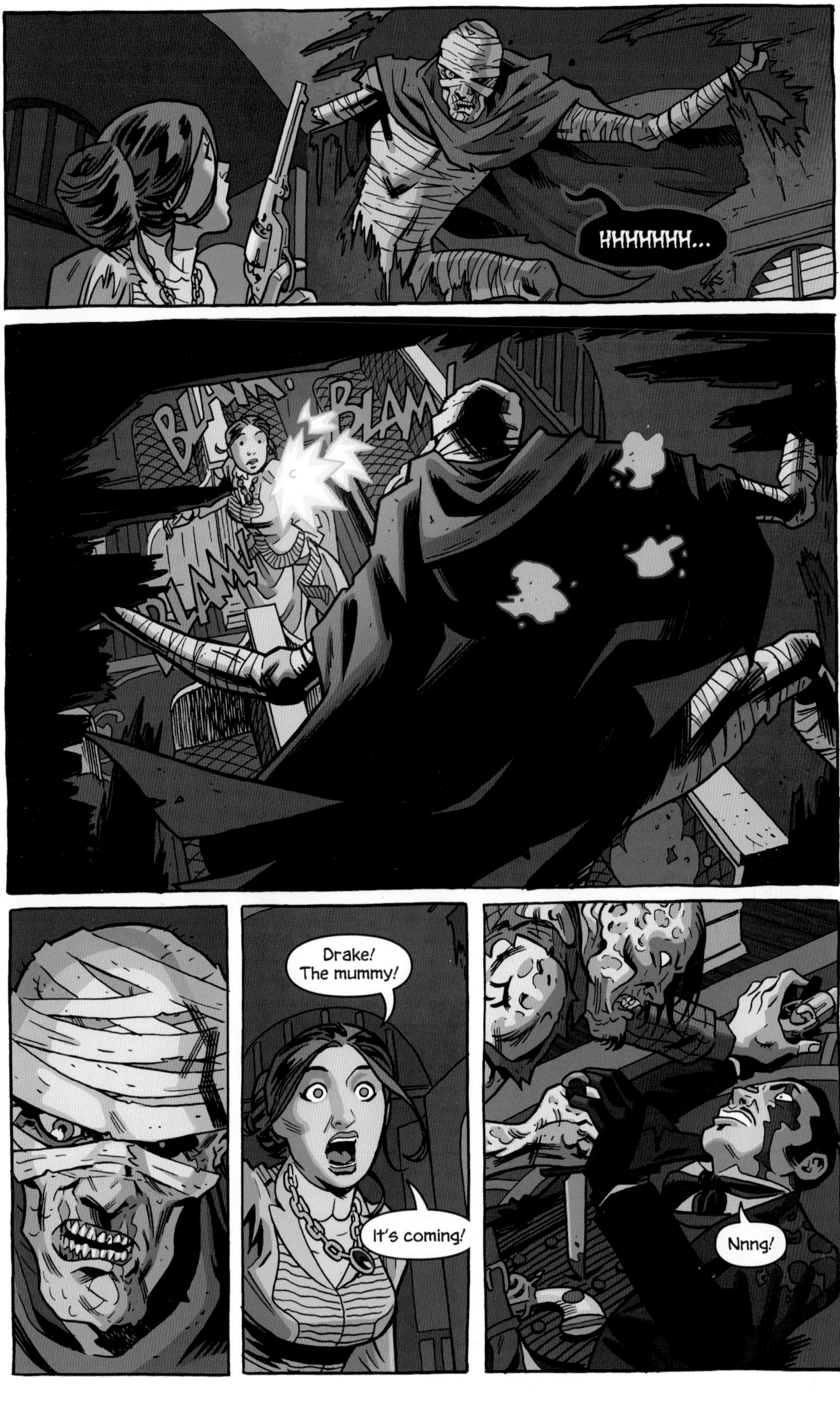
HHHHHHH...
BLAM! BLAM! BLAM!
Drake! The mummy!
It's coming!
Nnng!

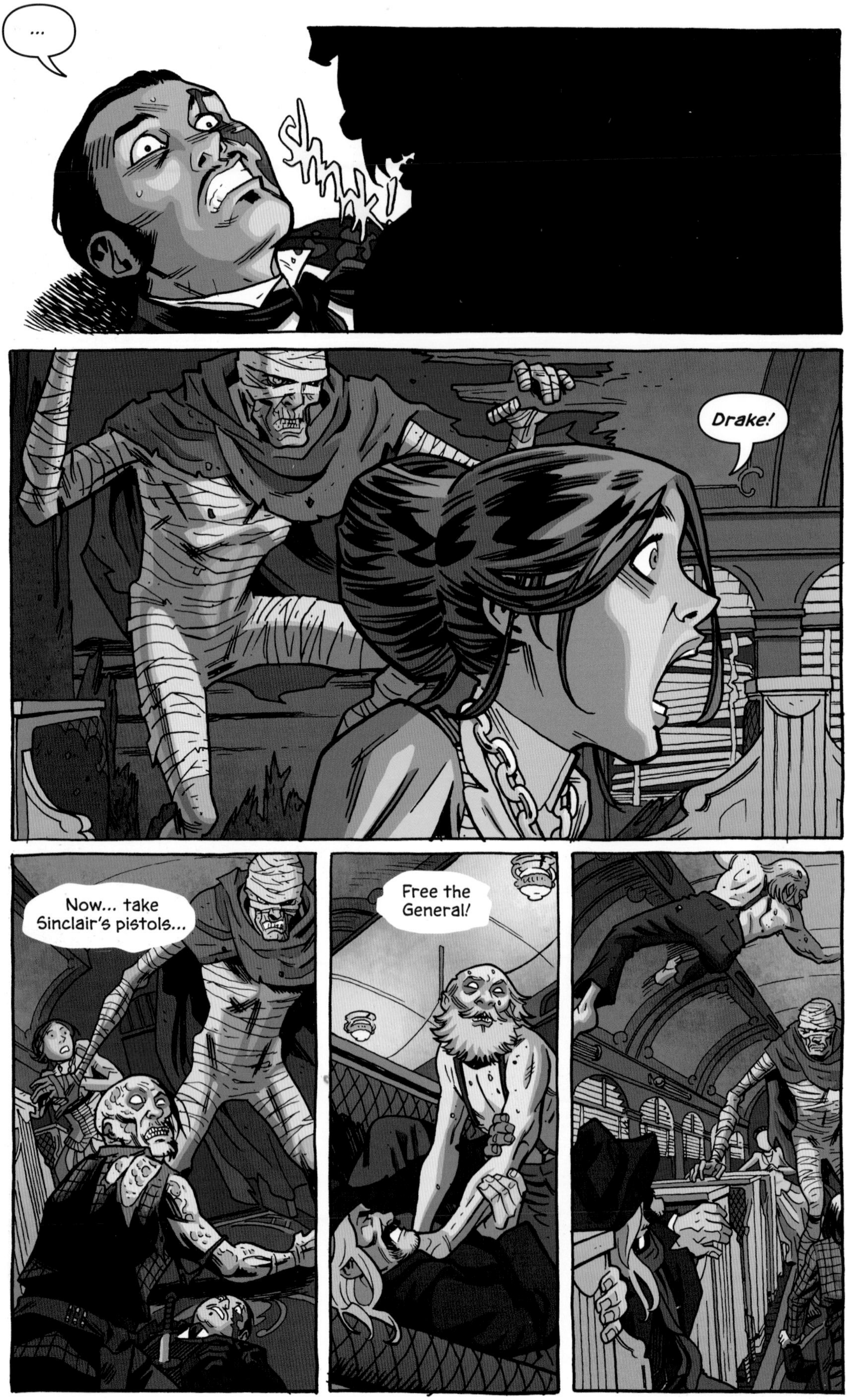
...
SHNNK!
Drake!
Now... take Sinclair's pistols...
Free the General!

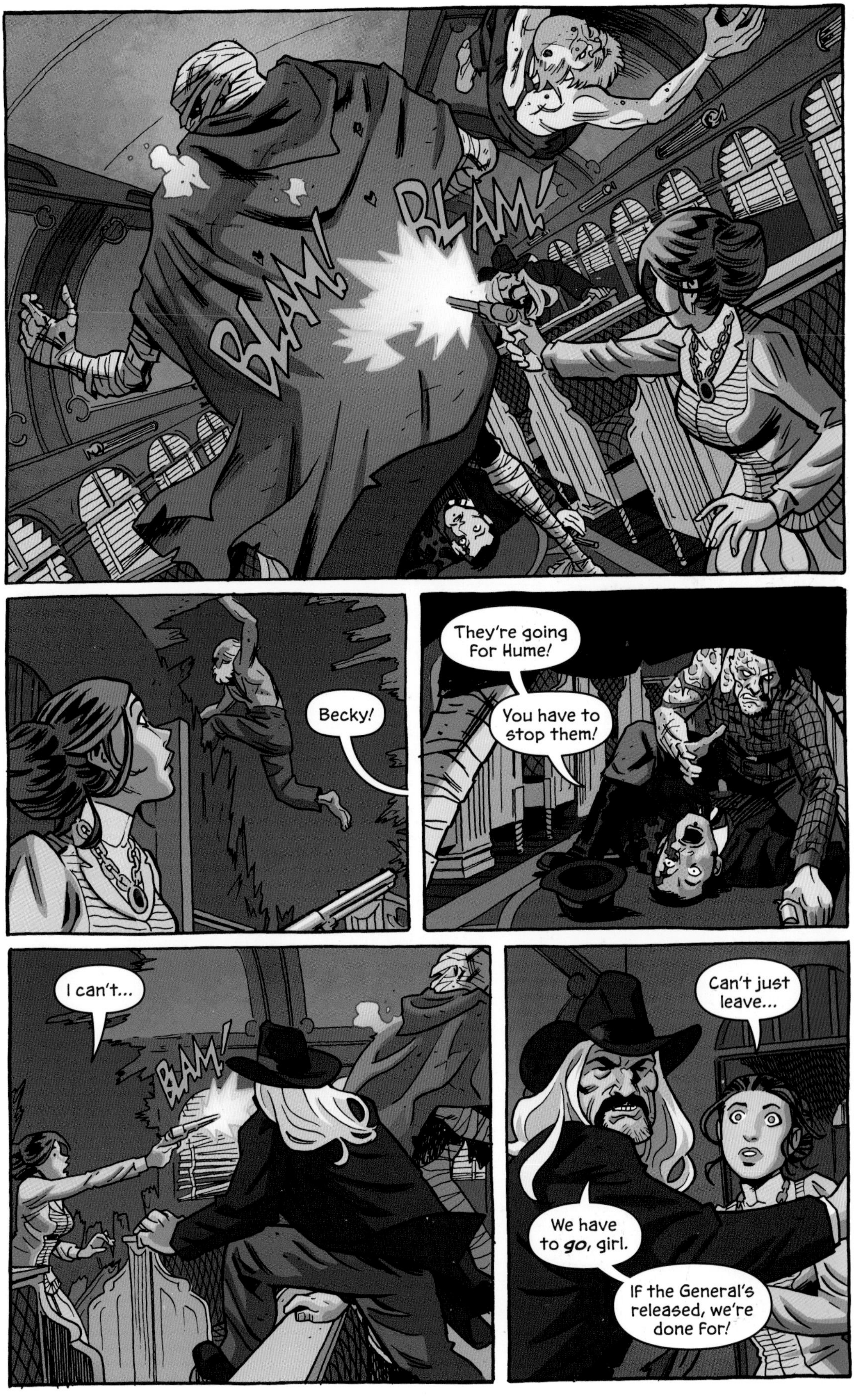
BLAM!
BLAM!
Becky!
They're going for Hume!
You have to stop them!
I can't...
BLAM!
Can't just leave...
We have to go, girl.
If the General's released, we're done for!

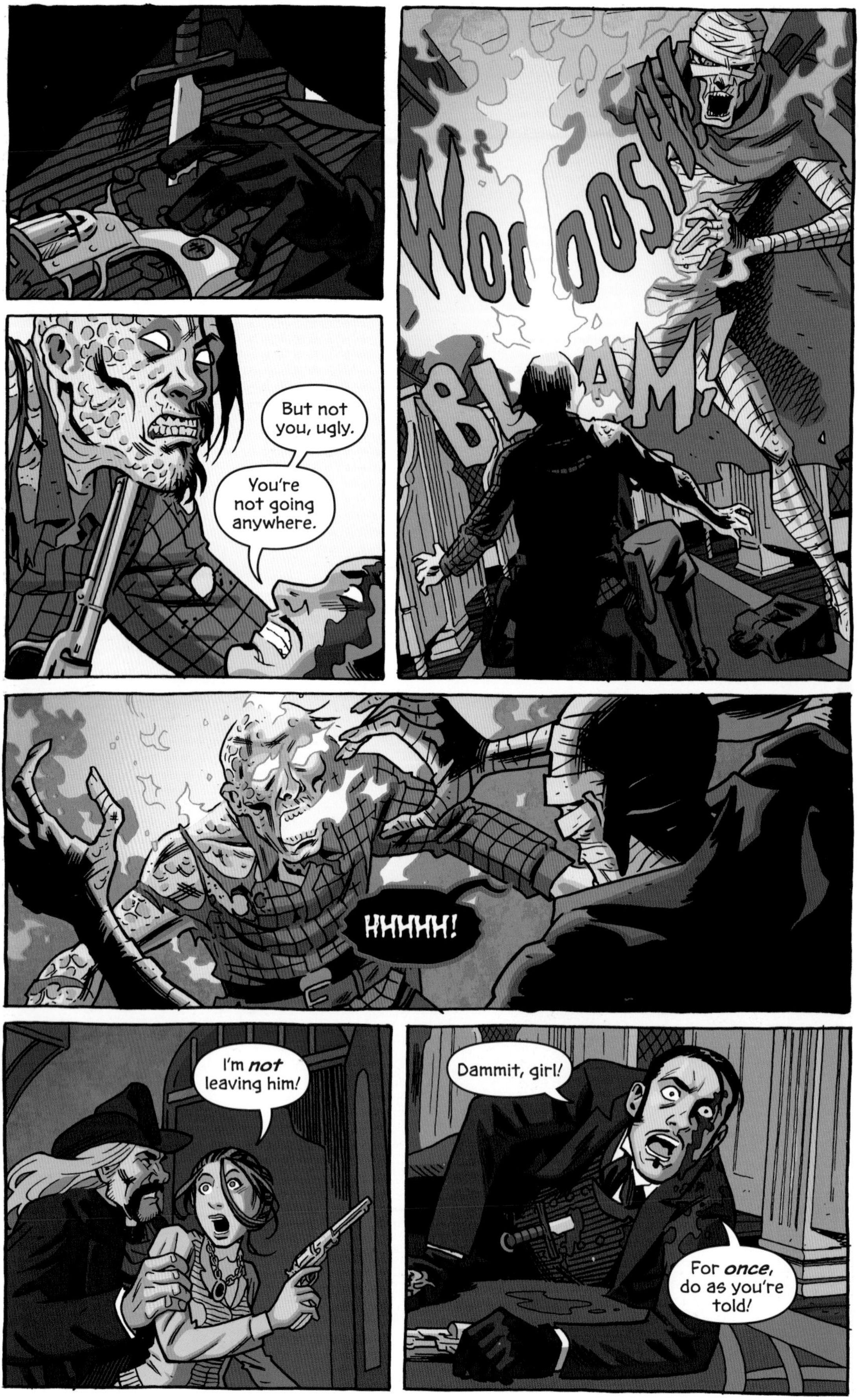
WOOOOSH!
BLAM!
But not you, ugly.
You're not going anywhere.
HHHHH!
I'm *not* leaving him!
Dammit, girl!
For *once*, do as you're told!

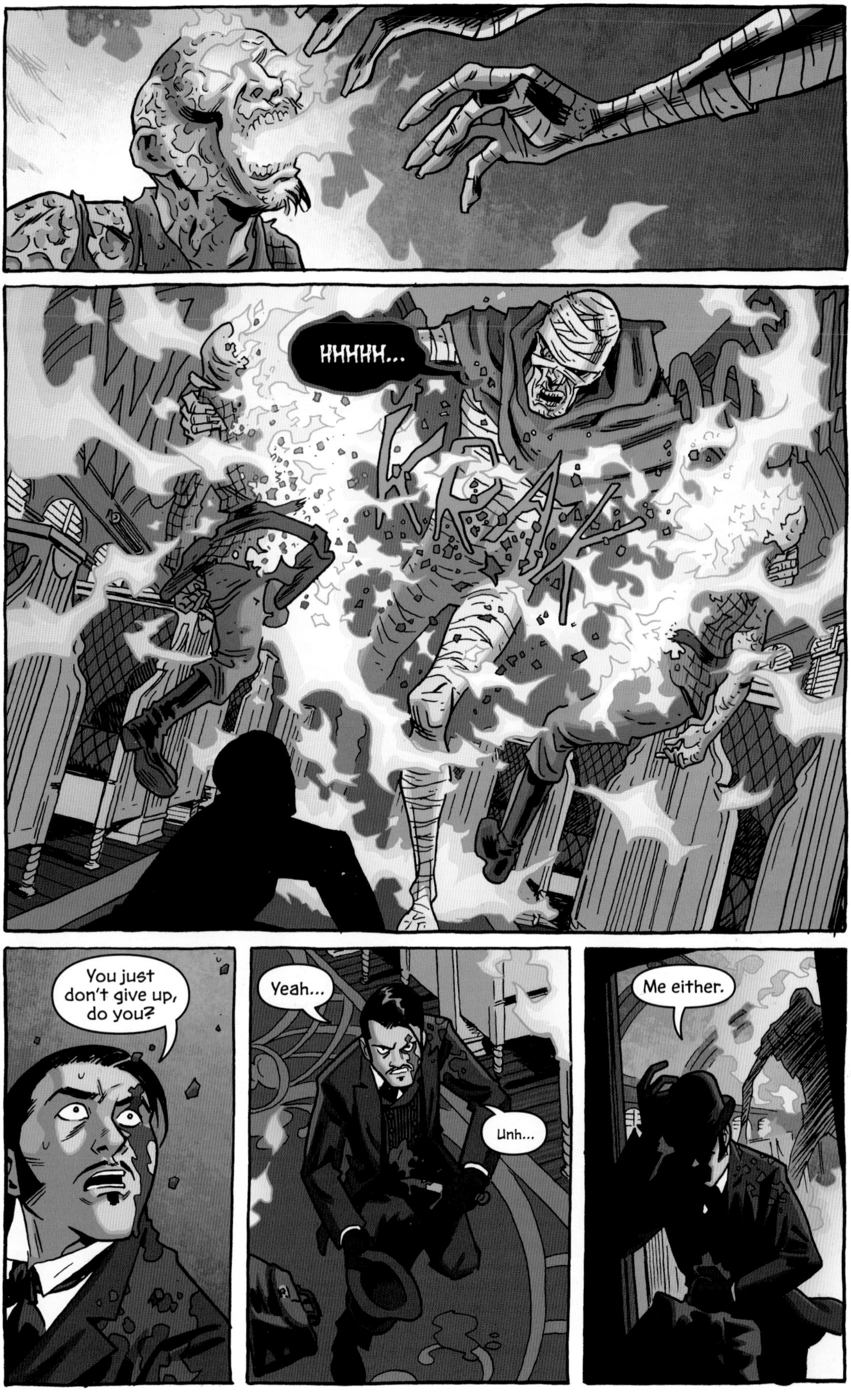
HHHHH...
KRAK
You just don't give up, do you?
Yeah...
Unh...
Me either.

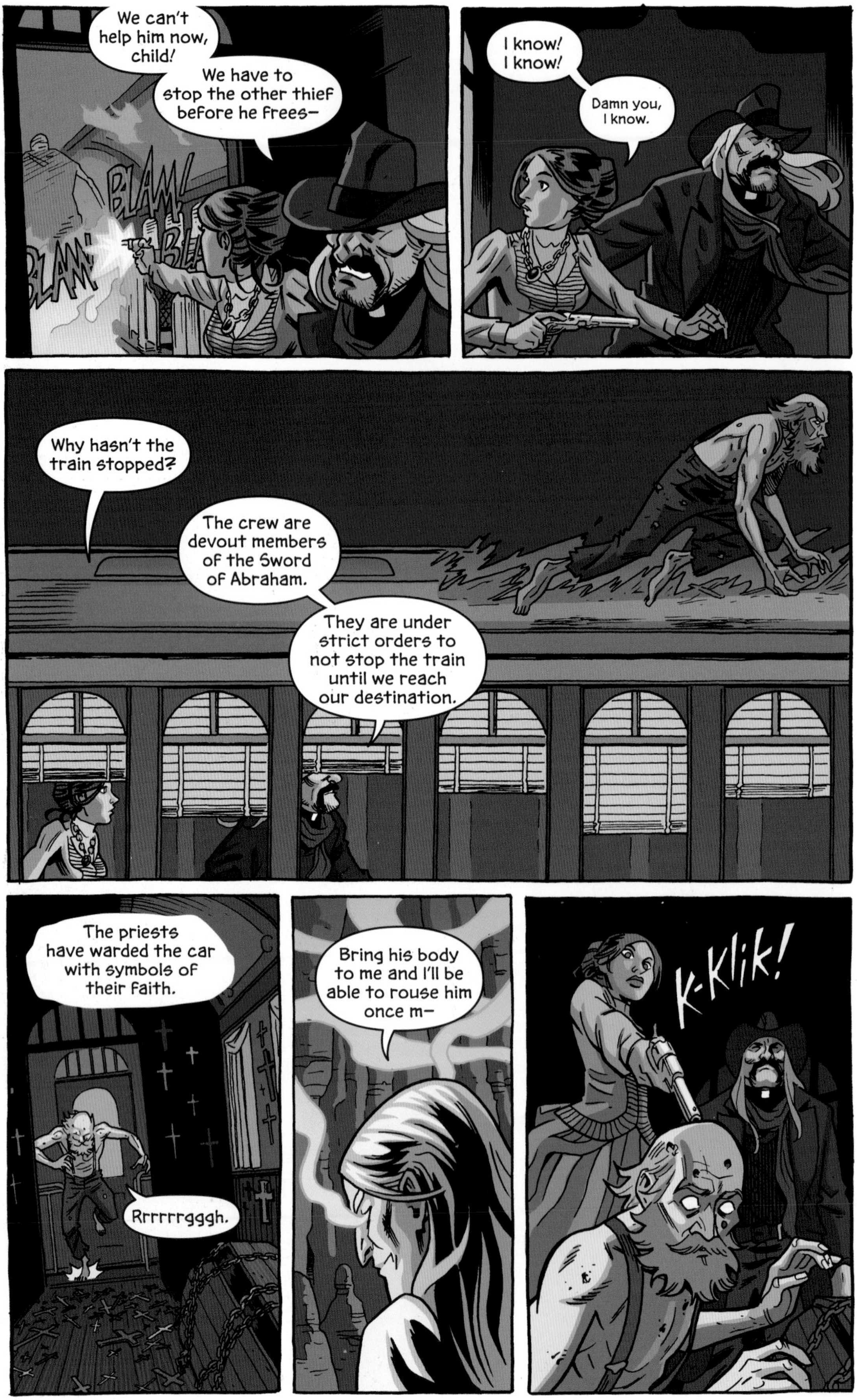
We can't help him now, child!
We have to stop the other thief before he frees–
BLAM!
BLAM!
I know! I know!
Damn you, I know.
Why hasn't the train stopped?
The crew are devout members of the Sword of Abraham.
They are under strict orders to not stop the train until we reach our destination.
The priests have warded the car with symbols of their faith.
Rrrrrrgggh.
Bring his body to me and I'll be able to rouse him once m–
K-Klik!

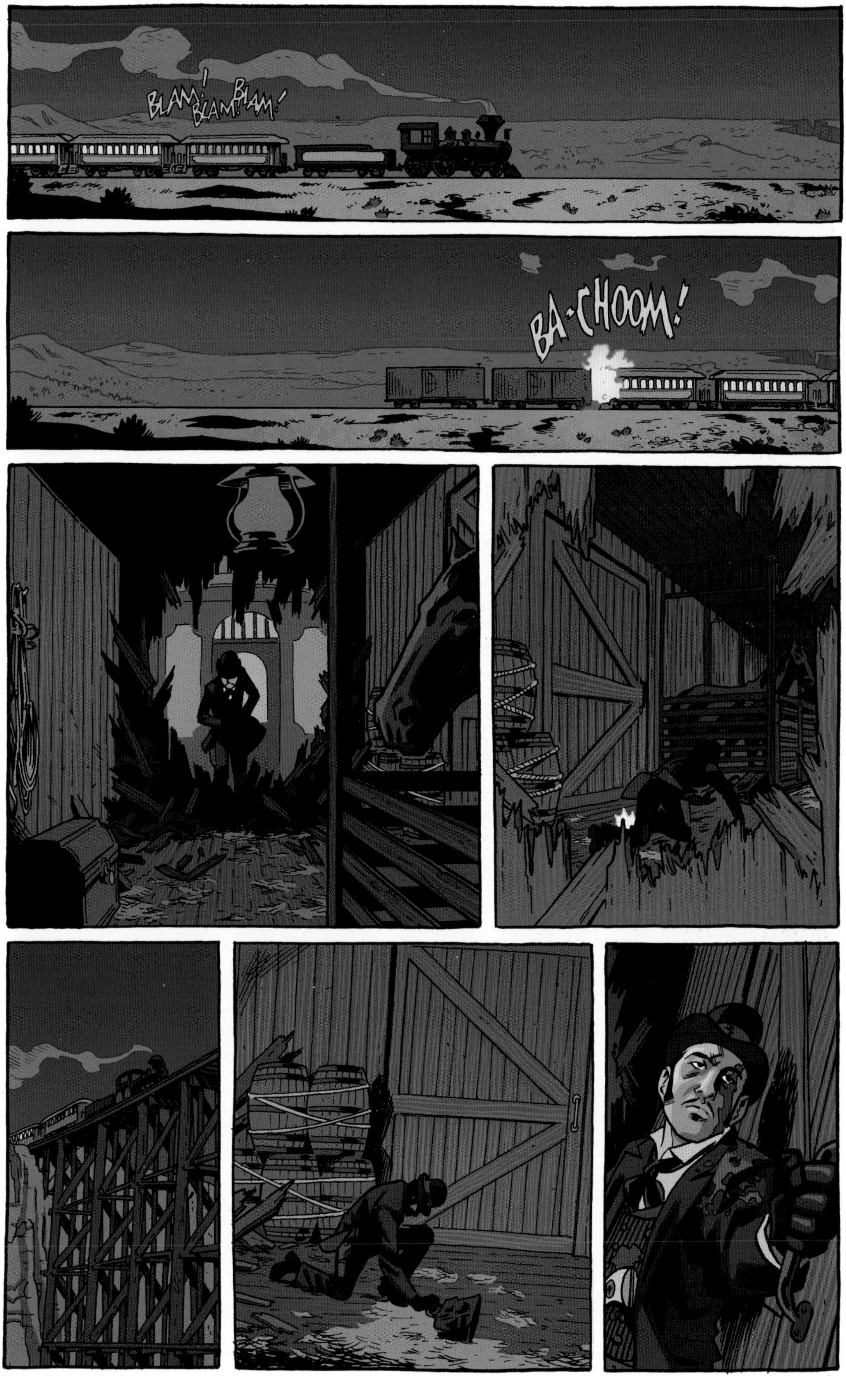
BLAM! BLAM! BLAM!
BA-CHOOM!

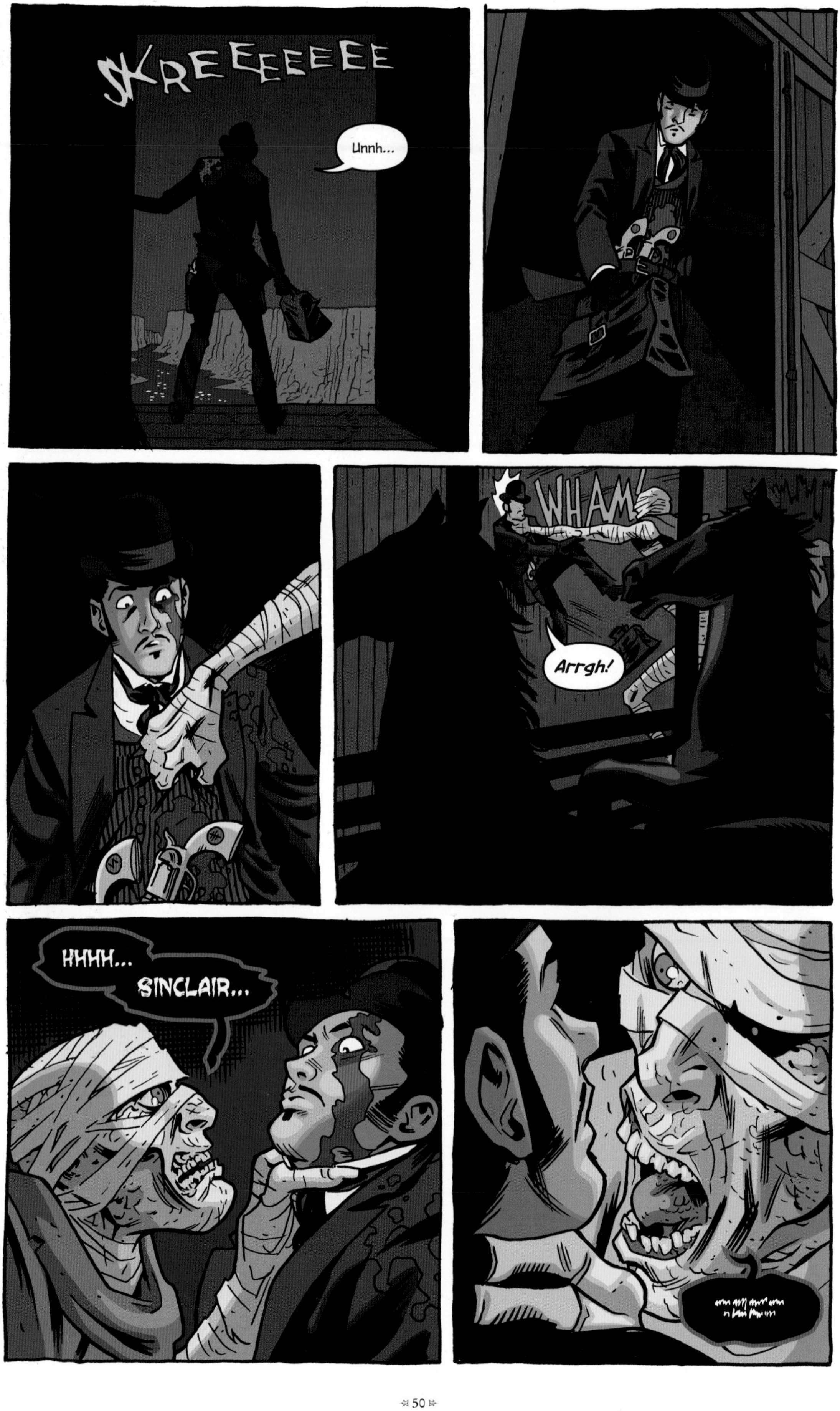
SKREEEEEEEE
Unnh...
WHAM!
Arrgh!
HHHH...
SINCLAIR...

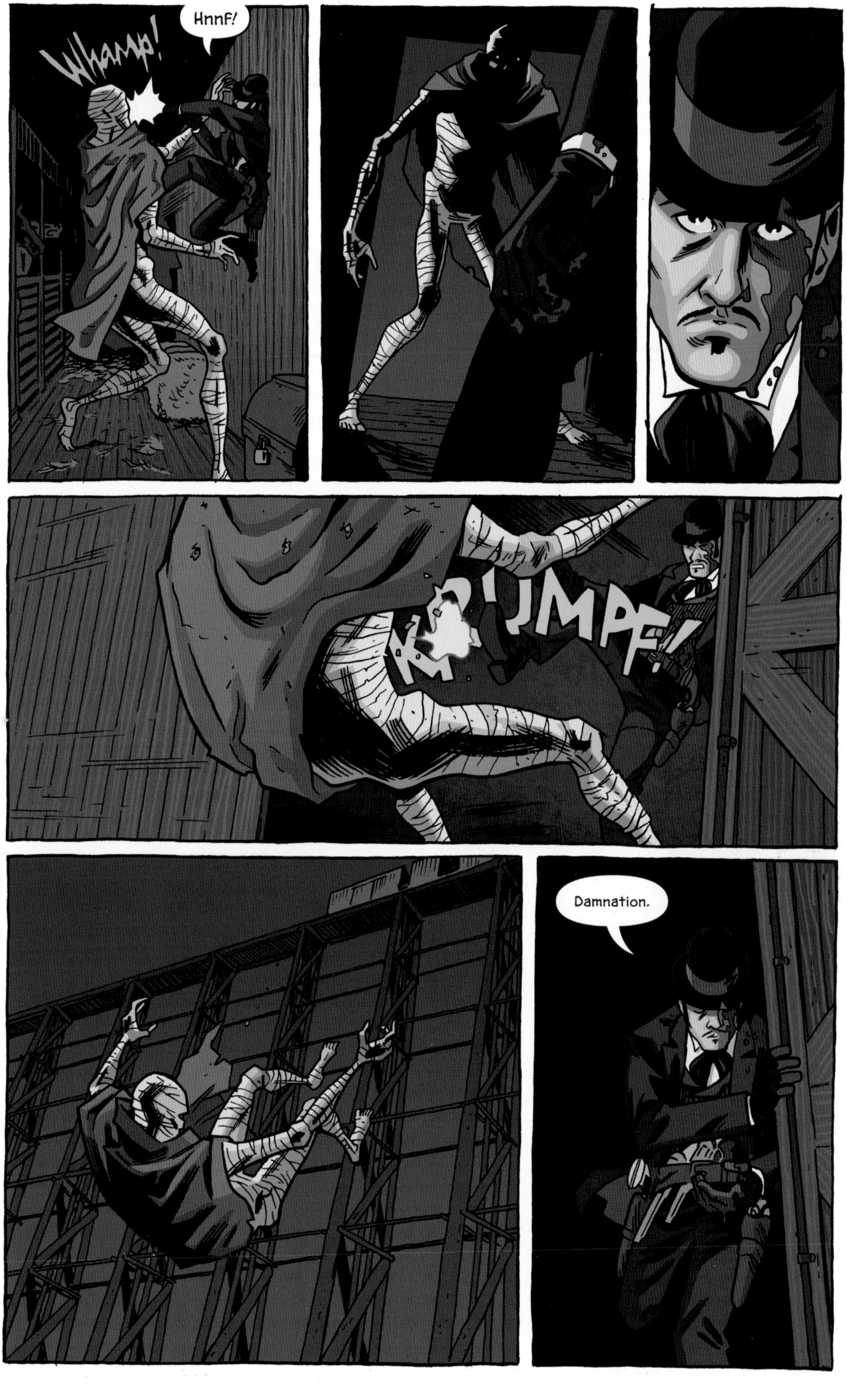
Whamp!
Hnnf!
KRUMPF!
Damnation.

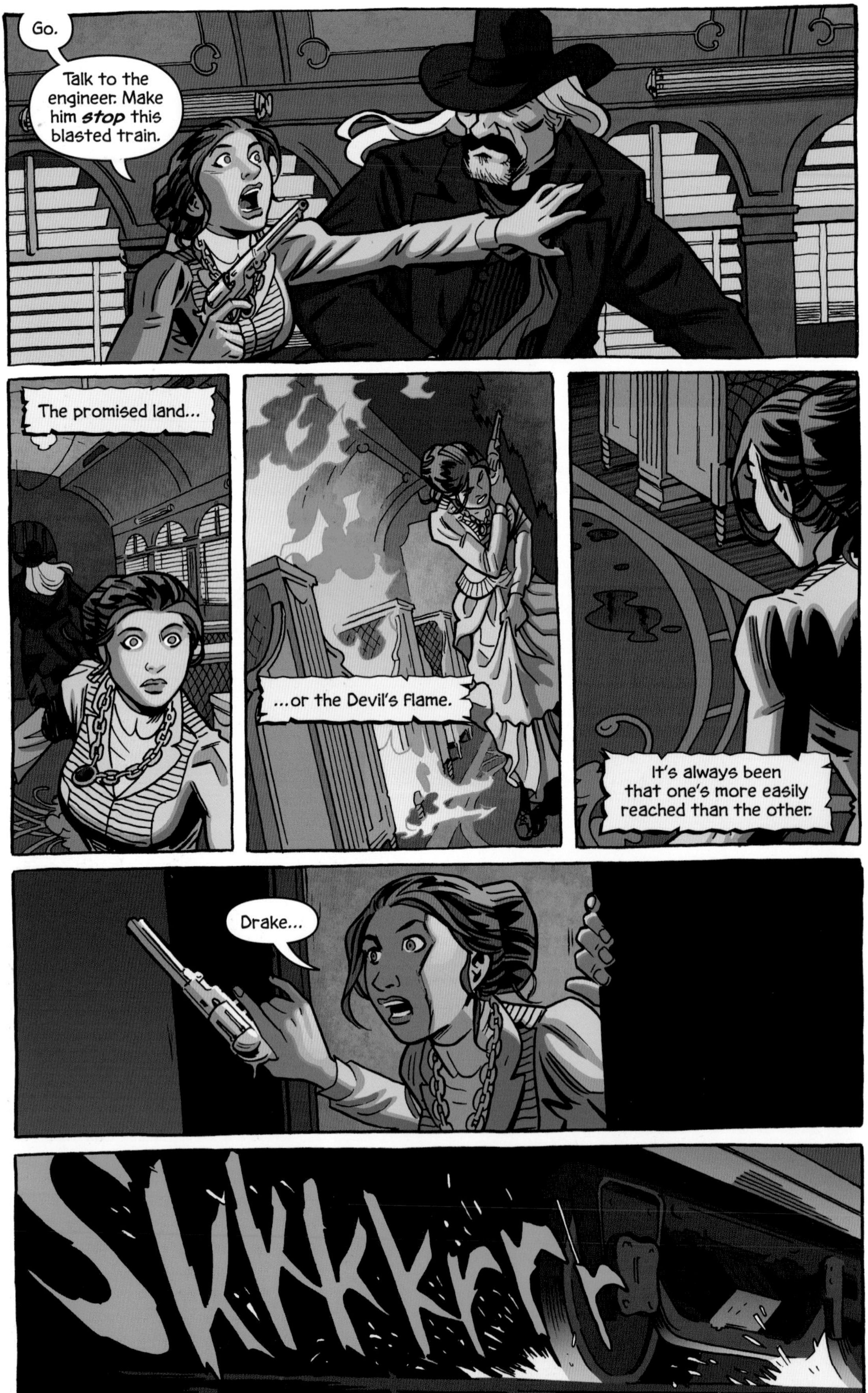
Go.
Talk to the engineer. Make him *stop* this blasted train.
The promised land...
...or the Devil's Flame.
It's always been that one's more easily reached than the other.
Drake...
SKKKrrr

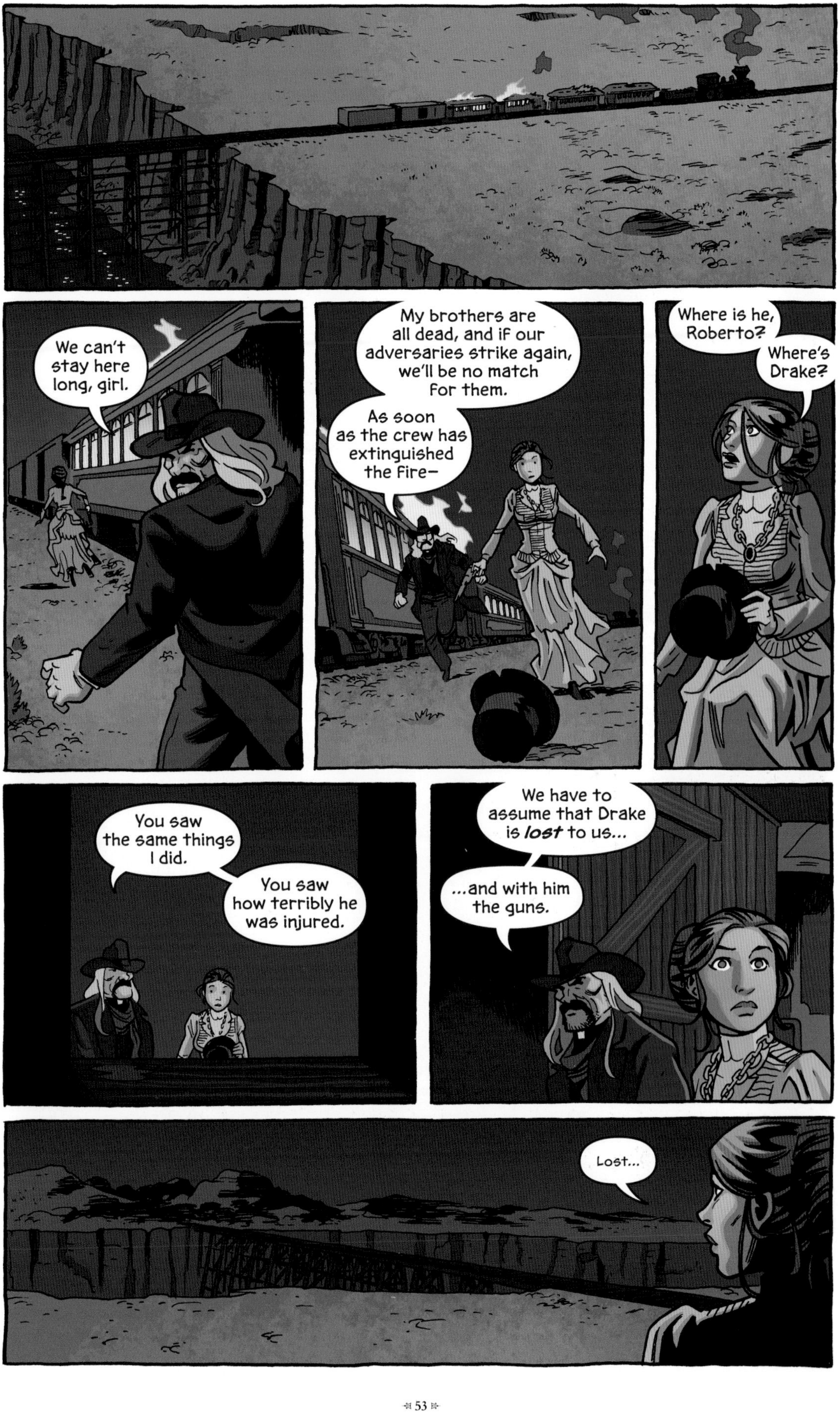
We can't stay here long, girl.
My brothers are all dead, and if our adversaries strike again, we'll be no match for them.
As soon as the crew has extinguished the fire—
Where is he, Roberto?
Where's Drake?
You saw the same things I did.
You saw how terribly he was injured.
We have to assume that Drake is *lost* to us...
...and with him the guns.
Lost...

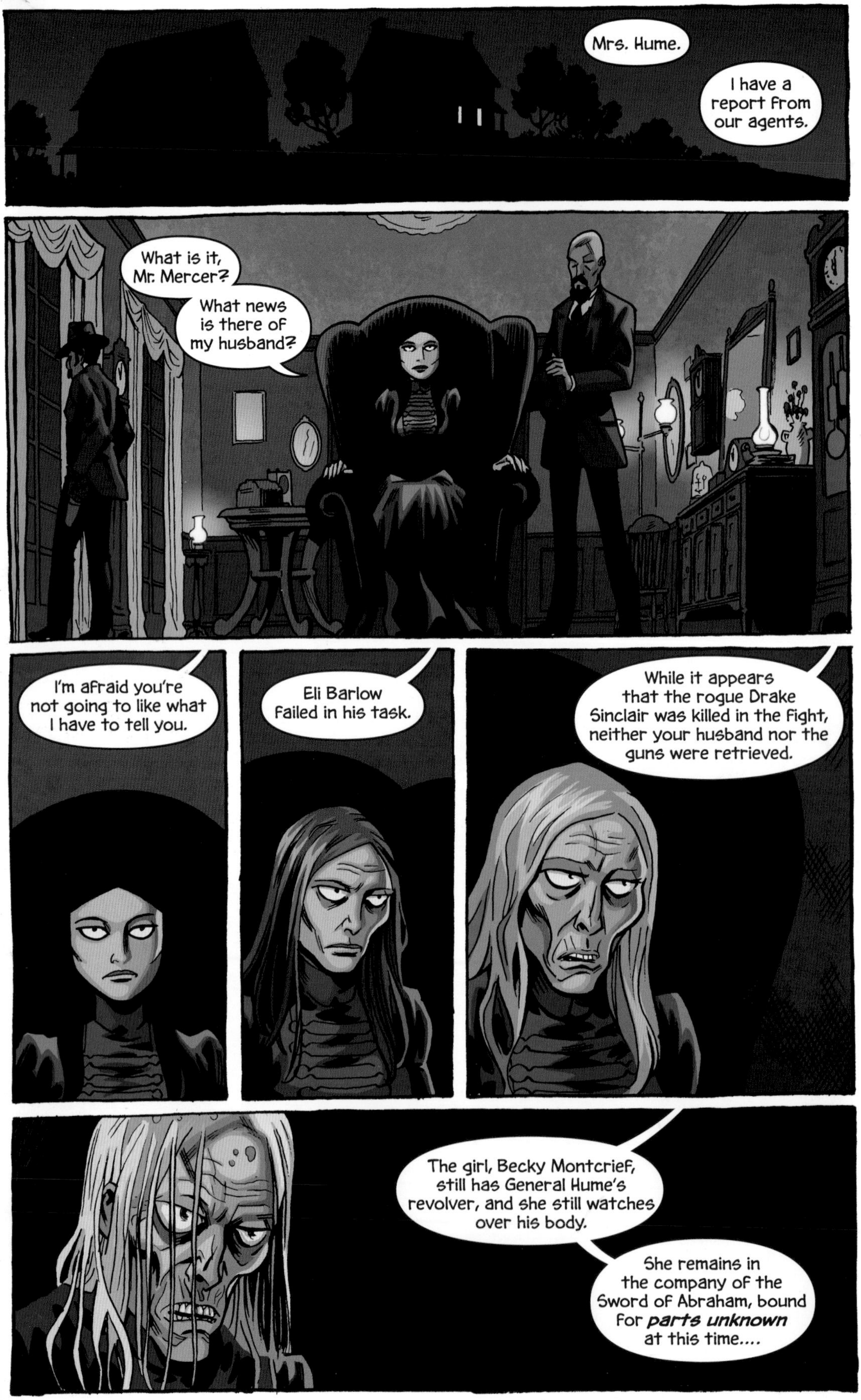
Mrs. Hume.
I have a report from our agents.
What is it, Mr. Mercer?
What news is there of my husband?
I'm afraid you're not going to like what I have to tell you.
Eli Barlow failed in his task.
While it appears that the rogue Drake Sinclair was killed in the fight, neither your husband nor the guns were retrieved.
The girl, Becky Montcrief, still has General Hume's revolver, and she still watches over his body.
She remains in the company of the Sword of Abraham, bound for *parts unknown* at this time....

CHAPTER
THREE

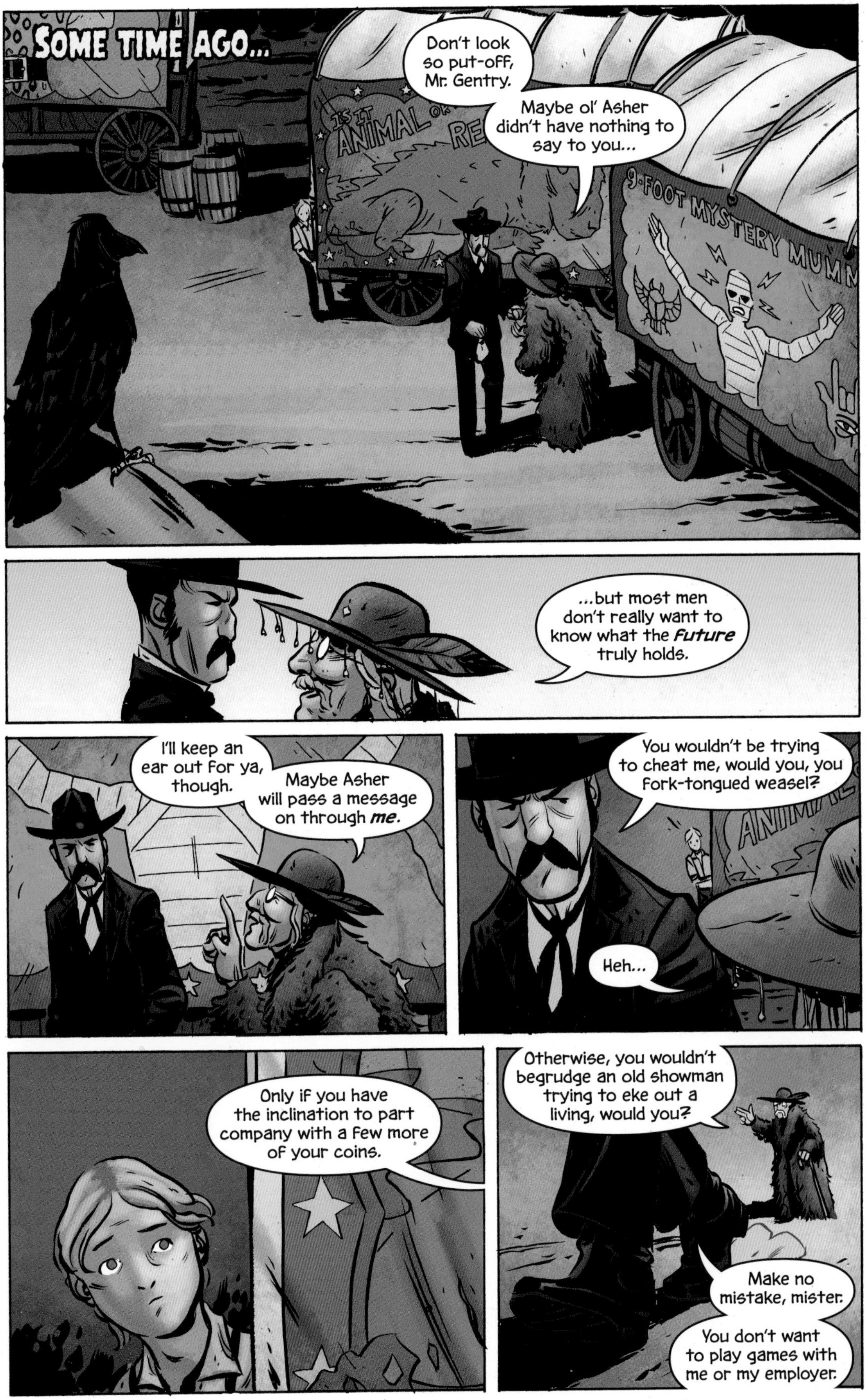
SOME TIME AGO...
Don't look so put-off, Mr. Gentry.
Maybe ol' Asher didn't have nothing to say to you...
...but most men don't really want to know what the *Future* truly holds.
I'll keep an ear out for ya, though.
Maybe Asher will pass a message on through *me.*
You wouldn't be trying to cheat me, would you, you fork-tongued weasel?
Heh...
Only if you have the inclination to part company with a few more of your coins.
Otherwise, you wouldn't begrudge an old showman trying to eke out a living, would you?
Make no mistake, mister.
You don't want to play games with me or my employer.

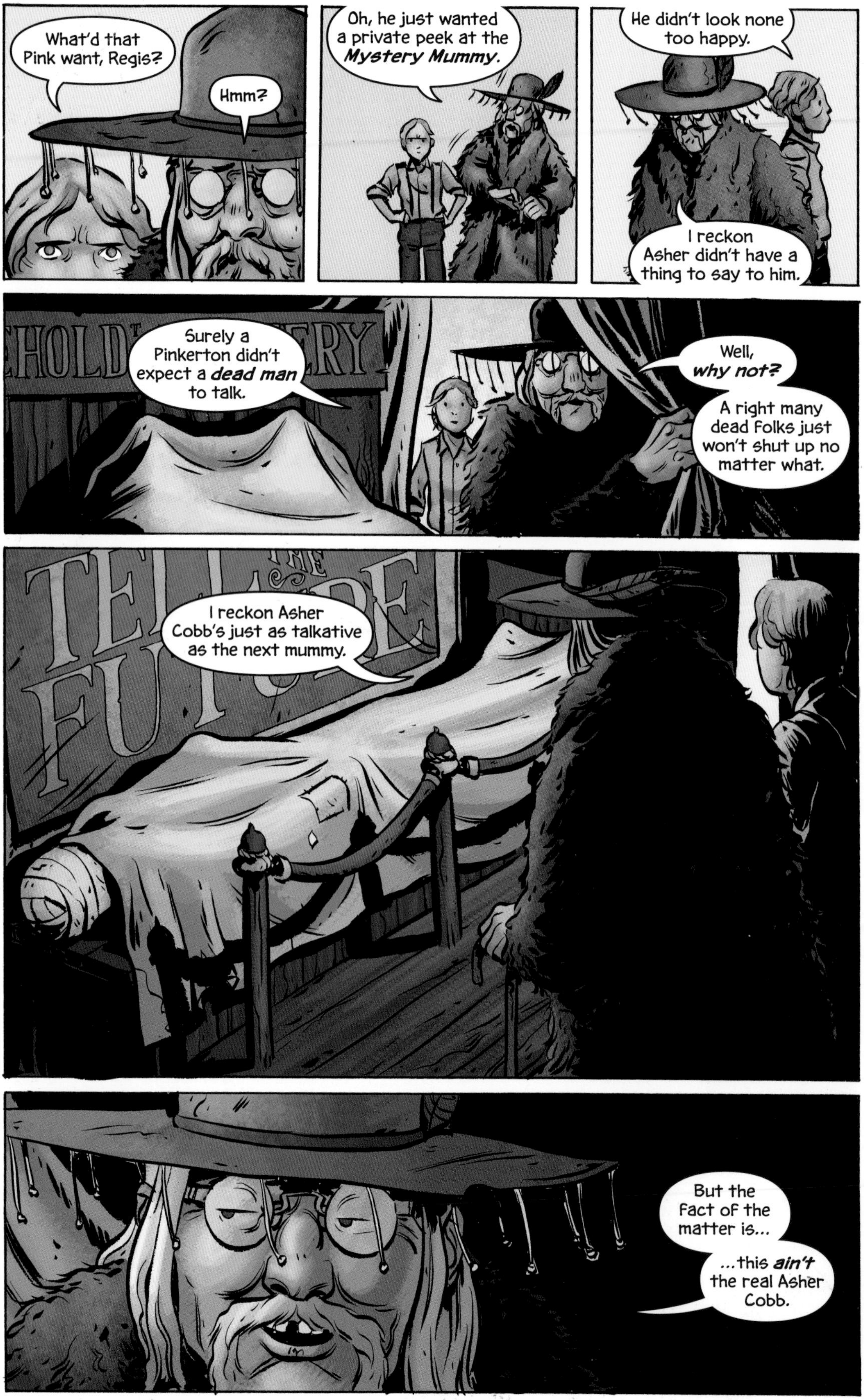
What'd that Pink want, Regis?
Hmm?
Oh, he just wanted a private peek at the *Mystery Mummy.*
He didn't look none too happy.
I reckon Asher didn't have a thing to say to him.
Surely a Pinkerton didn't expect a *dead man* to talk.
Well, *why not?*
A right many dead folks just won't shut up no matter what.
I reckon Asher Cobb's just as talkative as the next mummy.
But the fact of the matter is...
...this *ain't* the real Asher Cobb.

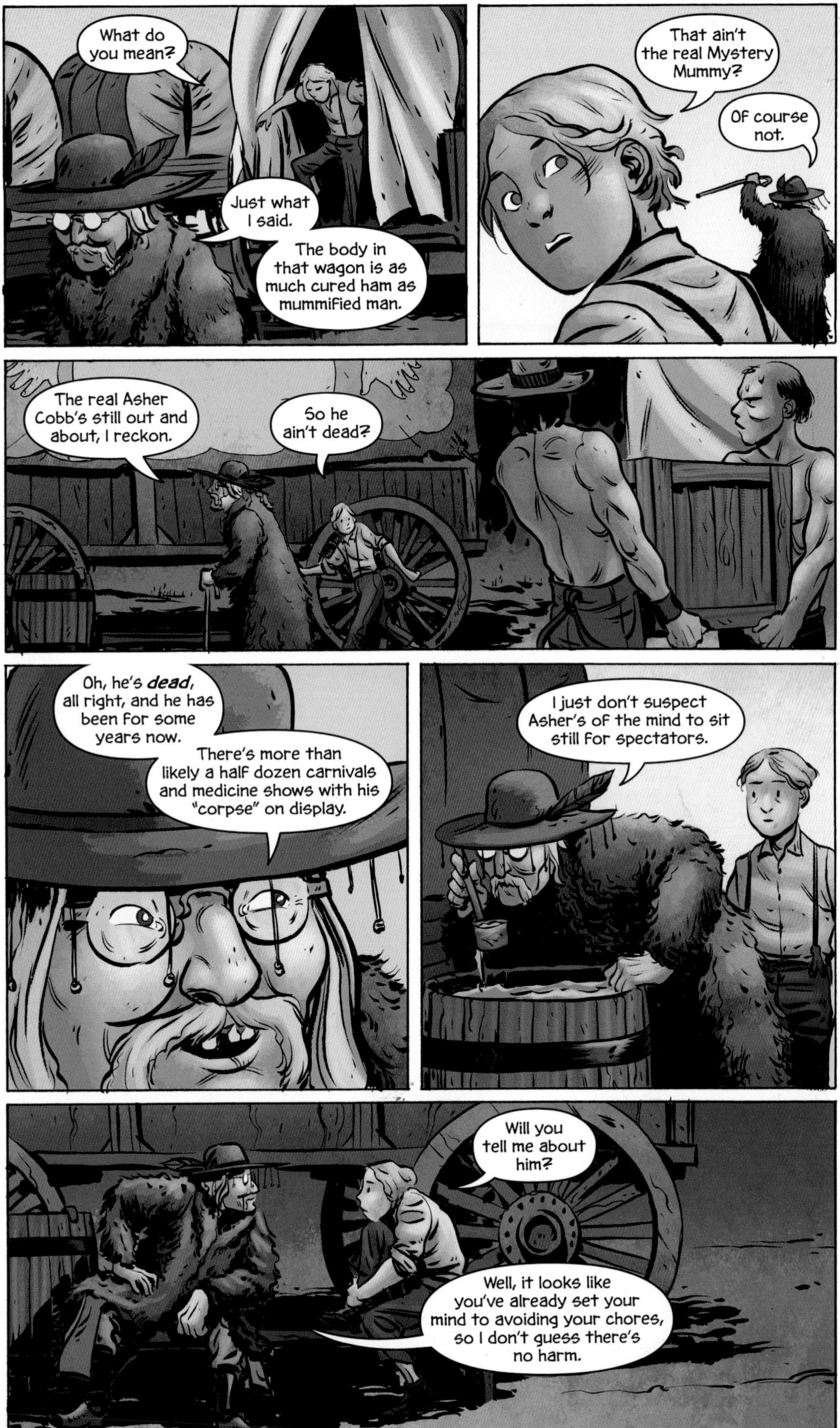
What do you mean?
Just what I said.
The body in that wagon is as much cured ham as mummified man.
That ain't the real Mystery Mummy?
Of course not.
The real Asher Cobb's still out and about, I reckon.
So he ain't dead?
Oh, he's *dead*, all right, and he has been for some years now.
There's more than likely a half dozen carnivals and medicine shows with his "corpse" on display.
I just don't suspect Asher's of the mind to sit still for spectators.
Will you tell me about him?
Well, it looks like you've already set your mind to avoiding your chores, so I don't guess there's no harm.

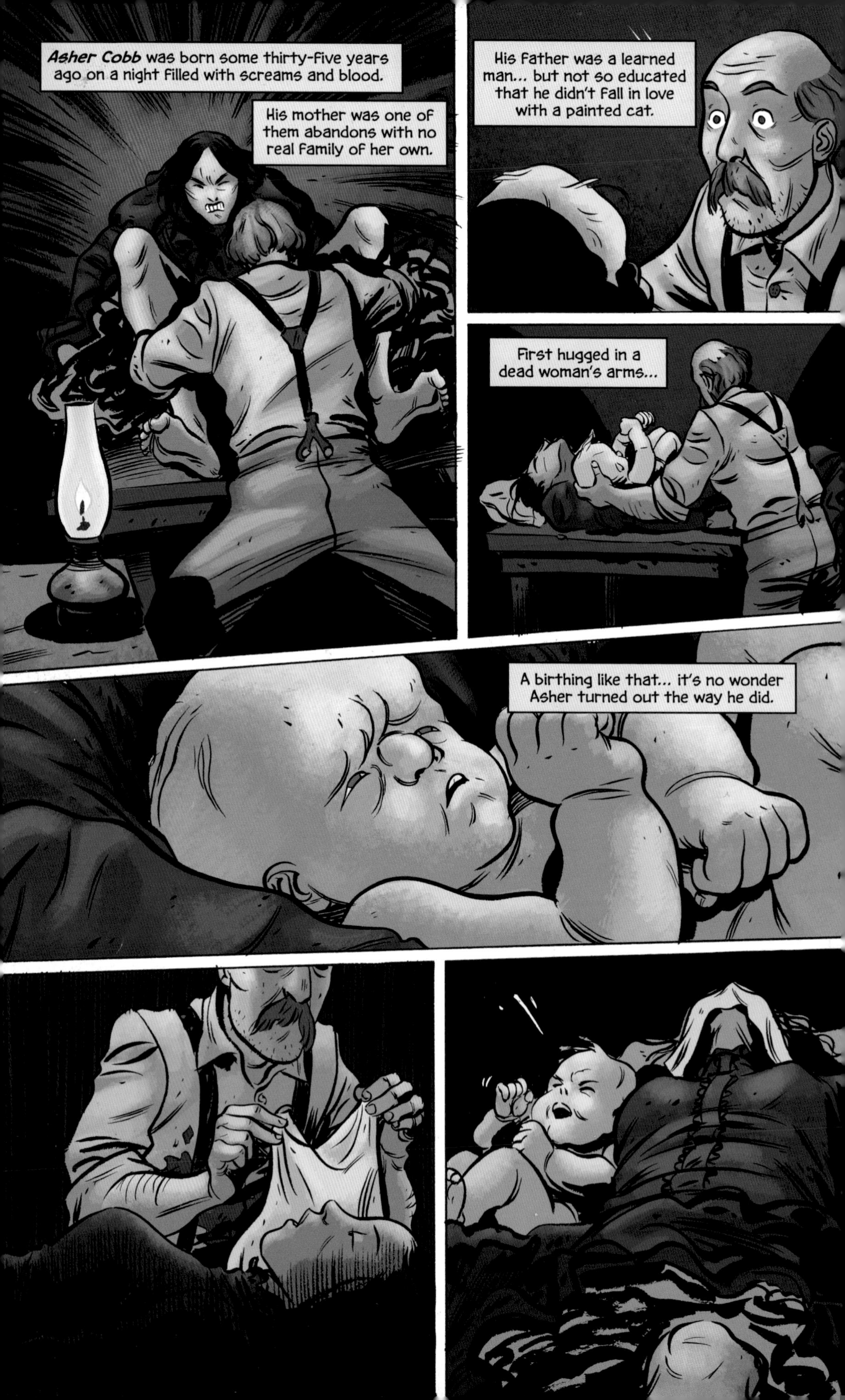
Asher Cobb was born some thirty-five years ago on a night filled with screams and blood.
His mother was one of them abandons with no real family of her own.
His father was a learned man... but not so educated that he didn't fall in love with a painted cat.
First hugged in a dead woman's arms...
A birthing like that... it's no wonder Asher turned out the way he did.

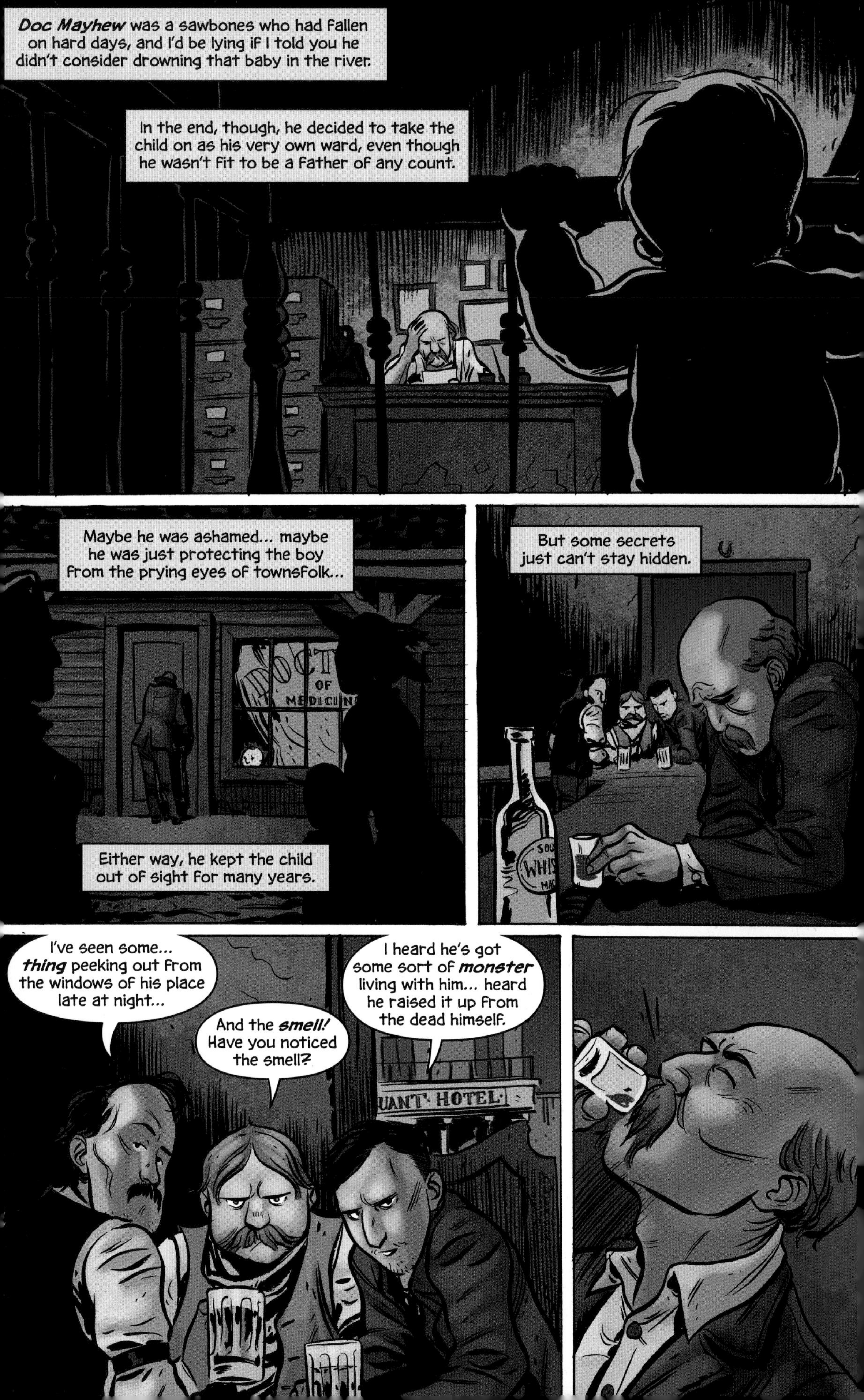

Doc Mayhew was a sawbones who had fallen on hard days, and I'd be lying if I told you he didn't consider drowning that baby in the river.
In the end, though, he decided to take the child on as his very own ward, even though he wasn't fit to be a father of any count.
Maybe he was ashamed... maybe he was just protecting the boy from the prying eyes of townsfolk...
OCT
OF
MEDICIN
Either way, he kept the child out of sight for many years.
But some secrets just can't stay hidden.
WHIS
I've seen some... thing peeking out from the windows of his place late at night...
And the smell! Have you noticed the smell?
I heard he's got some sort of monster living with him... heard he raised it up from the dead himself.
UANT HOTEL

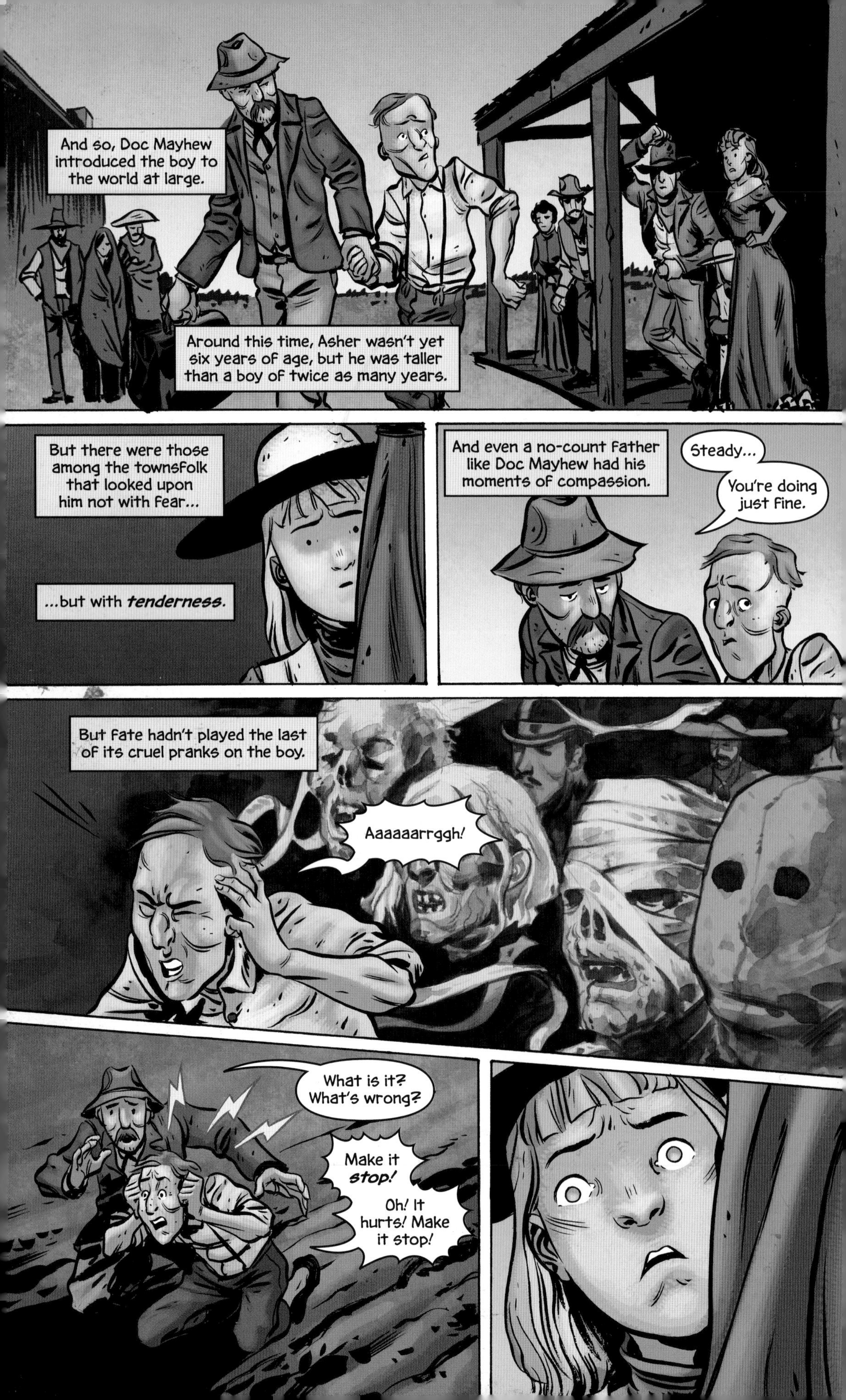
And so, Doc Mayhew introduced the boy to the world at large.
Around this time, Asher wasn't yet six years of age, but he was taller than a boy of twice as many years.
But there were those among the townsfolk that looked upon him not with fear...
...but with *tenderness.*
And even a no-count father like Doc Mayhew had his moments of compassion.
Steady...
You're doing just fine.
But fate hadn't played the last of its cruel pranks on the boy.
Aaaaaarrggh!
What is it? What's wrong?
Make it *stop!*
Oh! It hurts! Make it stop!

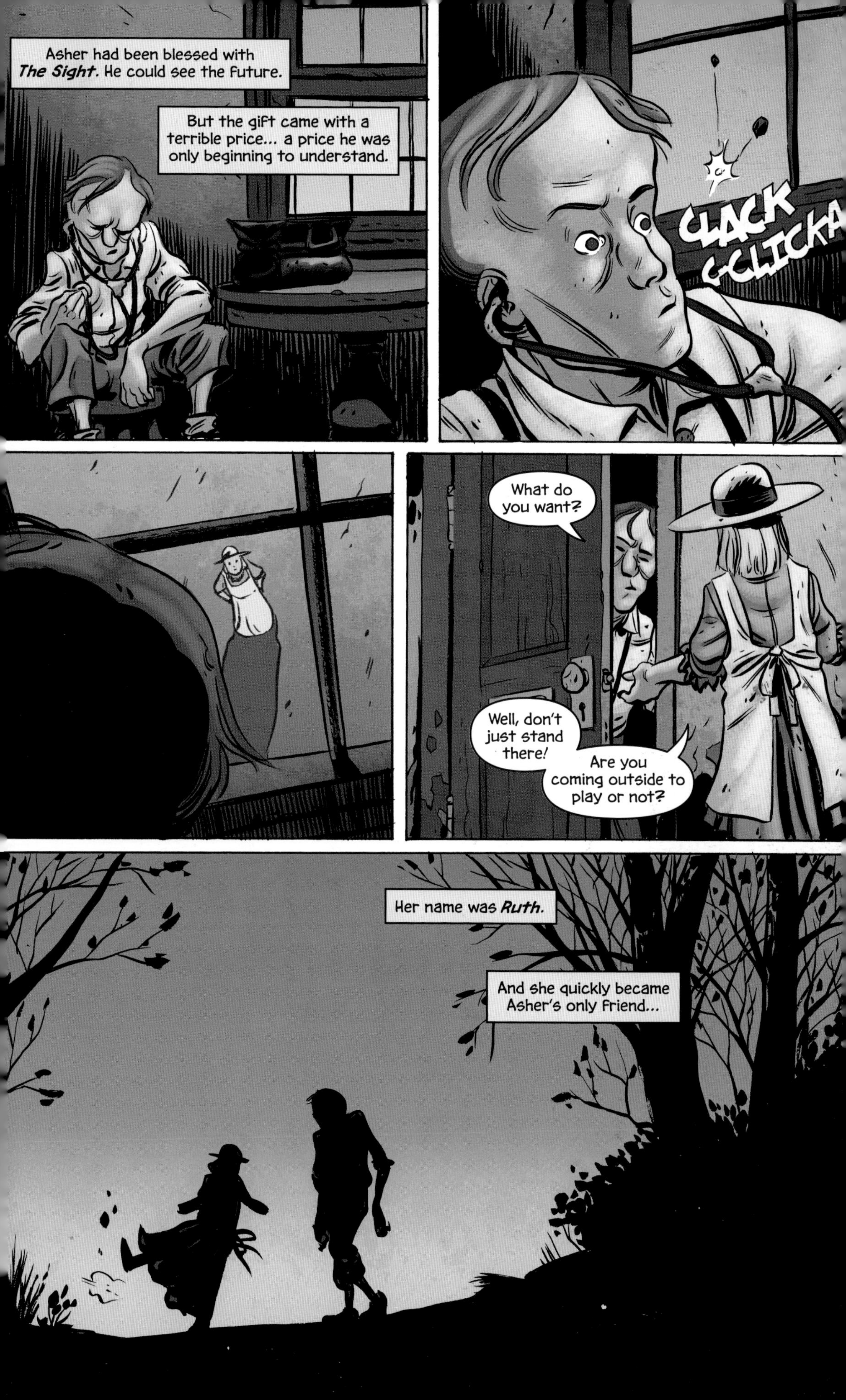
Asher had been blessed with *The Sight*. He could see the future.
But the gift came with a terrible price... a price he was only beginning to understand.
CLACK
C-CLICKA
What do you want?
Well, don't just stand there!
Are you coming outside to play or not?
Her name was *Ruth*.
And she quickly became Asher's only friend...

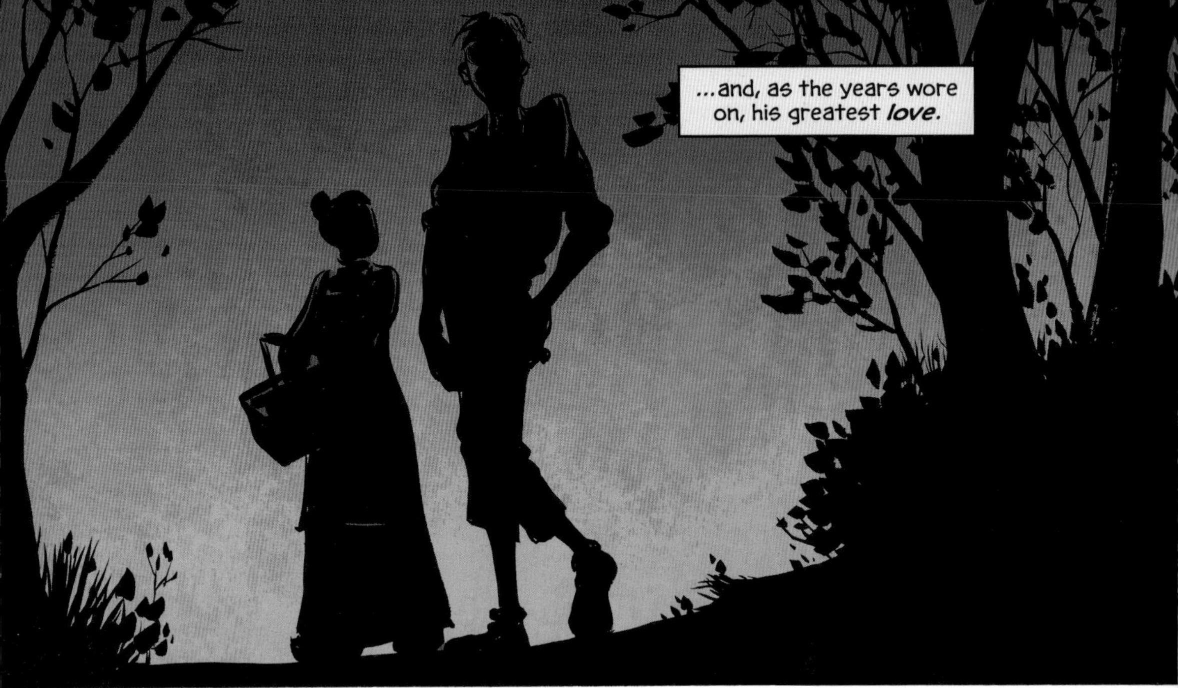
...and, as the years wore on, his greatest *love*.

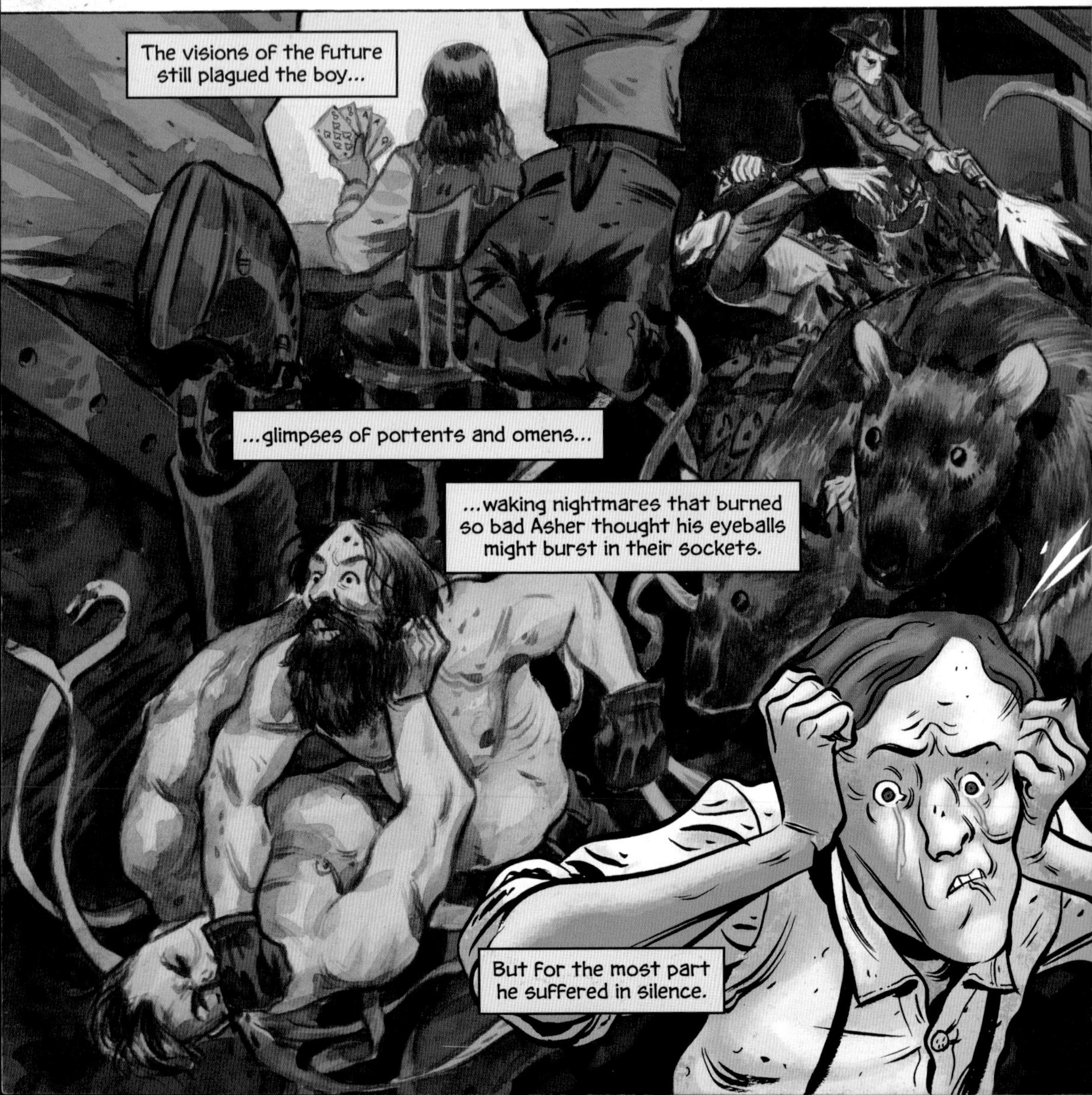
The visions of the future still plagued the boy...
...glimpses of portents and omens...
...waking nightmares that burned so bad Asher thought his eyeballs might burst in their sockets.
But for the most part he suffered in silence.

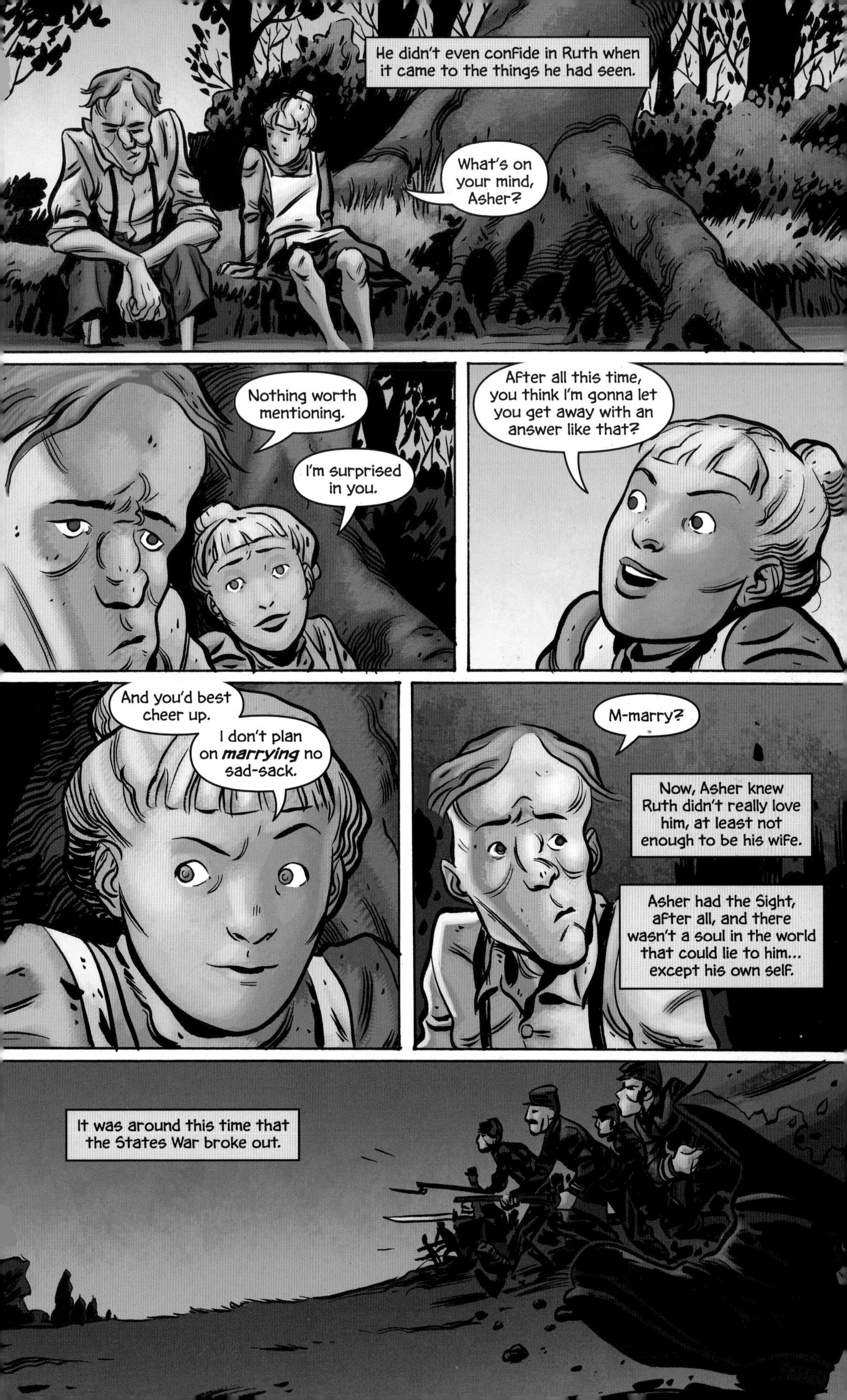
He didn't even confide in Ruth when it came to the things he had seen.
What's on your mind, Asher?
Nothing worth mentioning.
I'm surprised in you.
After all this time, you think I'm gonna let you get away with an answer like that?
And you'd best cheer up.
I don't plan on *marrying* no sad-sack.
M-marry?
Now, Asher knew Ruth didn't really love him, at least not enough to be his wife.
Asher had the Sight, after all, and there wasn't a soul in the world that could lie to him... except his own self.
It was around this time that the States War broke out.

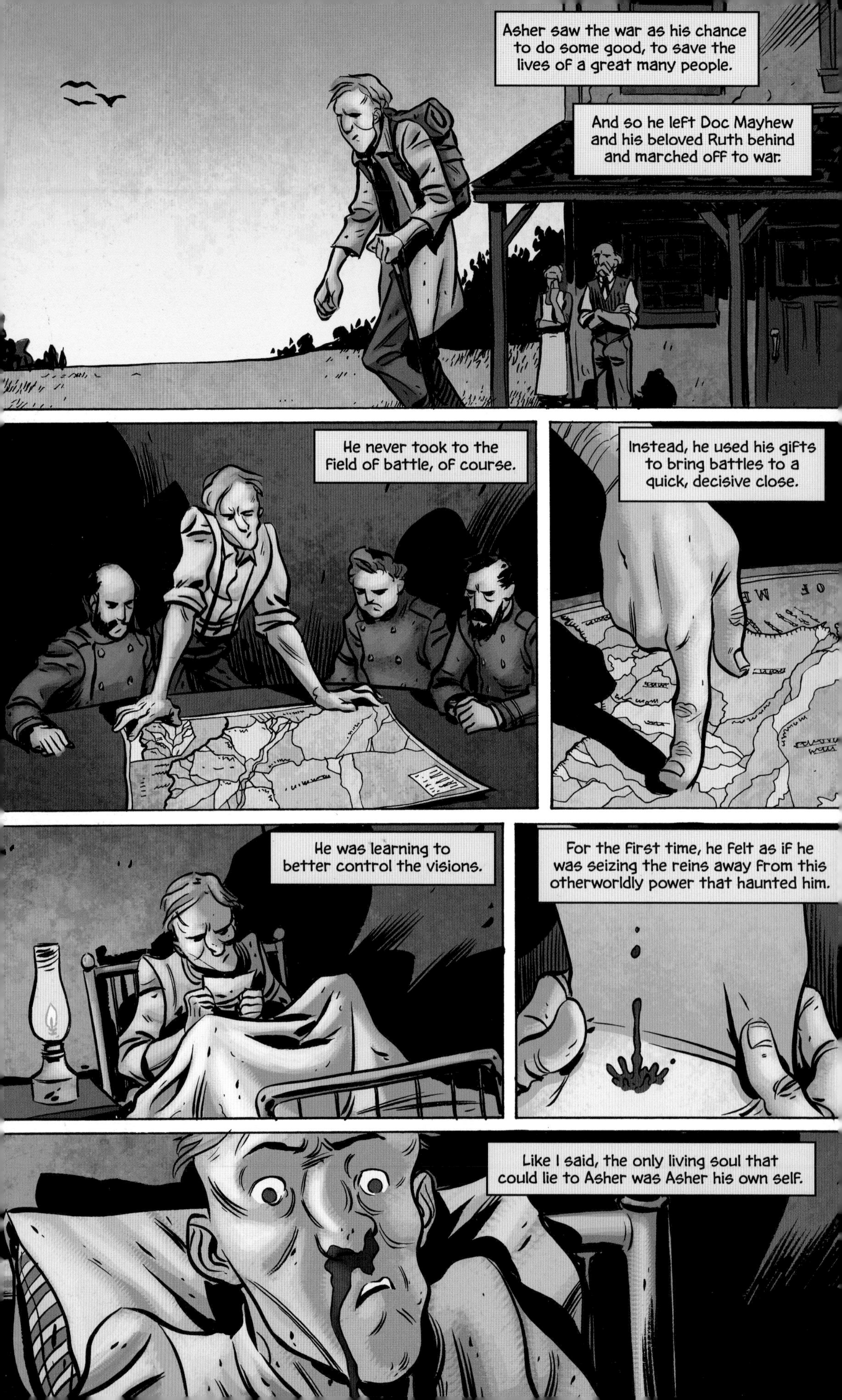
Asher saw the war as his chance to do some good, to save the lives of a great many people.
And so he left Doc Mayhew and his beloved Ruth behind and marched off to war.
He never took to the field of battle, of course.
Instead, he used his gifts to bring battles to a quick, decisive close.
He was learning to better control the visions.
For the first time, he felt as if he was seizing the reins away from this otherworldly power that haunted him.
Like I said, the only living soul that could lie to Asher was Asher his own self.

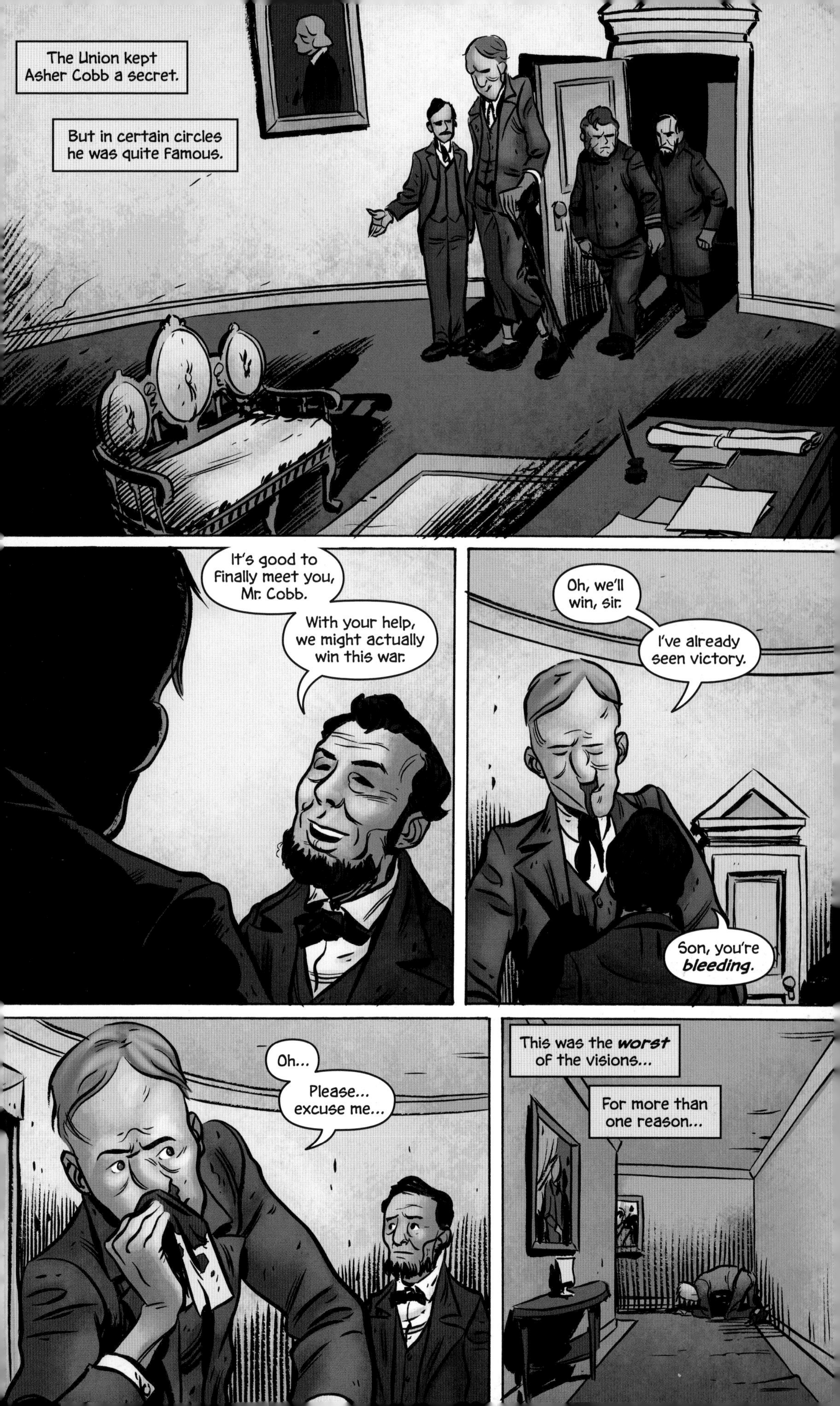
The Union kept Asher Cobb a secret.
But in certain circles he was quite famous.
It's good to finally meet you, Mr. Cobb.
With your help, we might actually win this war.
Oh, we'll win, sir.
I've already seen victory.
Son, you're *bleeding*.
Oh...
Please... excuse me...
This was the *worst* of the visions...
For more than one reason...

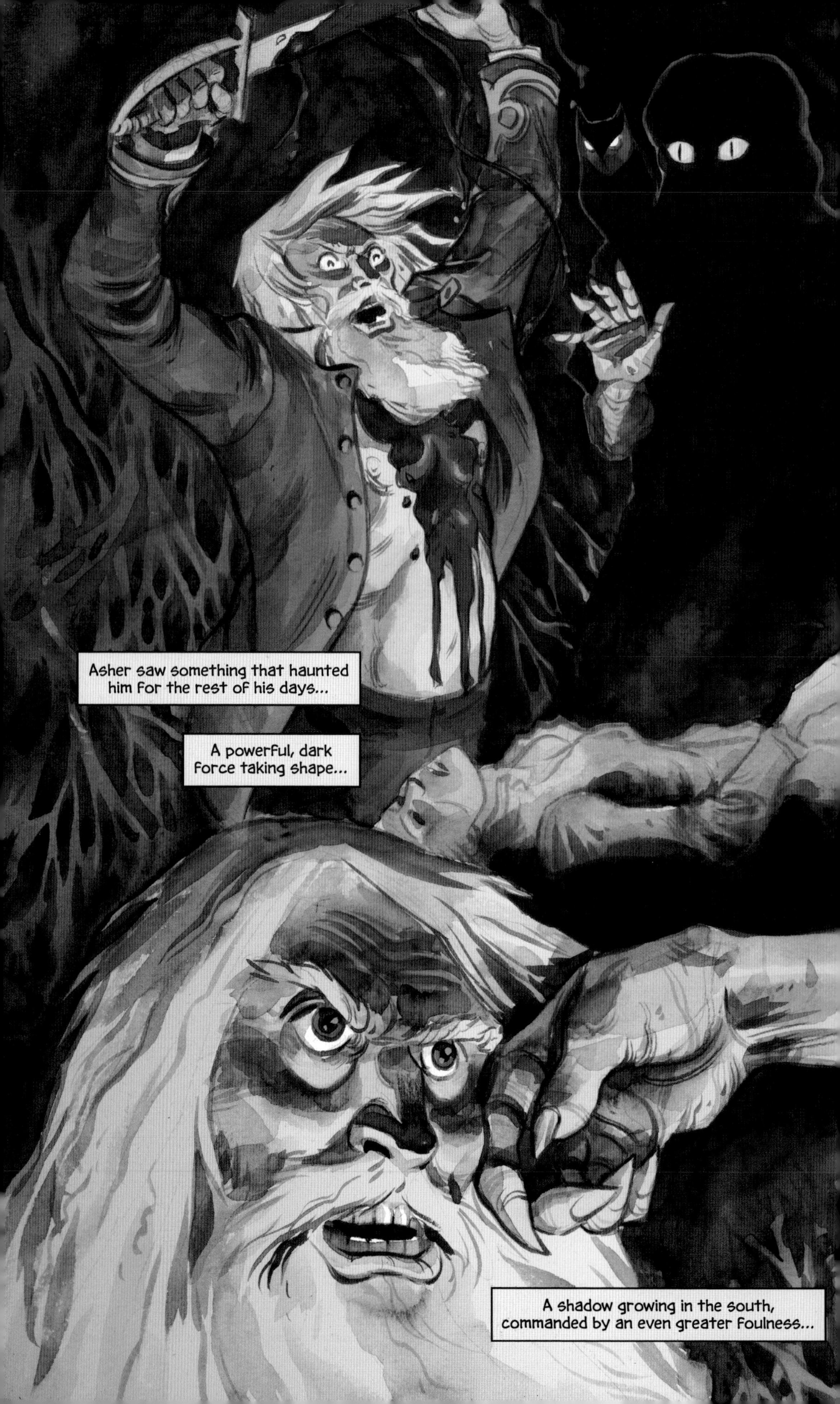
Asher saw something that haunted him for the rest of his days...
A powerful, dark force taking shape...
A shadow growing in the south, commanded by an even greater foulness...

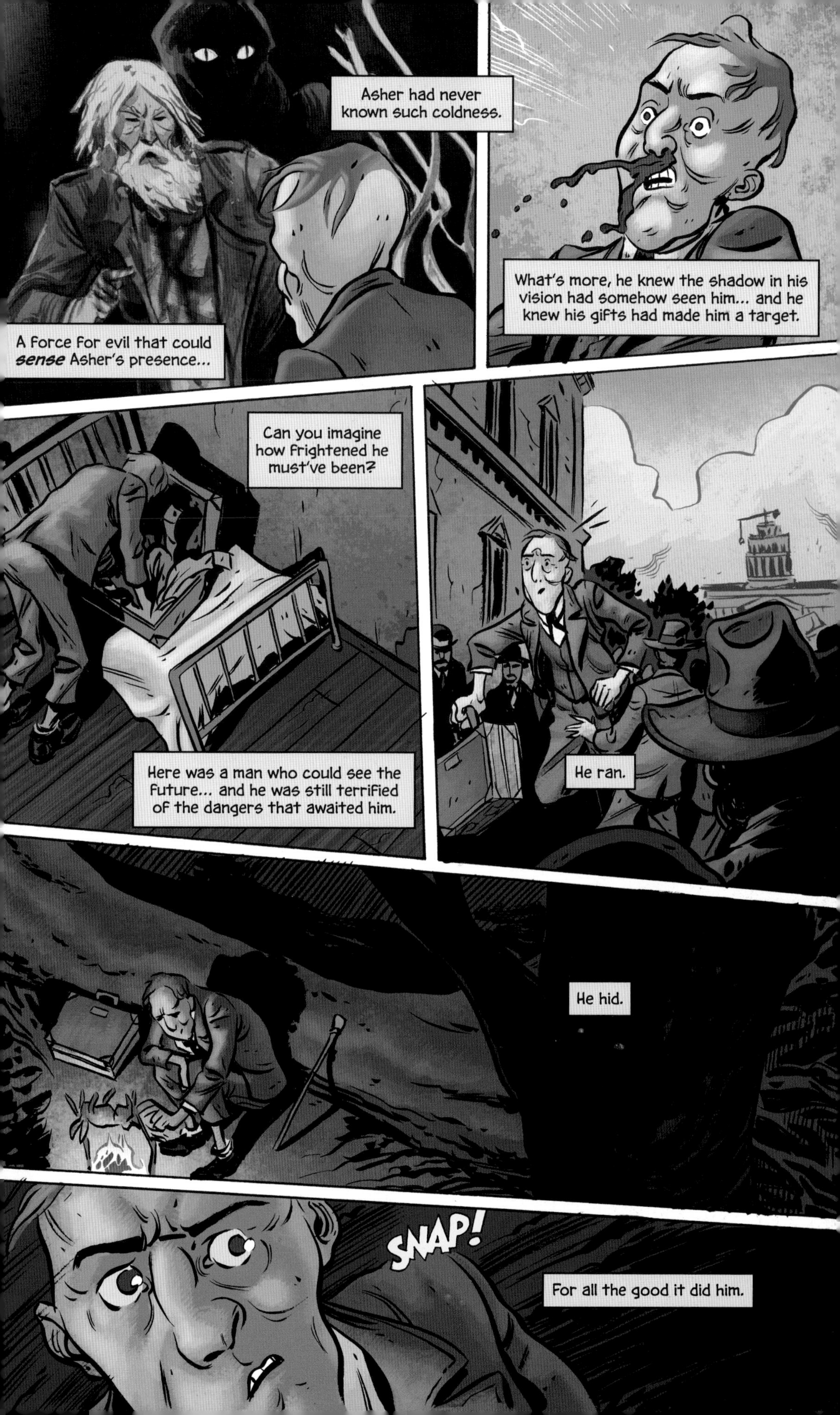
Asher had never known such coldness.
A force for evil that could *sense* Asher's presence...
What's more, he knew the shadow in his vision had somehow seen him... and he knew his gifts had made him a target.
Can you imagine how frightened he must've been?
Here was a man who could see the future... and he was still terrified of the dangers that awaited him.
He ran.
He hid.
SNAP!
For all the good it did him.

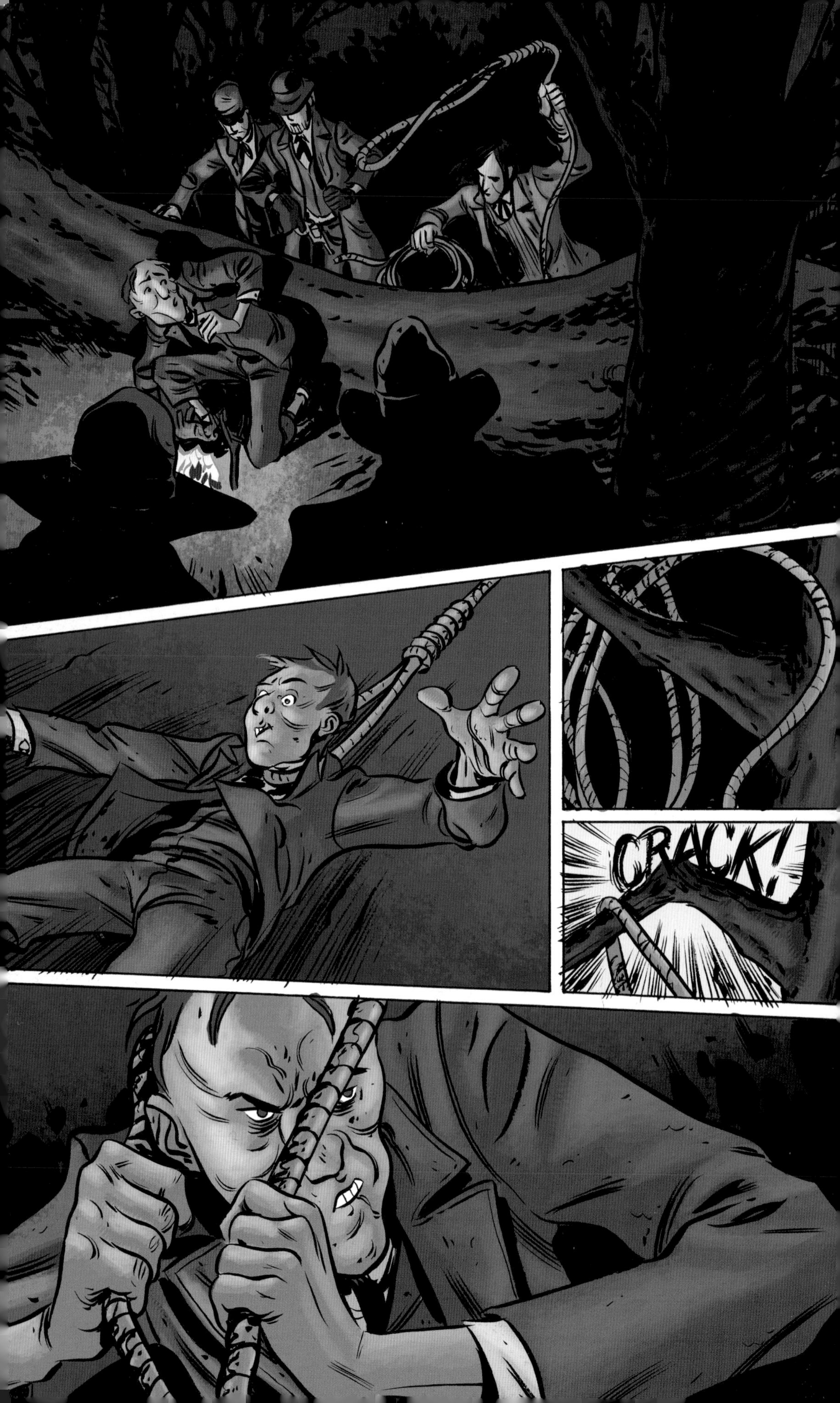
CRACK!

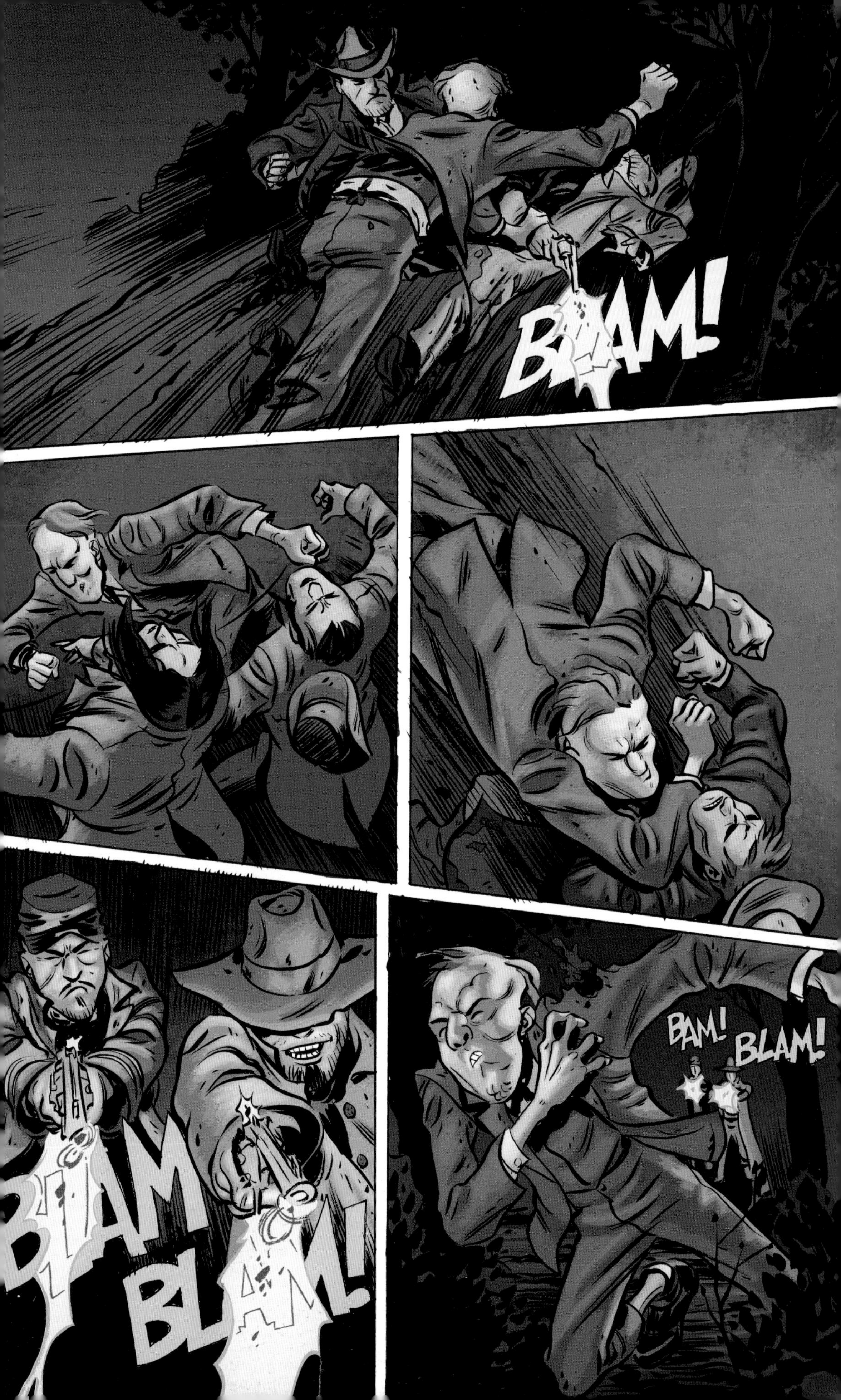
BLAM!
BAM! BLAM!
BAM!
BLAM!

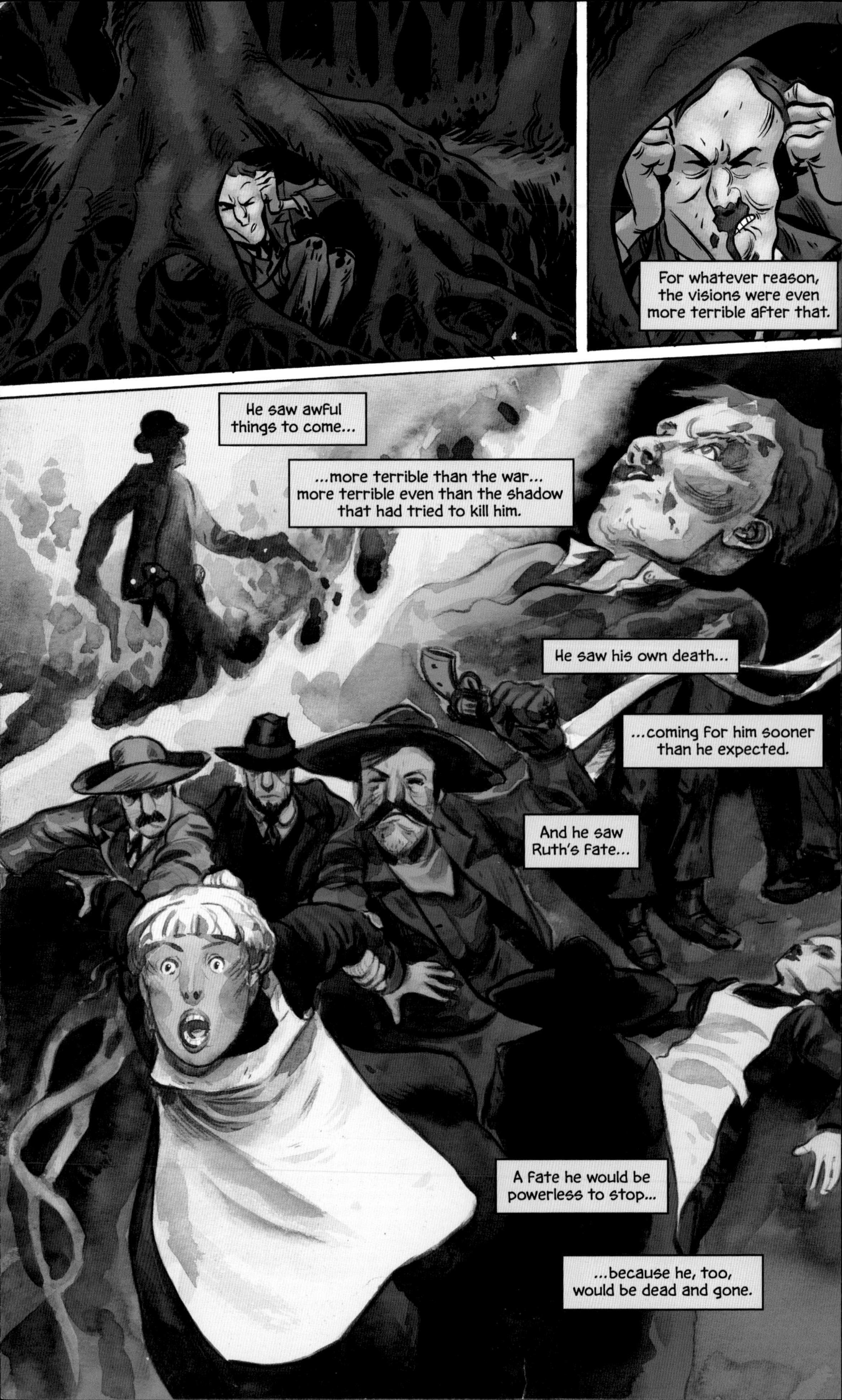
For whatever reason, the visions were even more terrible after that.
He saw awful things to come...
...more terrible than the war... more terrible even than the shadow that had tried to kill him.
He saw his own death...
...coming for him sooner than he expected.
And he saw Ruth's fate...
A fate he would be powerless to stop...
...because he, too, would be dead and gone.

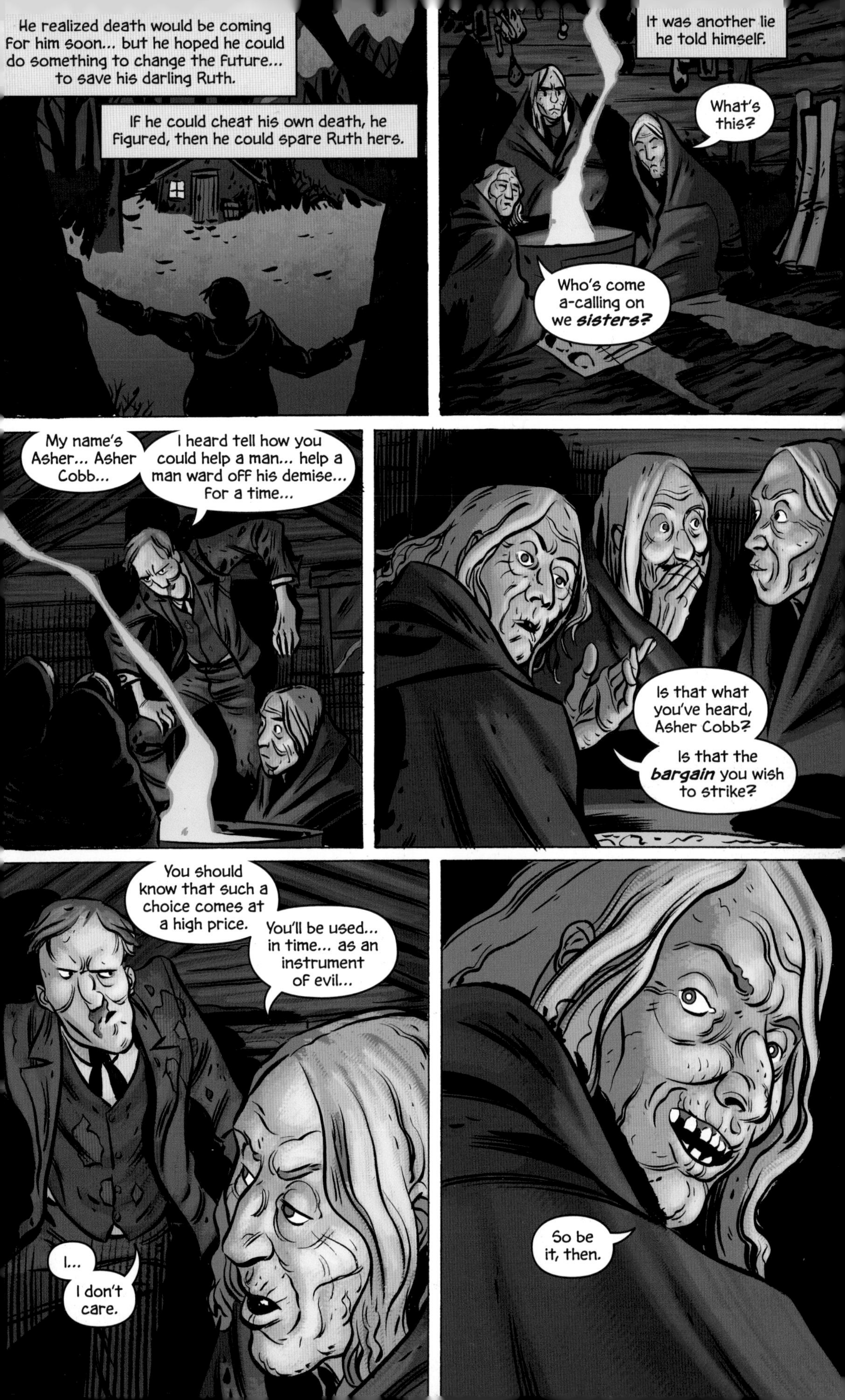
He realized death would be coming for him soon... but he hoped he could do something to change the future... to save his darling Ruth.
If he could cheat his own death, he figured, then he could spare Ruth hers.
It was another lie he told himself.
What's this?
Who's come a-calling on we *sisters?*
My name's Asher... Asher Cobb...
I heard tell how you could help a man... help a man ward off his demise... for a time...
Is that what you've heard, Asher Cobb?
Is that the *bargain* you wish to strike?
You should know that such a choice comes at a high price.
You'll be used... in time... as an instrument of evil...
I... I don't care.
So be it, then.

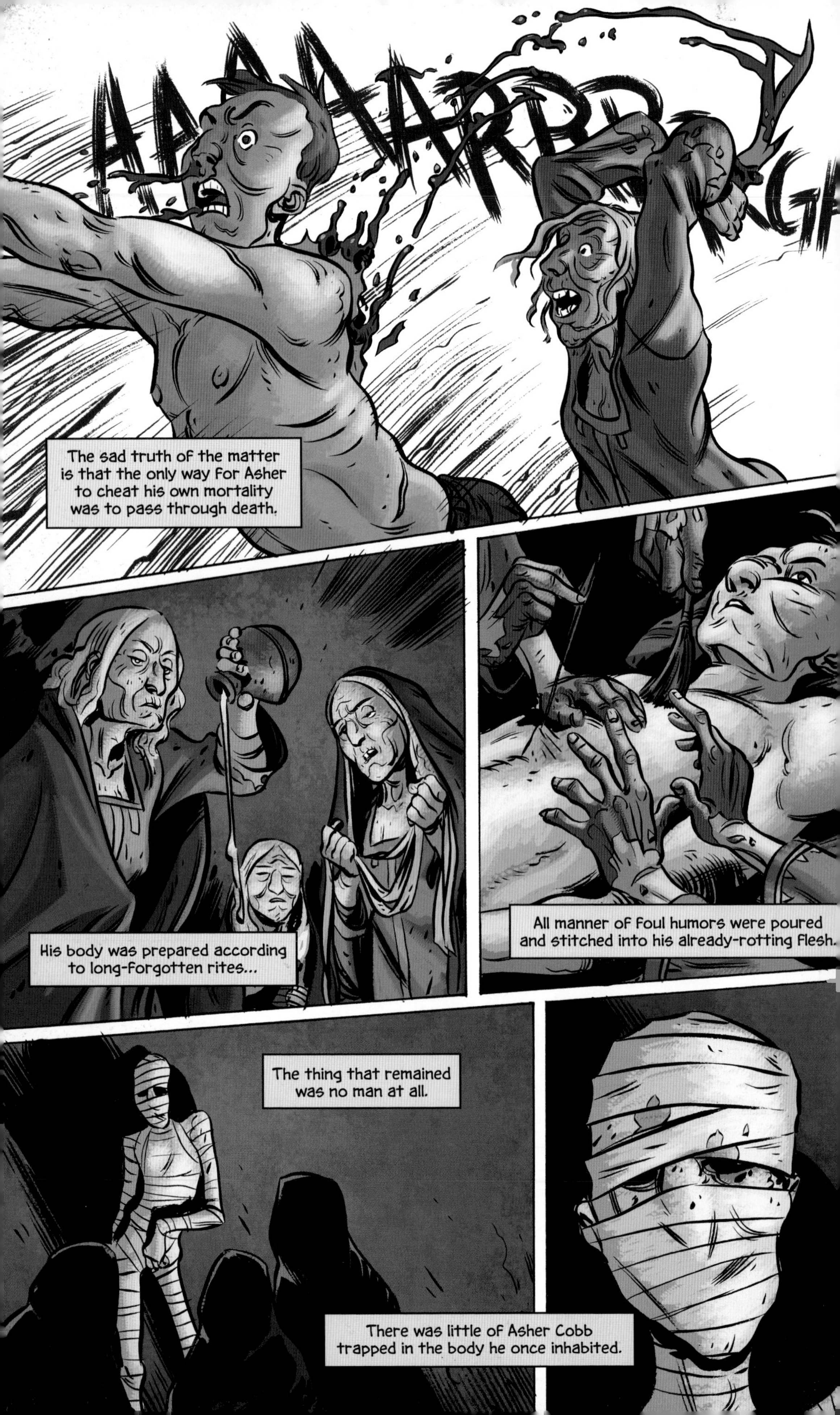

The sad truth of the matter is that the only way for Asher to cheat his own mortality was to pass through death.
His body was prepared according to long-forgotten rites...
All manner of foul humors were poured and stitched into his already-rotting flesh.
The thing that remained was no man at all.
There was little of Asher Cobb trapped in the body he once inhabited.

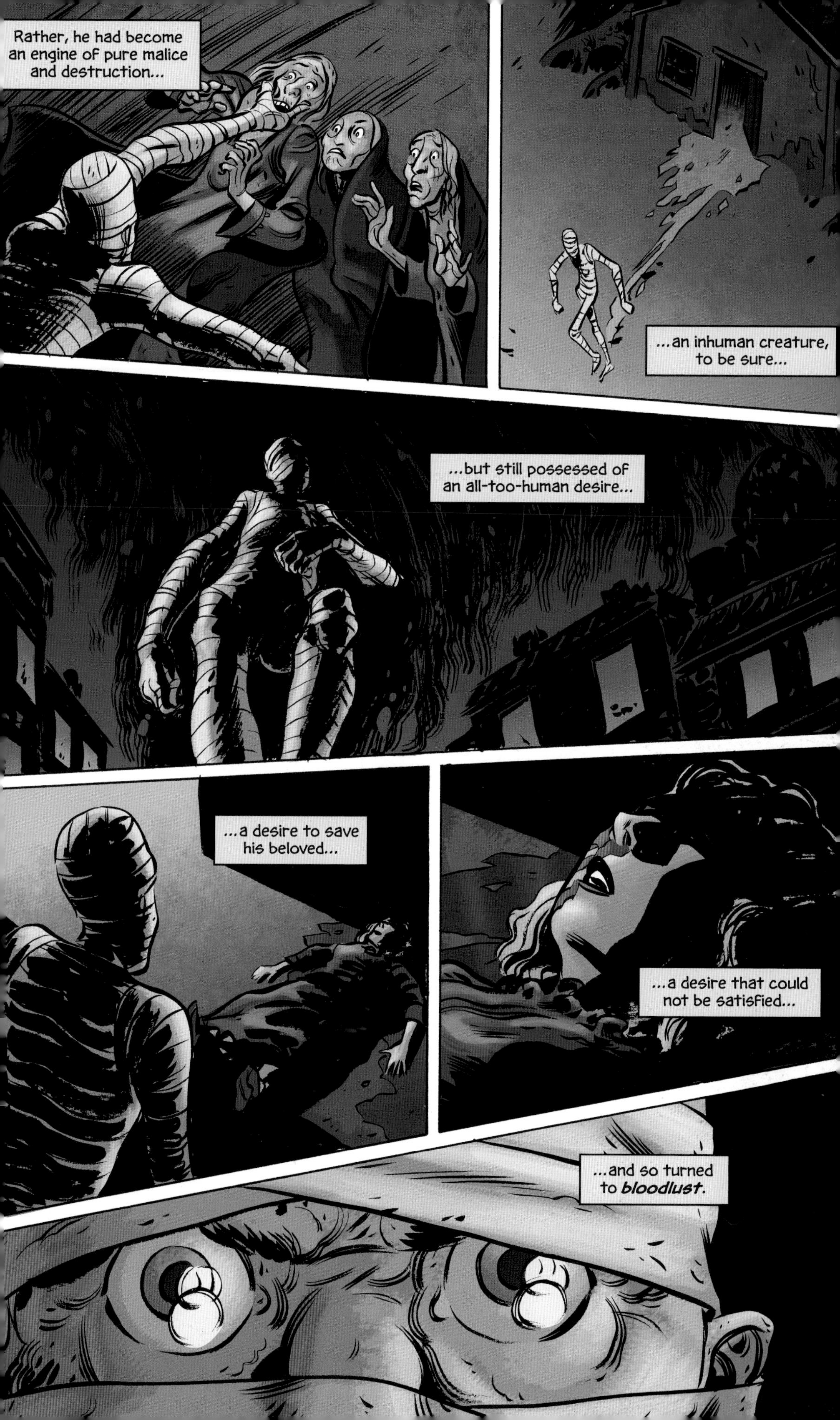
Rather, he had become an engine of pure malice and destruction...
...an inhuman creature, to be sure...
...but still possessed of an all-too-human desire...
...a desire to save his beloved...
...a desire that could not be satisfied...
...and so turned to *bloodlust*.

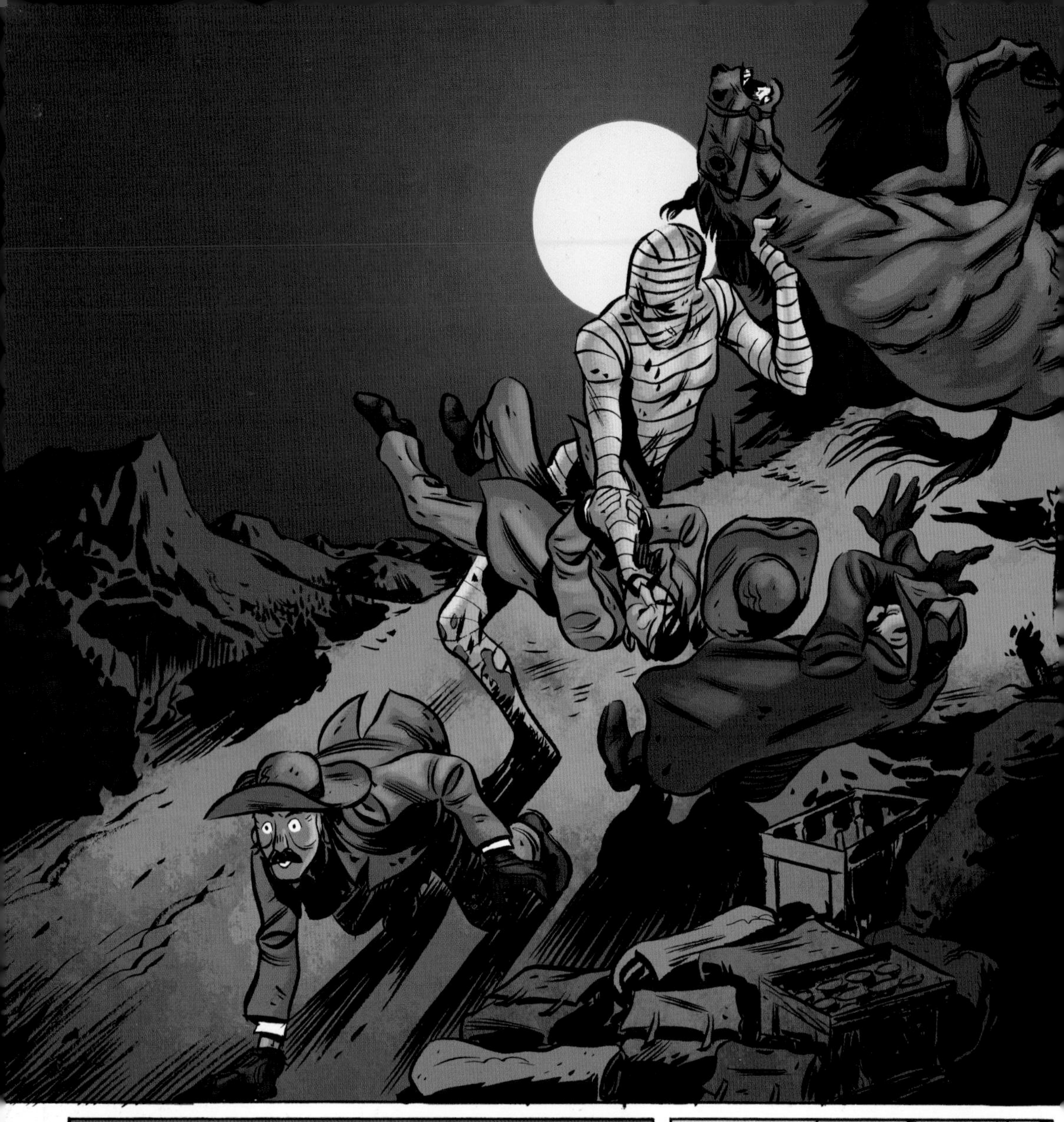

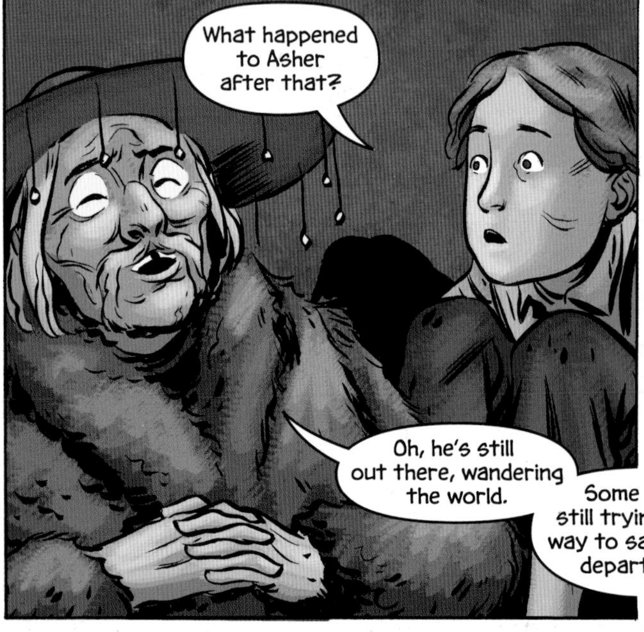

What happened to Asher after that?
Oh, he's still out there, wandering the world.
Some say he's still trying to find a way to save his dear, departed Ruth.

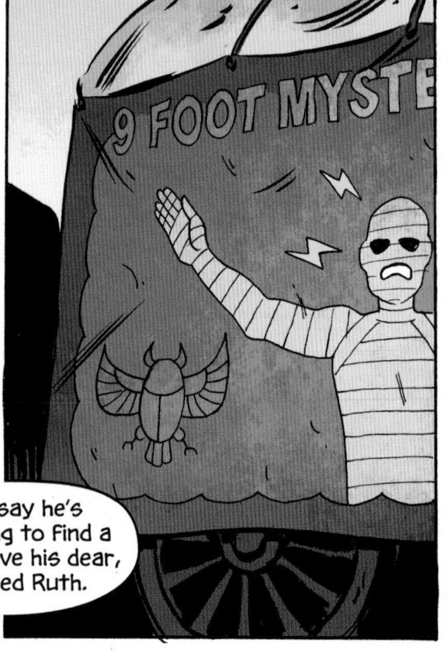

9 FOOT MYSTE

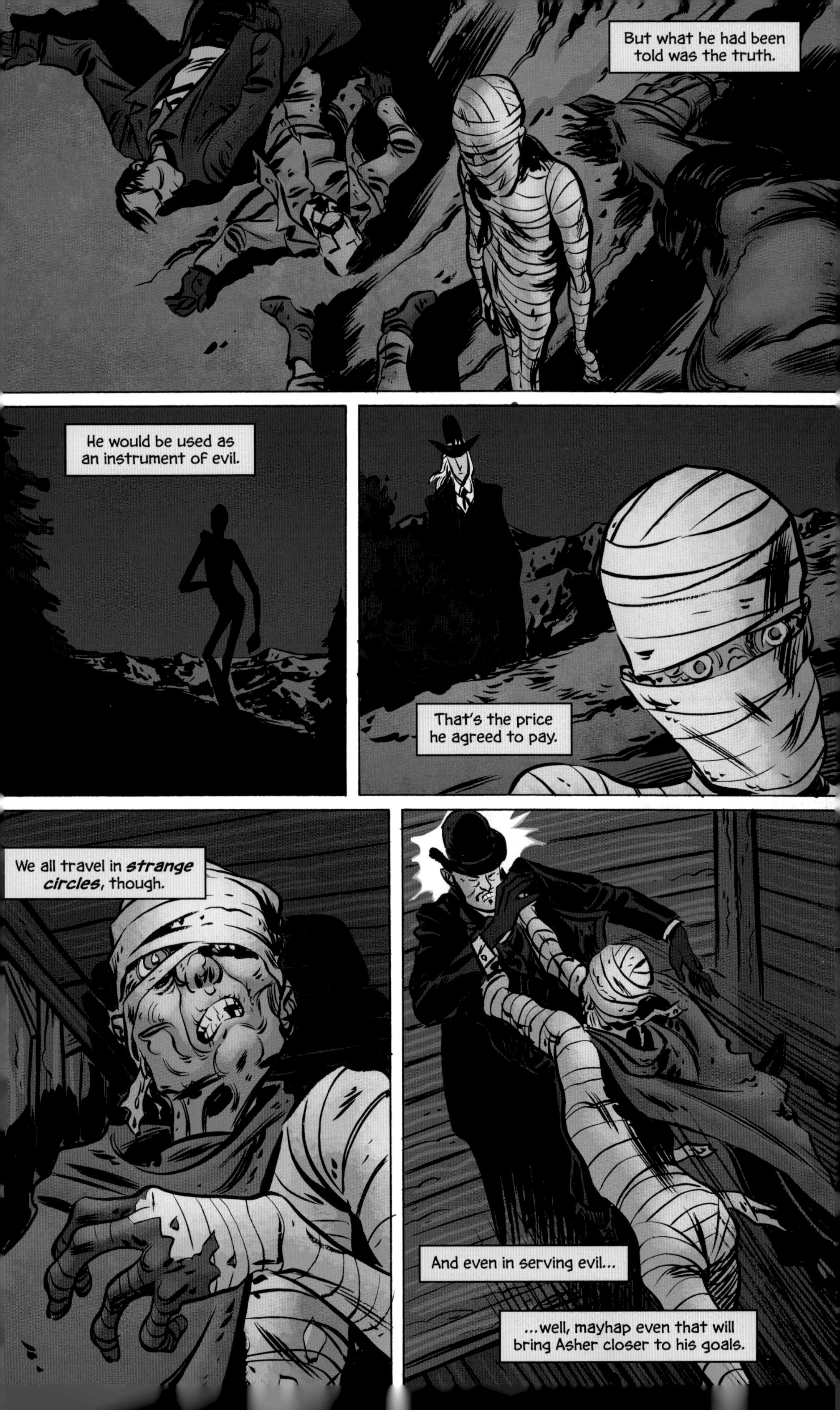
But what he had been told was the truth.
He would be used as an instrument of evil.
That's the price he agreed to pay.
We all travel in *strange circles*, though.
And even in serving evil...
...well, mayhap even that will bring Asher closer to his goals.

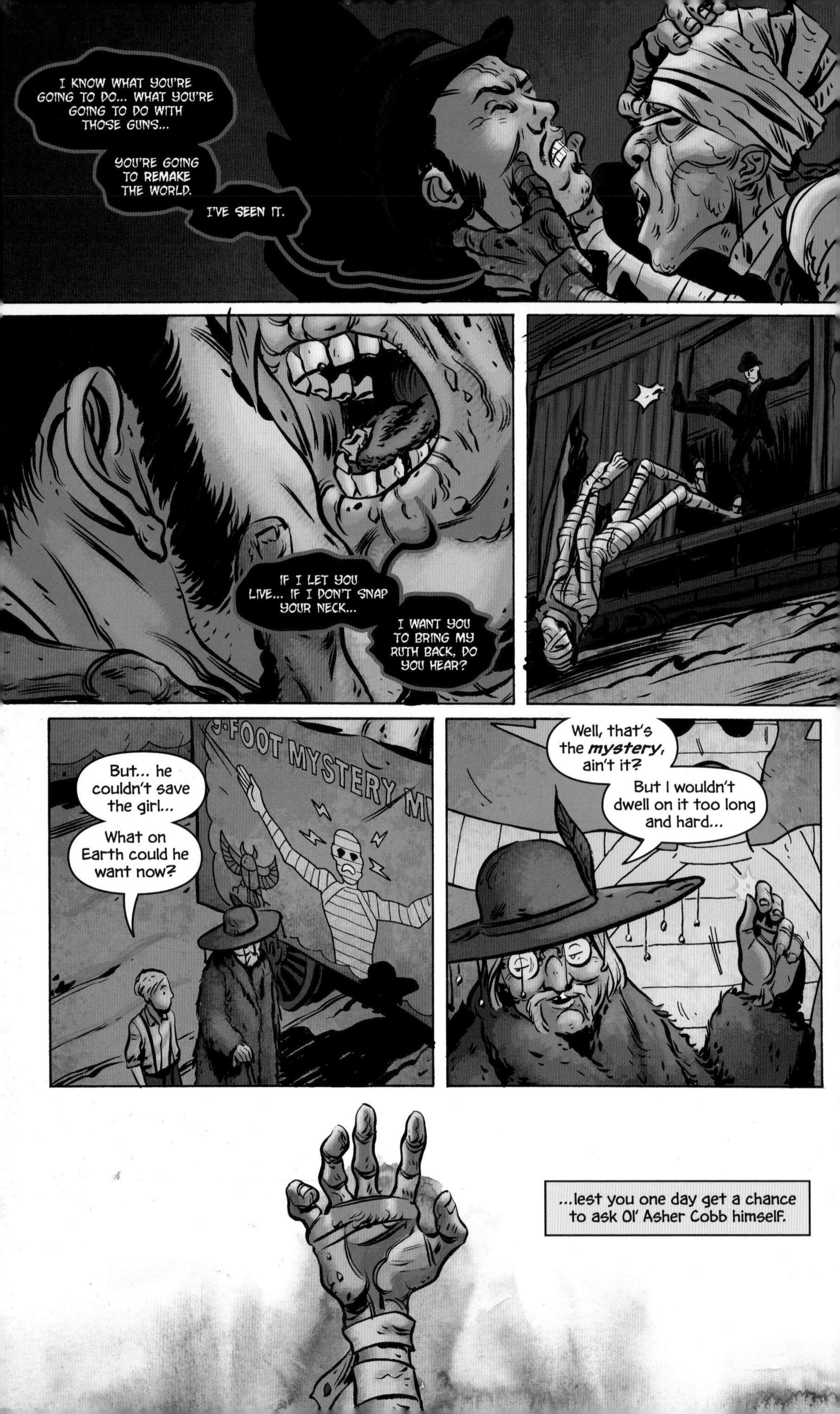

I KNOW WHAT YOU'RE GOING TO DO... WHAT YOU'RE GOING TO DO WITH THOSE GUNS...
YOU'RE GOING TO REMAKE THE WORLD.
I'VE SEEN IT.
IF I LET YOU LIVE... IF I DON'T SNAP YOUR NECK...
I WANT YOU TO BRING MY RUTH BACK, DO YOU HEAR?
-FOOT MYSTERY MU
But... he couldn't save the girl...
What on Earth could he want now?
Well, that's the *mystery*, ain't it?
But I wouldn't dwell on it too long and hard...
...lest you one day get a chance to ask Ol' Asher Cobb himself.

CHAPTER FOUR

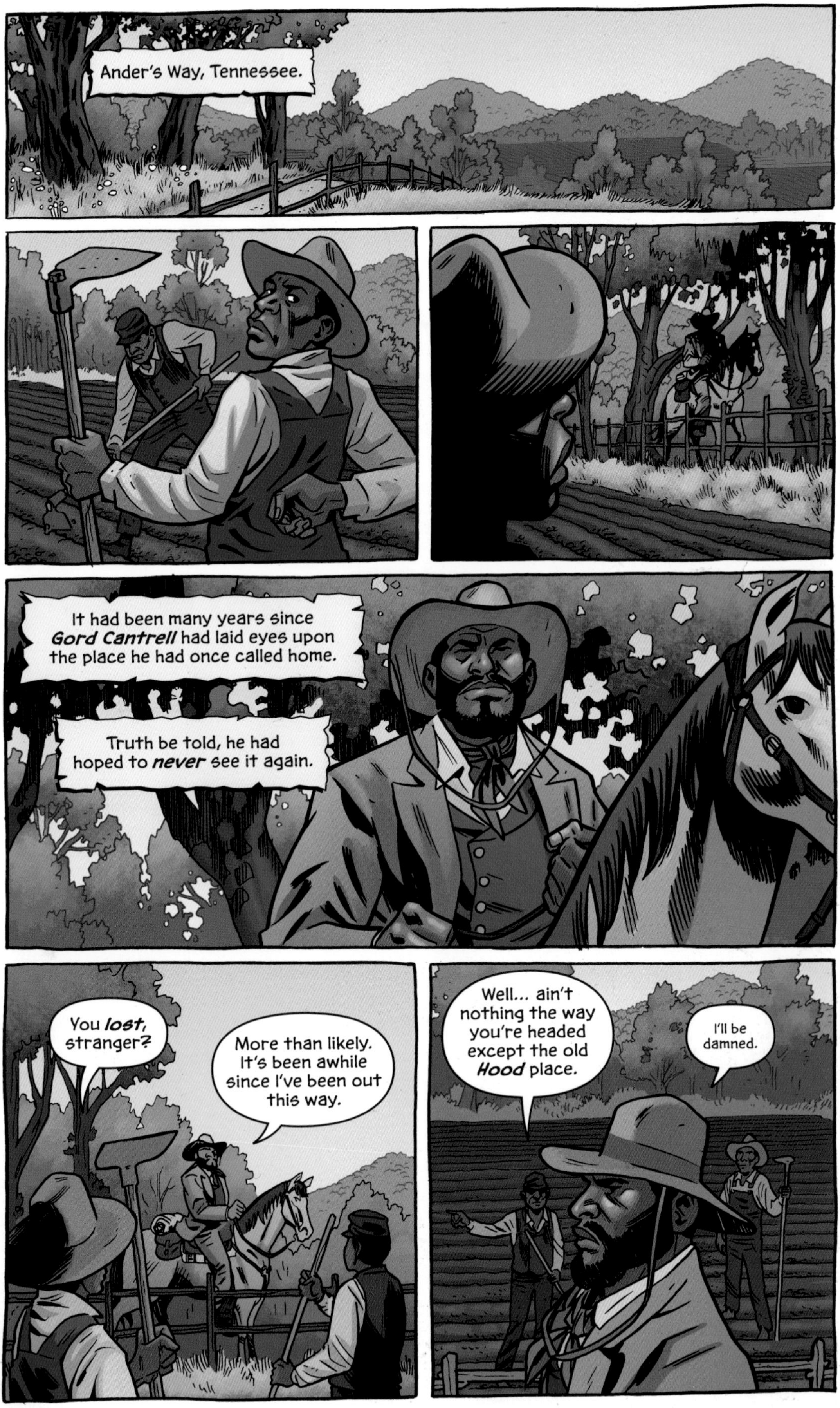
Ander's Way, Tennessee.
It had been many years since *Gord Cantrell* had laid eyes upon the place he had once called home.
Truth be told, he had hoped to *never* see it again.
You *lost*, stranger?
More than likely. It's been awhile since I've been out this way.
Well... ain't nothing the way you're headed except the old *Hood* place.
I'll be damned.

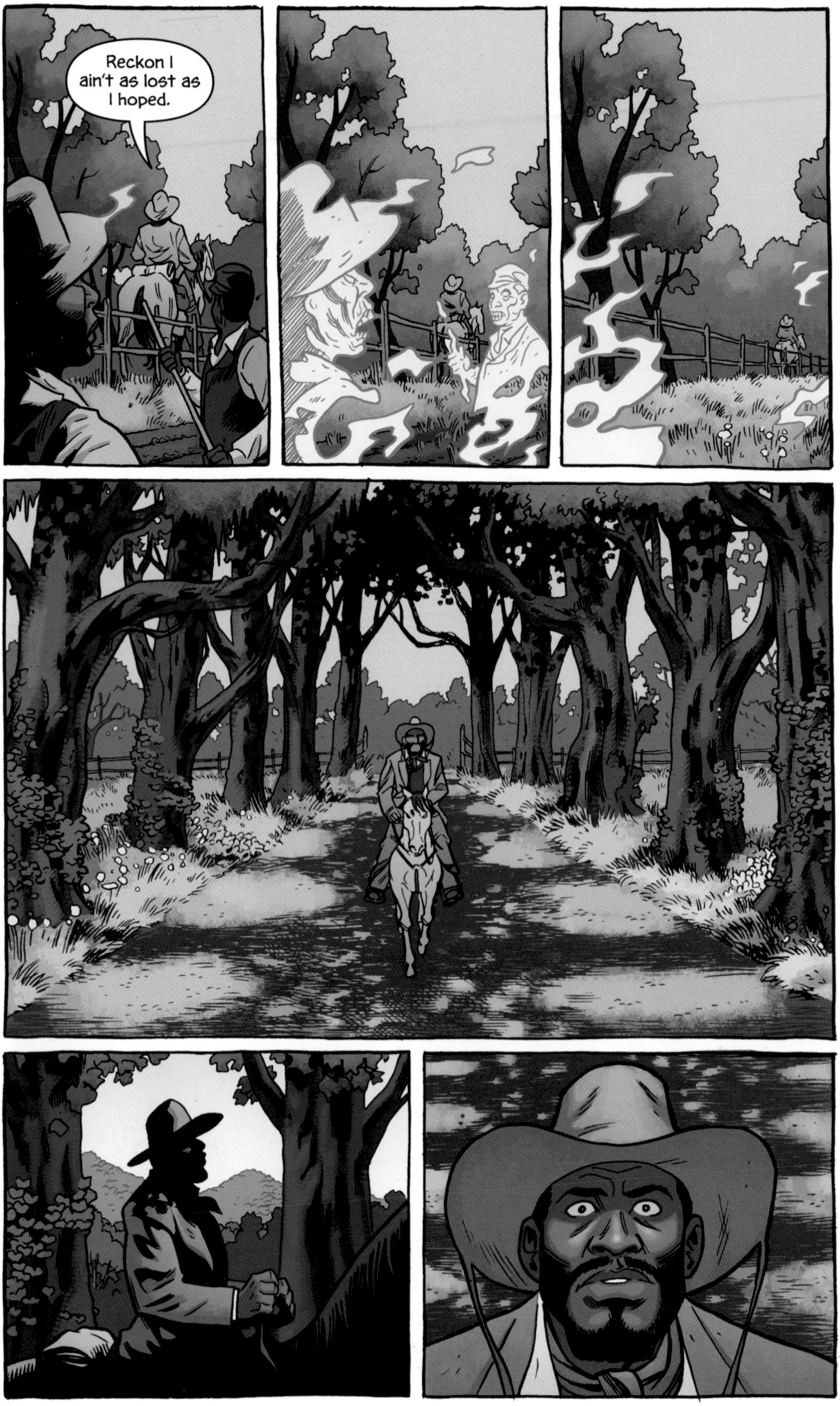
Reckon I ain't as lost as I hoped.

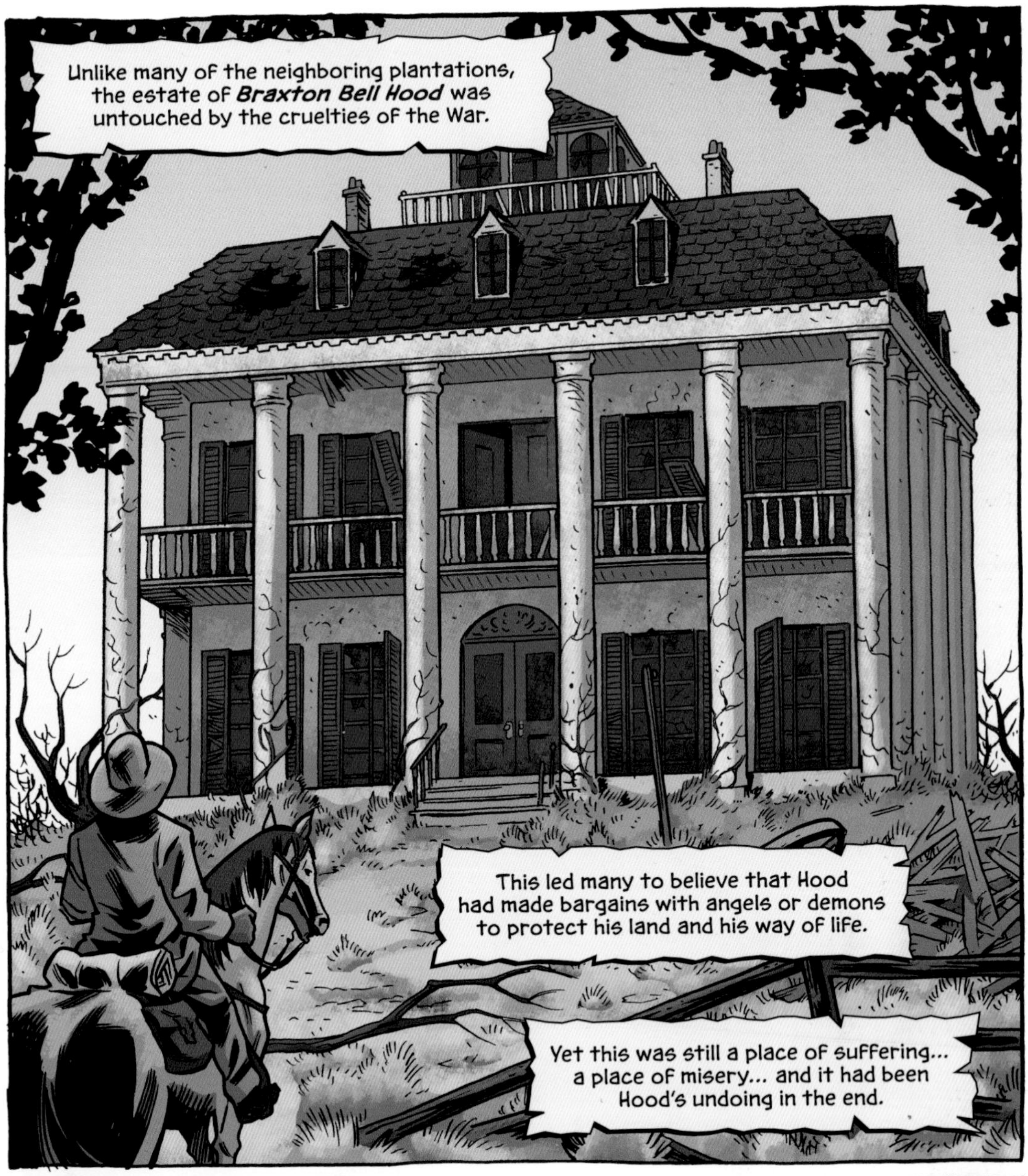
Unlike many of the neighboring plantations, the estate of ***Braxton Bell Hood*** was untouched by the cruelties of the War.
This led many to believe that Hood had made bargains with angels or demons to protect his land and his way of life.
Yet this was still a place of suffering... a place of misery... and it had been Hood's undoing in the end.

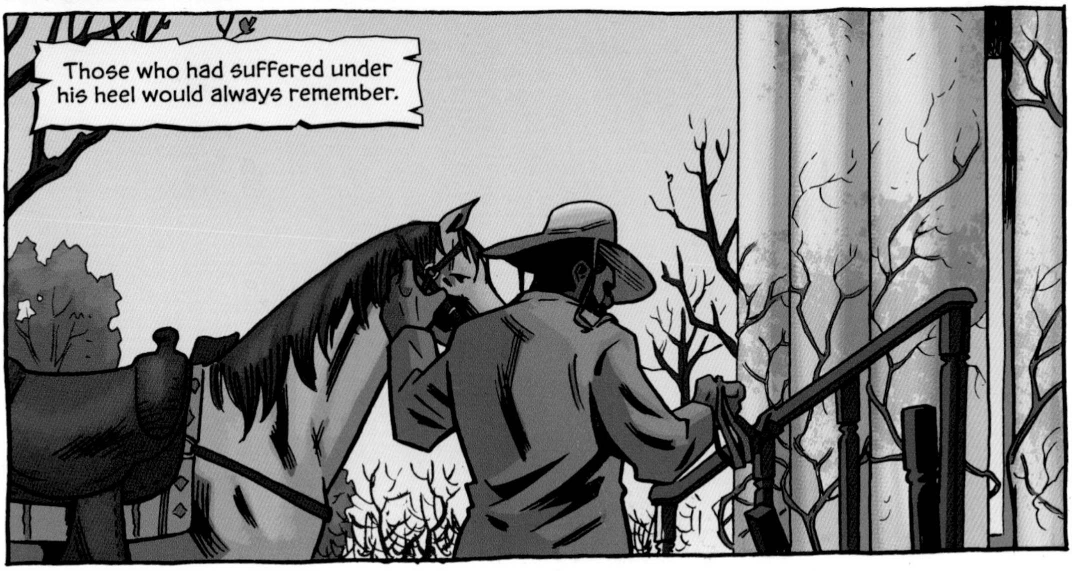
Those who had suffered under his heel would always remember.

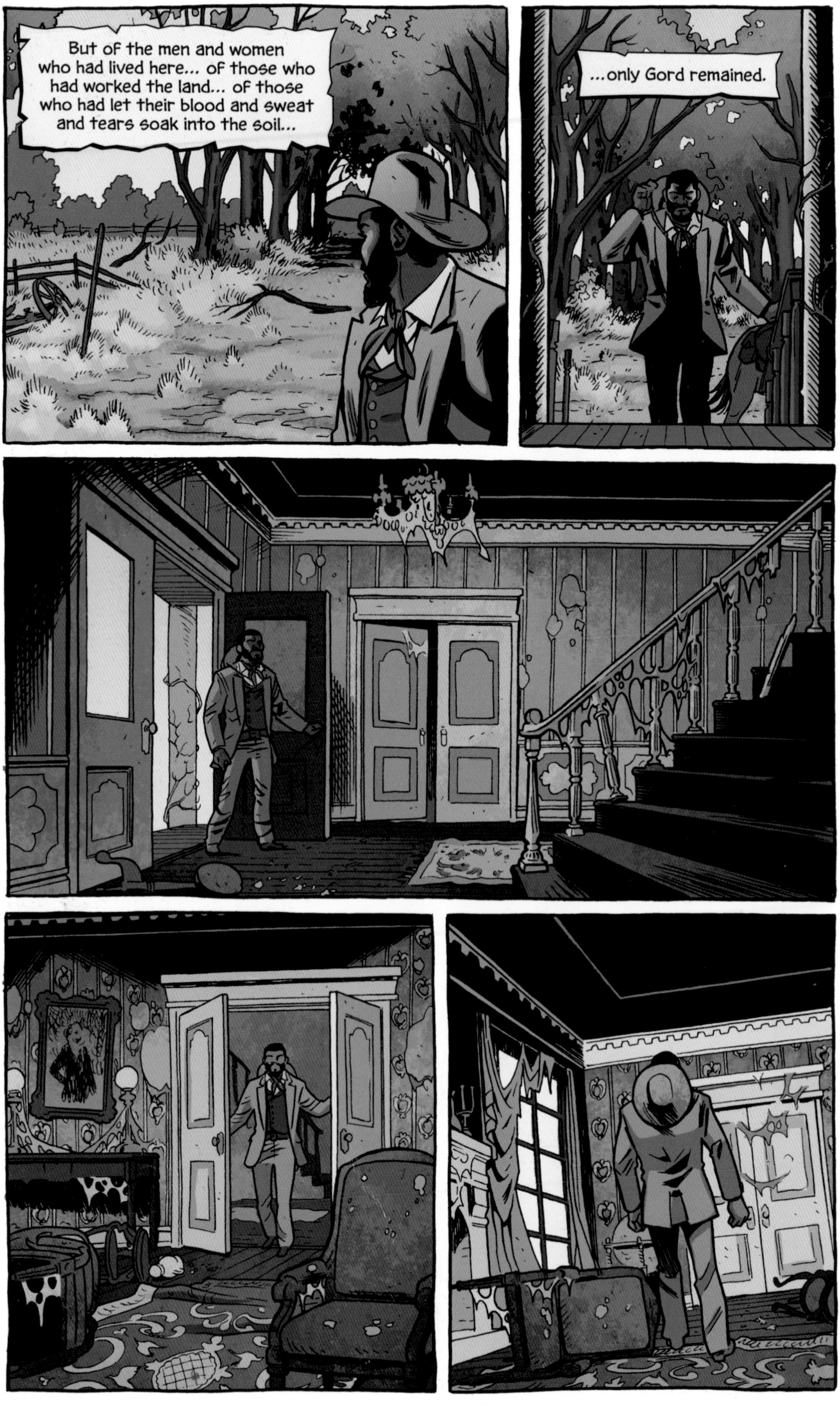
But of the men and women who had lived here... of those who had worked the land... of those who had let their blood and sweat and tears soak into the soil...
...only Gord remained.

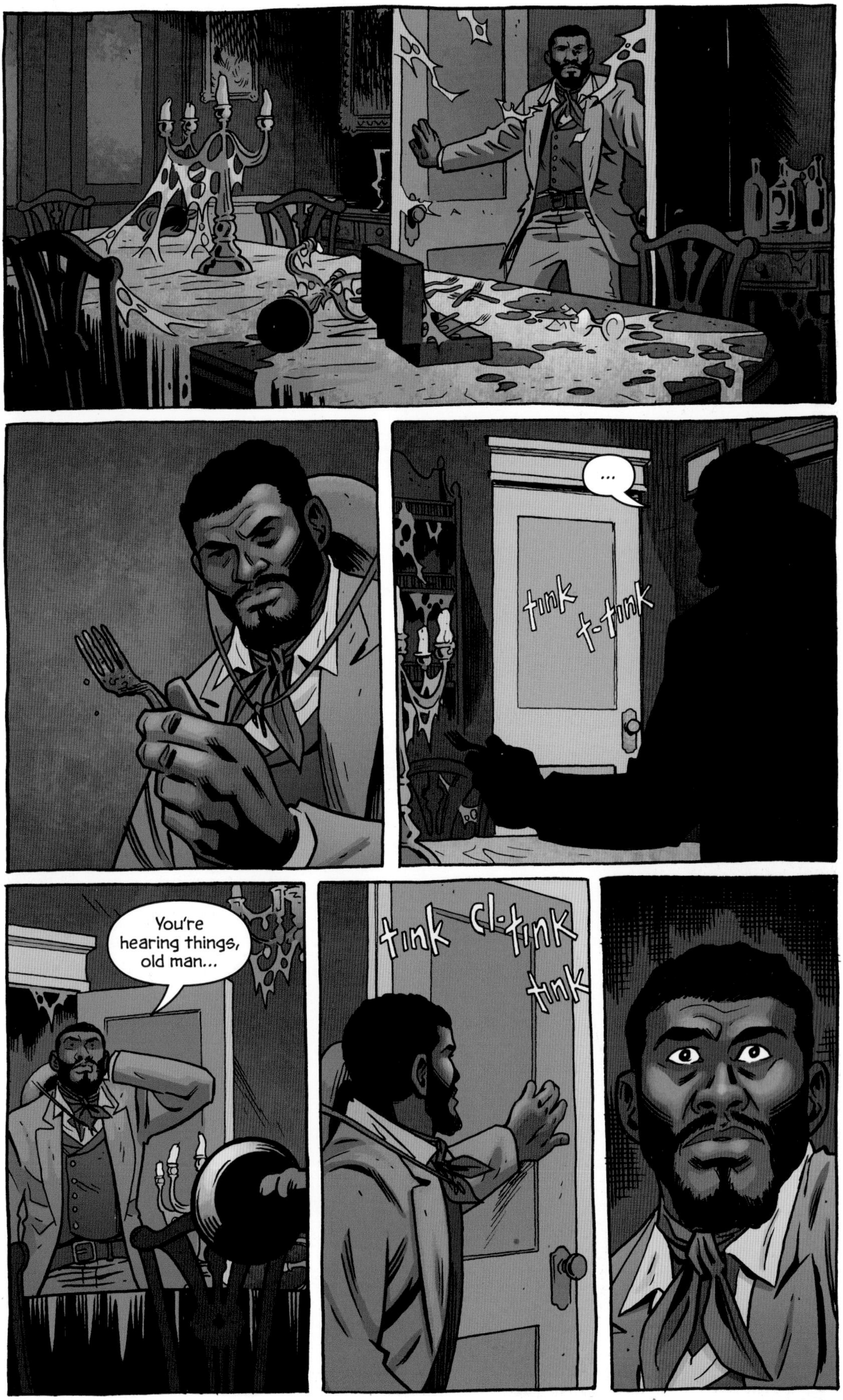
...
tink t-tink
You're hearing things, old man...
tink cl-tink tink
tink

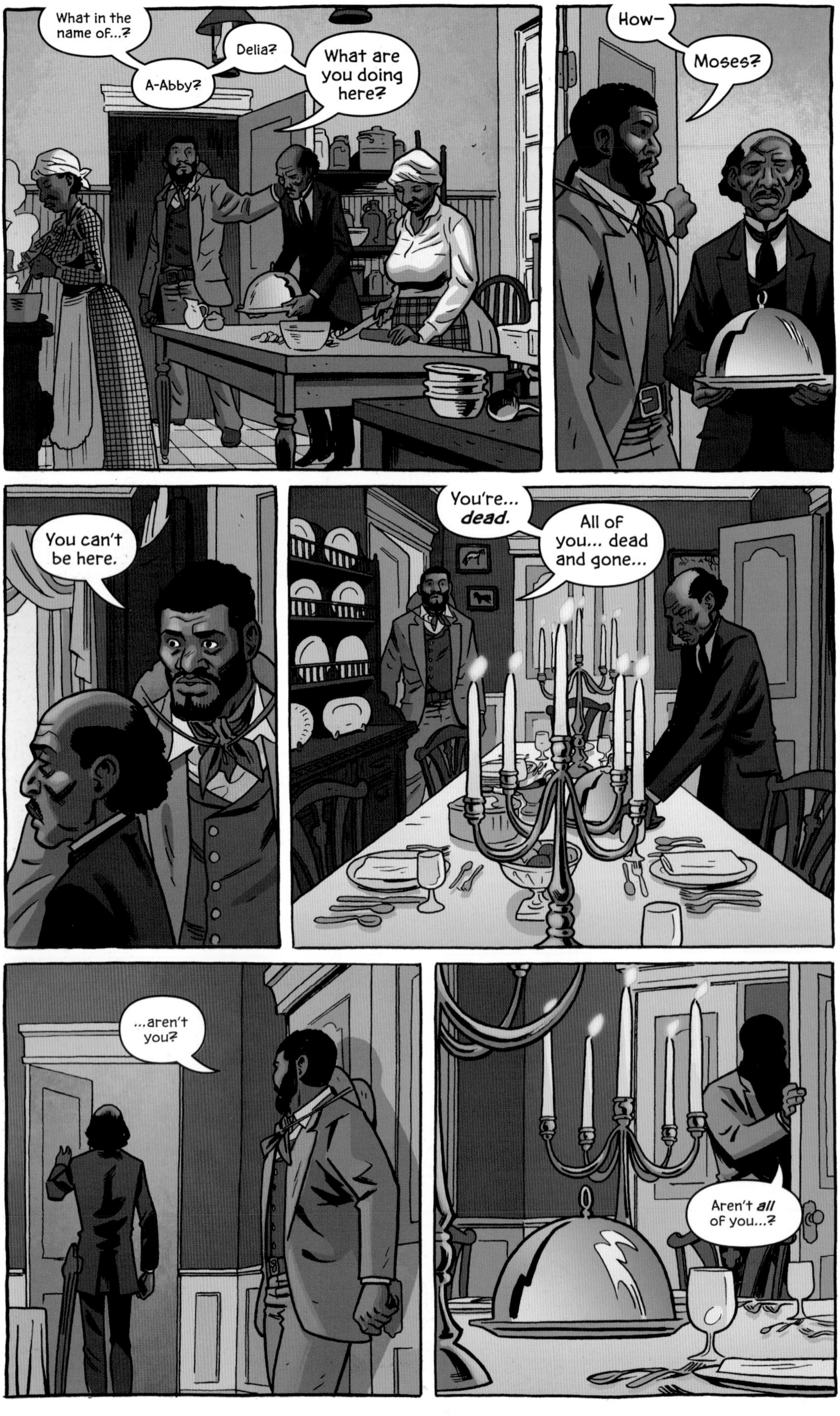
What in the name of...?
A-Abby?
Delia?
What are you doing here?
How—
Moses?
You can't be here.
You're... *dead.*
All of you... dead and gone...
...aren't you?
Aren't *all* of you...?

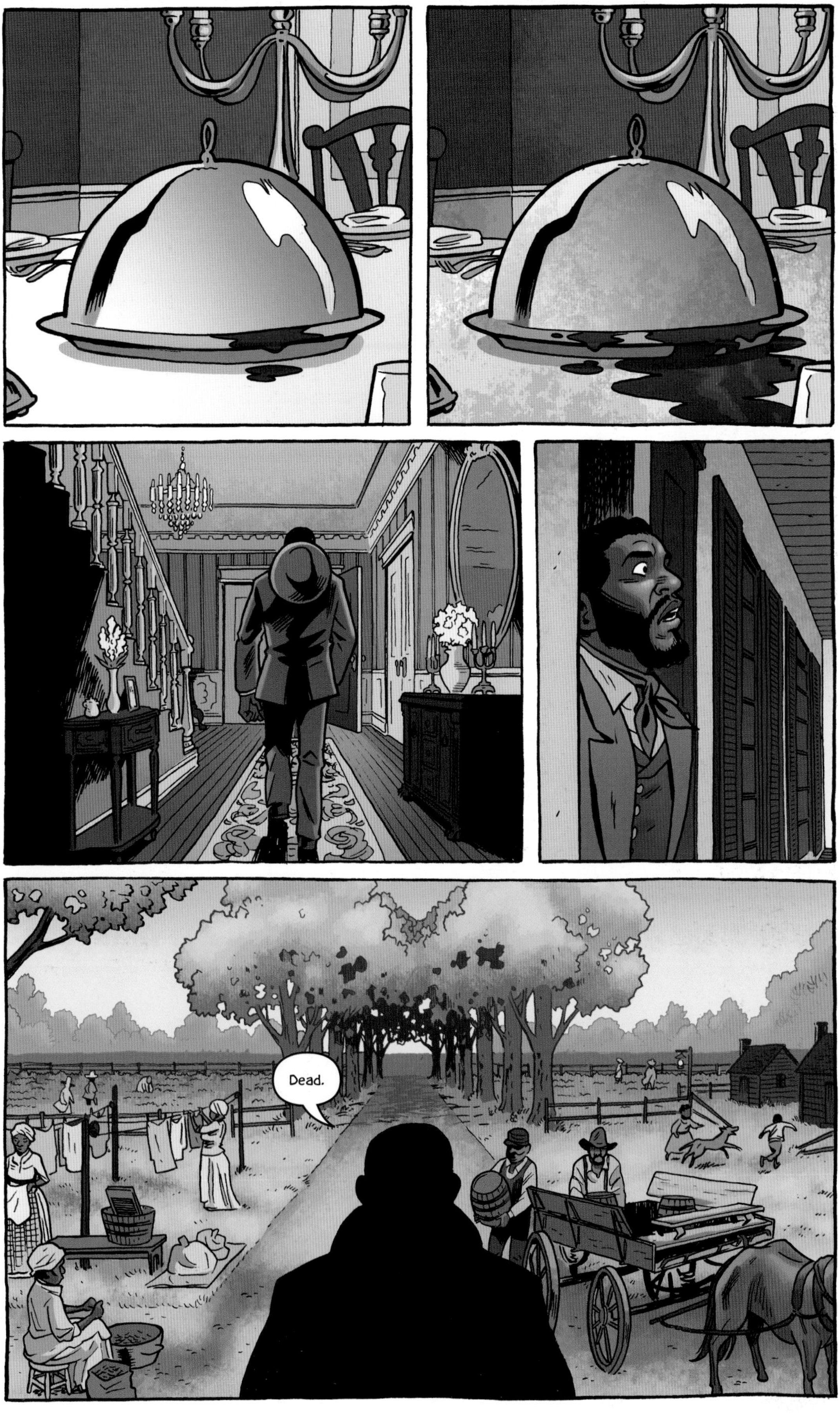
Dead.

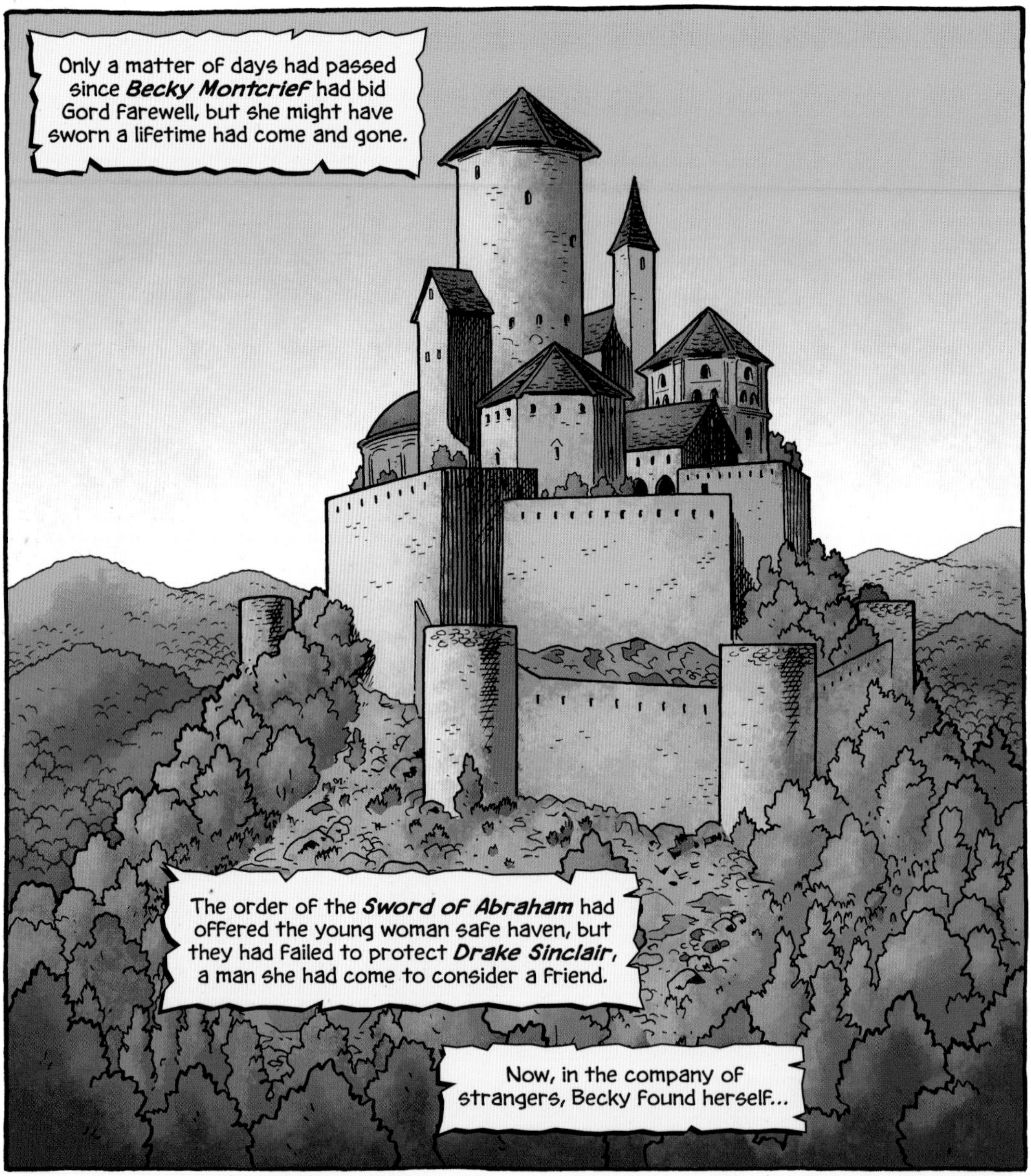
Only a matter of days had passed since Becky Montcrief had bid Gord Farewell, but she might have sworn a lifetime had come and gone.
The order of the Sword of Abraham had offered the young woman safe haven, but they had failed to protect Drake Sinclair, a man she had come to consider a friend.
Now, in the company of strangers, Becky found herself...

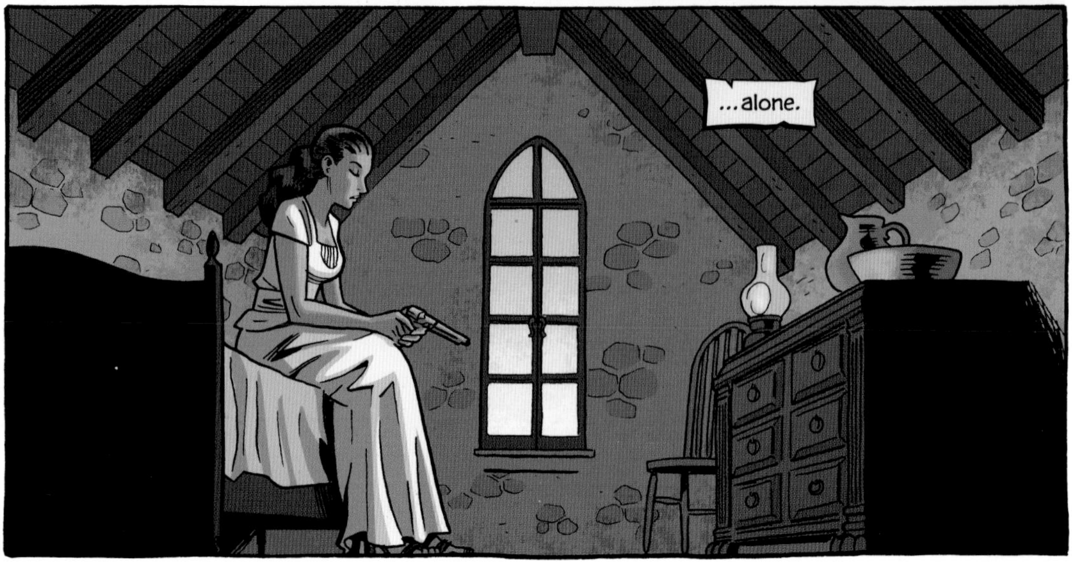
...alone.

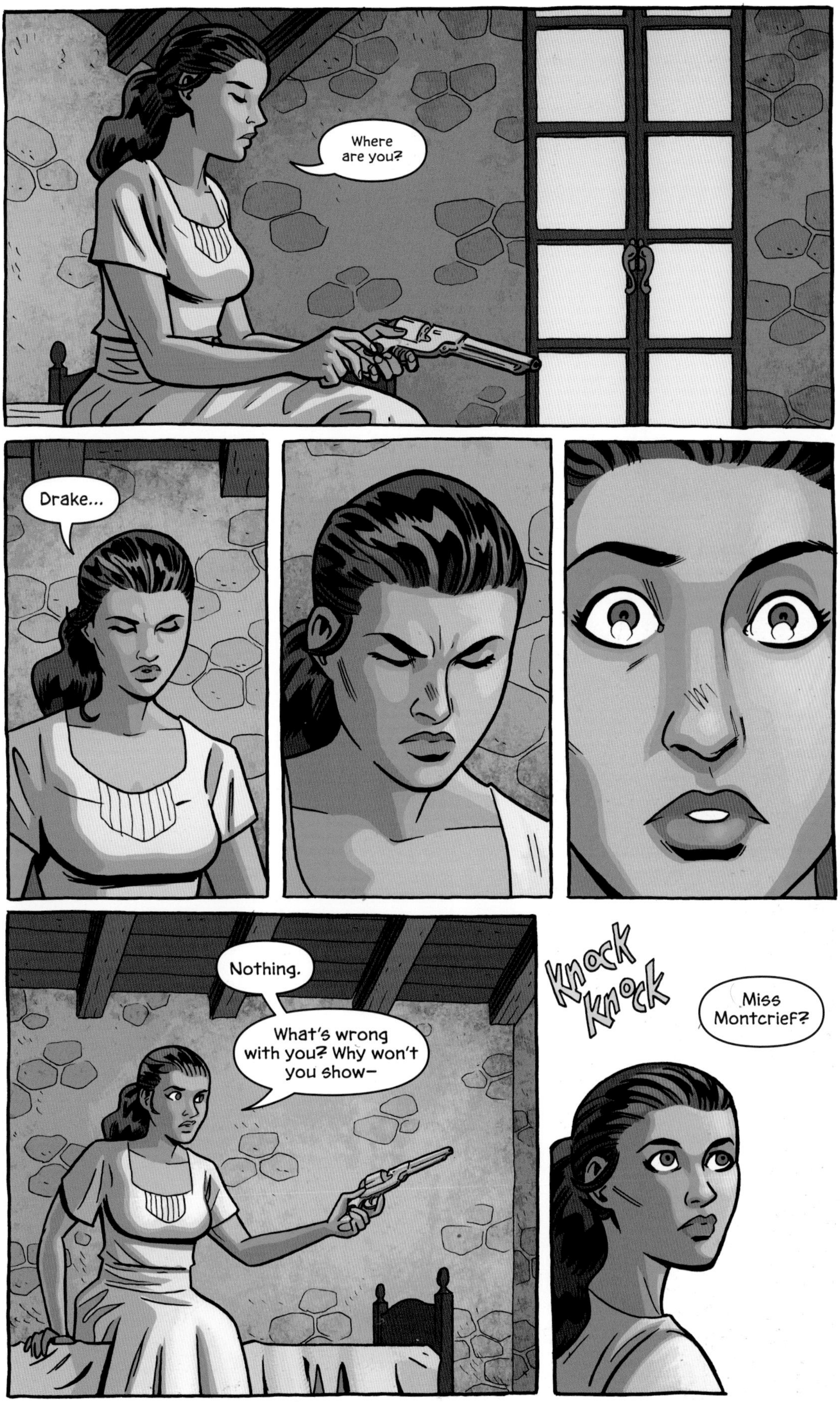
Where are you?
Drake...
Nothing.
What's wrong with you? Why won't you show—
KNOCK KNOCK
Miss Montcrief?

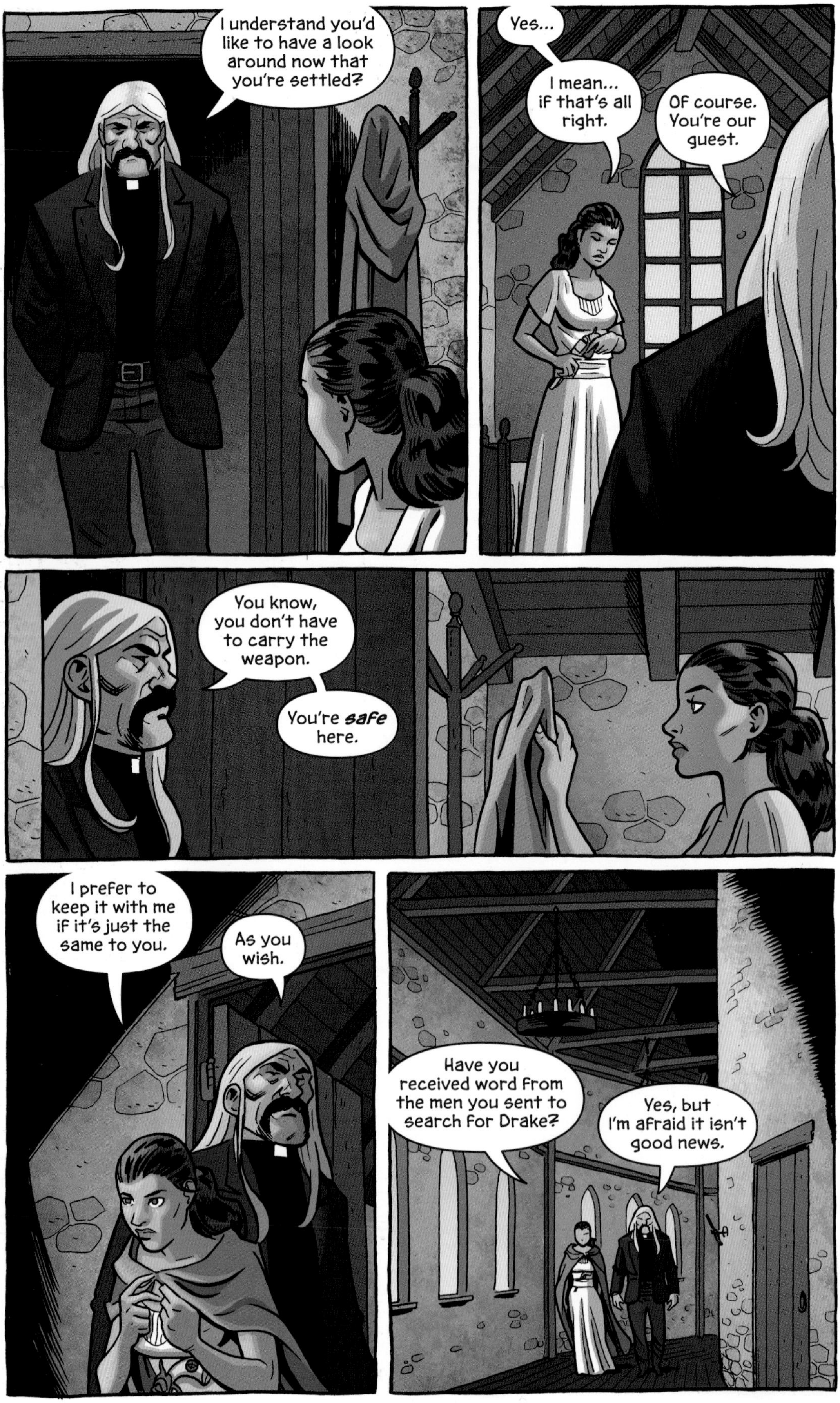

I understand you'd like to have a look around now that you're settled?
Yes...
I mean... if that's all right.
Of course. You're our guest.
You know, you don't have to carry the weapon.
You're *safe* here.
I prefer to keep it with me if it's just the same to you.
As you wish.
Have you received word from the men you sent to search for Drake?
Yes, but I'm afraid it isn't good news.

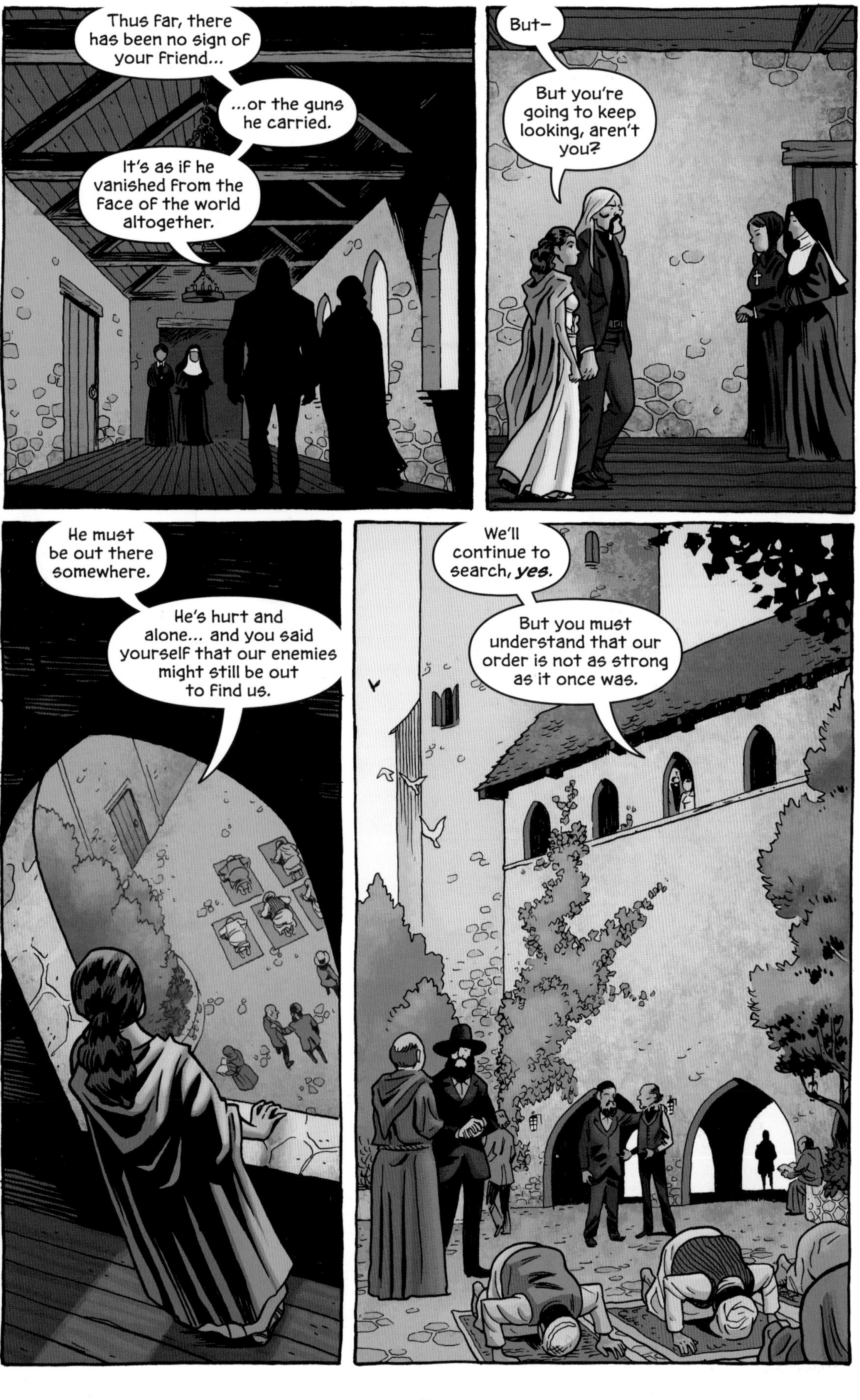

Thus far, there has been no sign of your friend...
...or the guns he carried.
It's as if he vanished from the face of the world altogether.
But–
But you're going to keep looking, aren't you?
He must be out there somewhere.
He's hurt and alone... and you said yourself that our enemies might still be out to find us.
We'll continue to search, *yes.*
But you must understand that our order is not as strong as it once was.

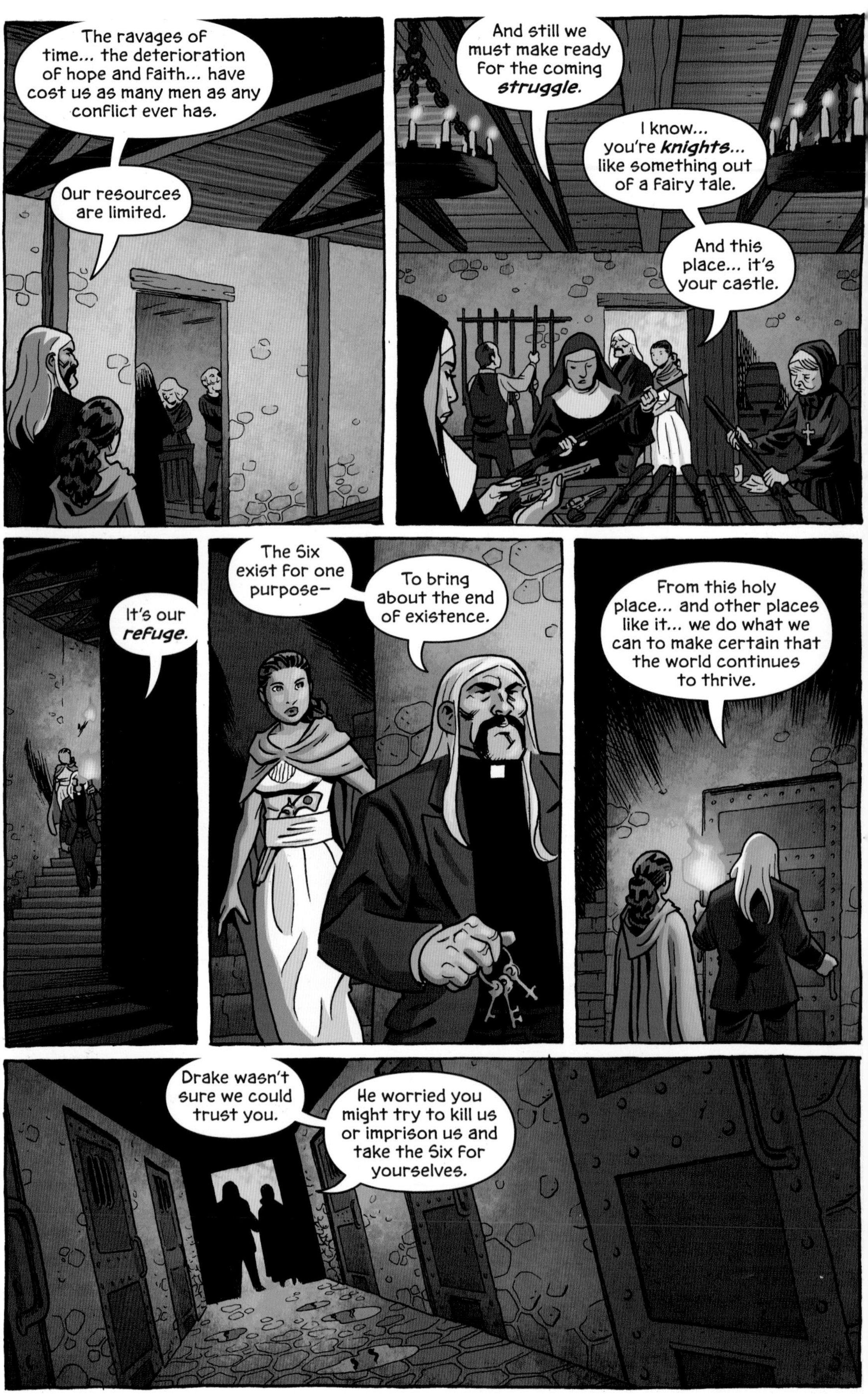
The ravages of time... the deterioration of hope and faith... have cost us as many men as any conflict ever has.
Our resources are limited.
And still we must make ready for the coming *struggle.*
I know... you're *knights...* like something out of a fairy tale.
And this place... it's your castle.
It's our *refuge.*
The Six exist for one purpose—
To bring about the end of existence.
From this holy place... and other places like it... we do what we can to make certain that the world continues to thrive.
Drake wasn't sure we could trust you.
He worried you might try to kill us or imprison us and take the Six for yourselves.

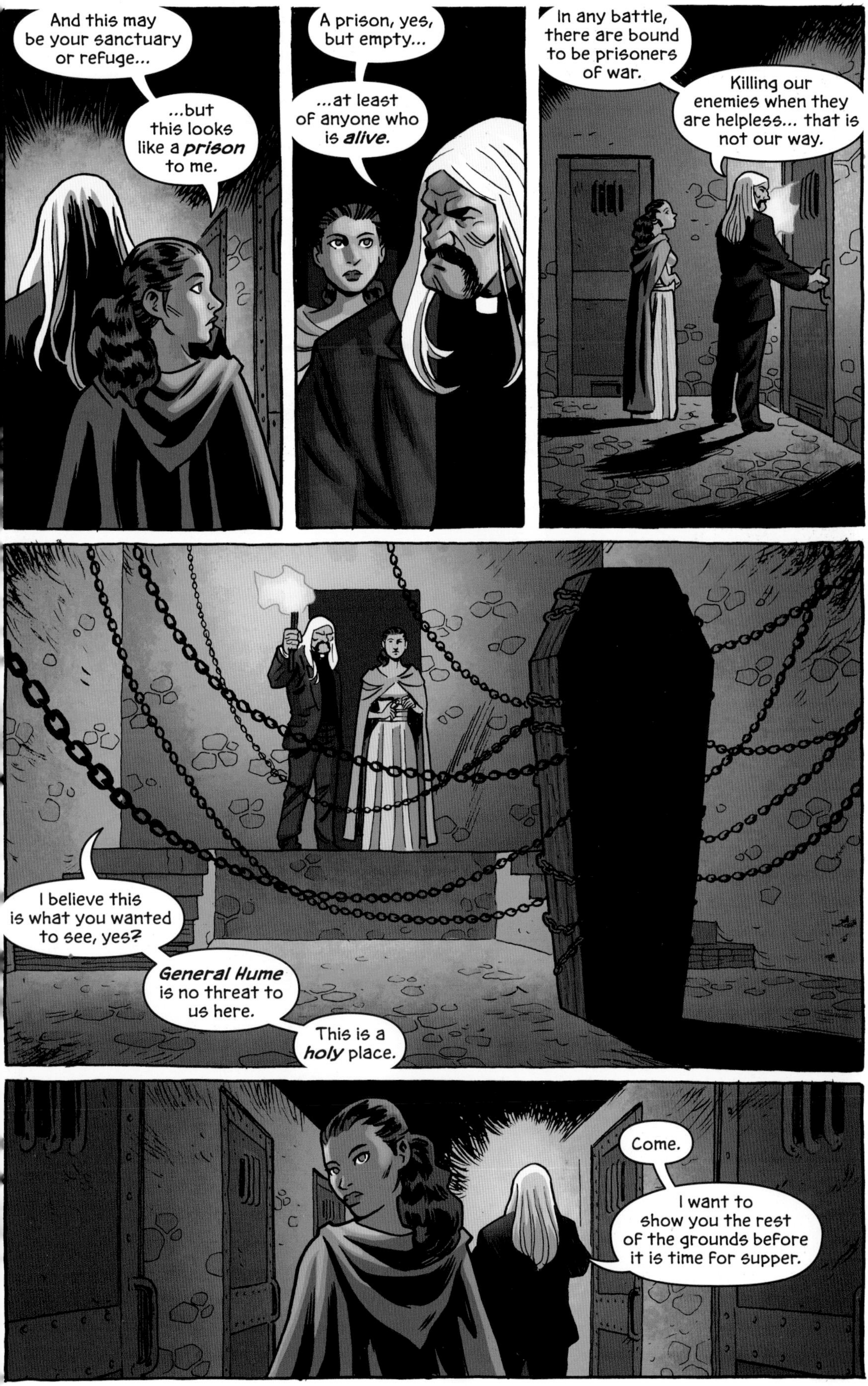
And this may be your sanctuary or refuge...
...but this looks like a *prison* to me.
A prison, yes, but empty...
...at least of anyone who is *alive.*
In any battle, there are bound to be prisoners of war.
Killing our enemies when they are helpless... that is not our way.
I believe this is what you wanted to see, yes?
General Hume is no threat to us here.
This is a *holy* place.
Come.
I want to show you the rest of the grounds before it is time for supper.

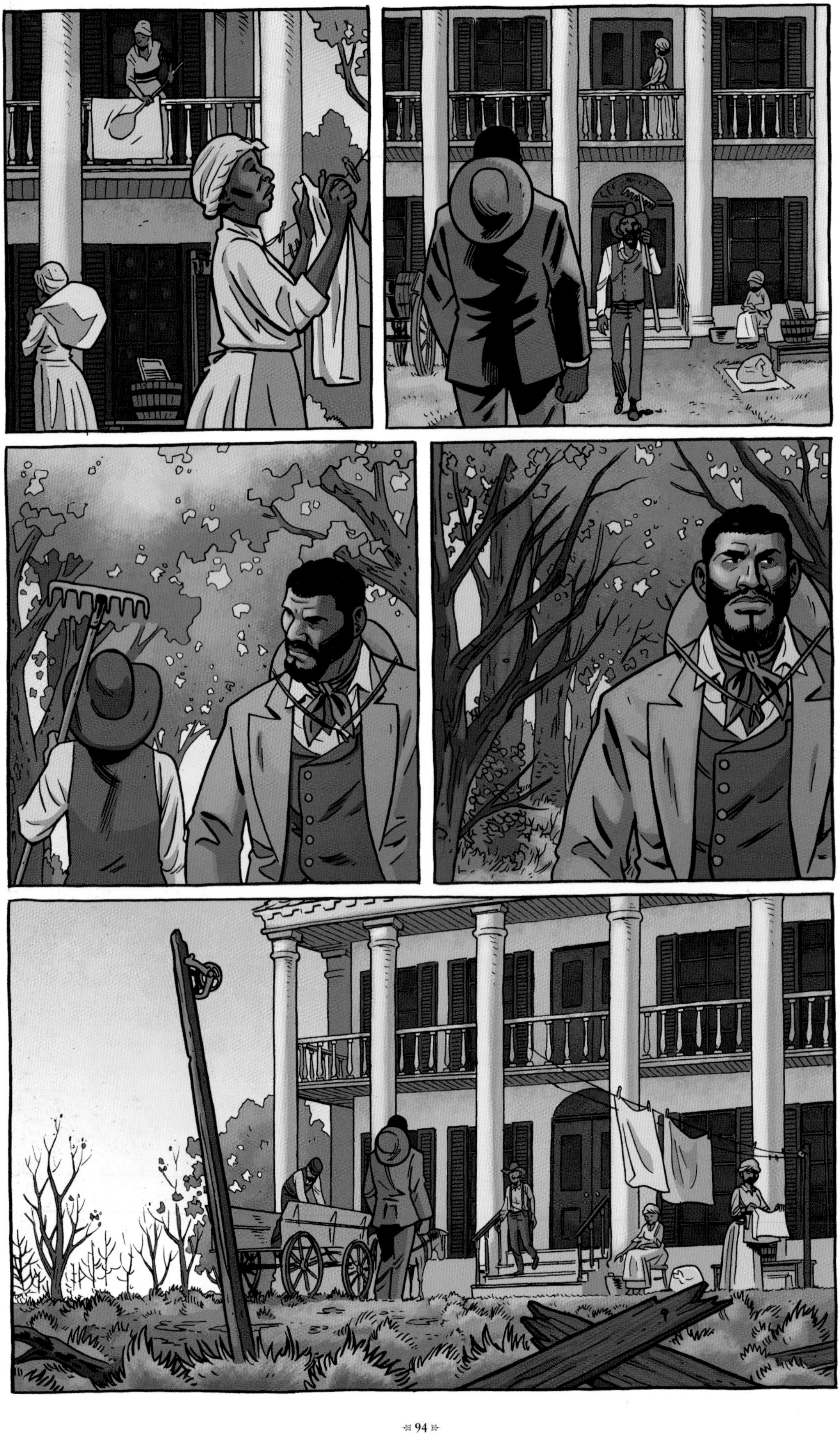

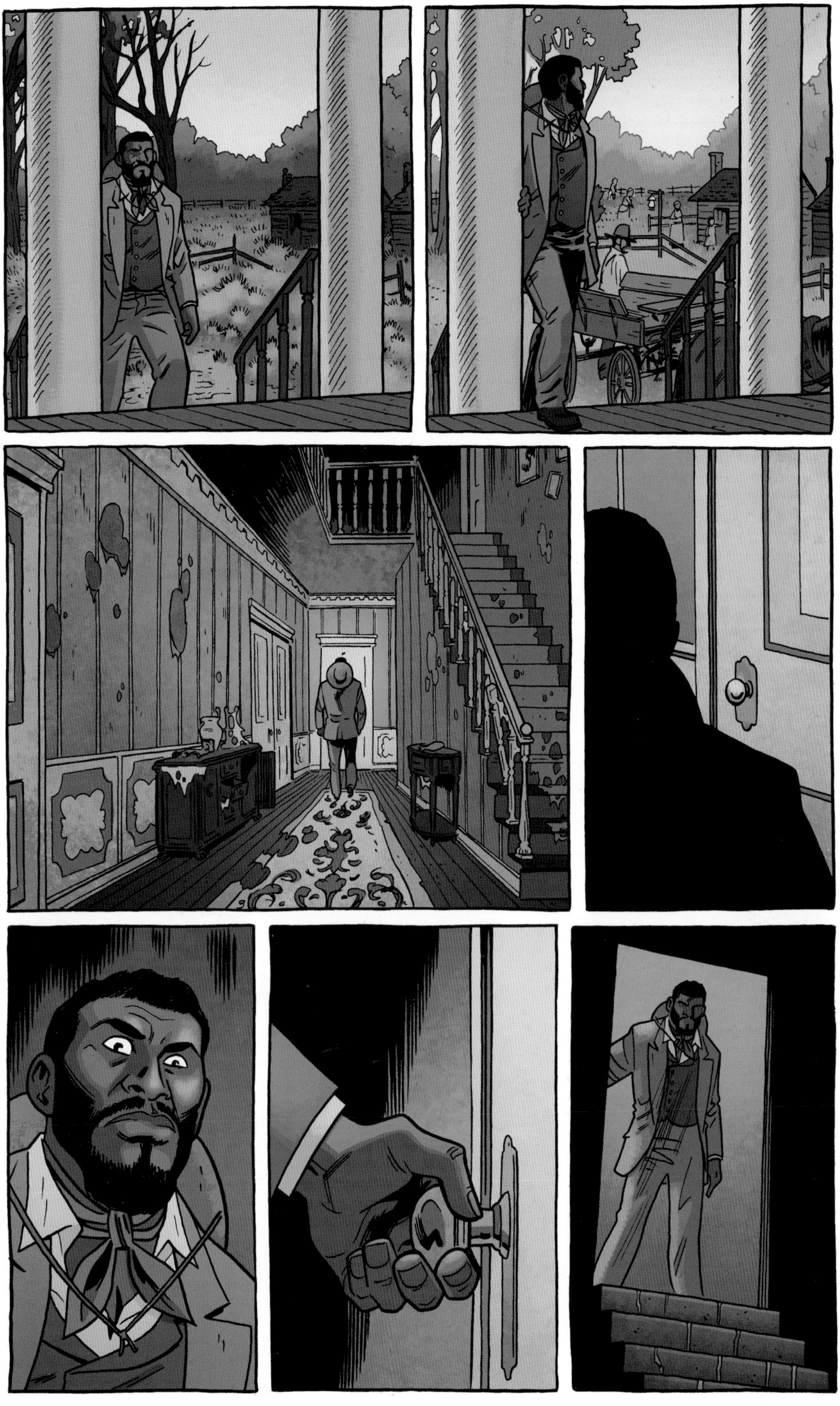

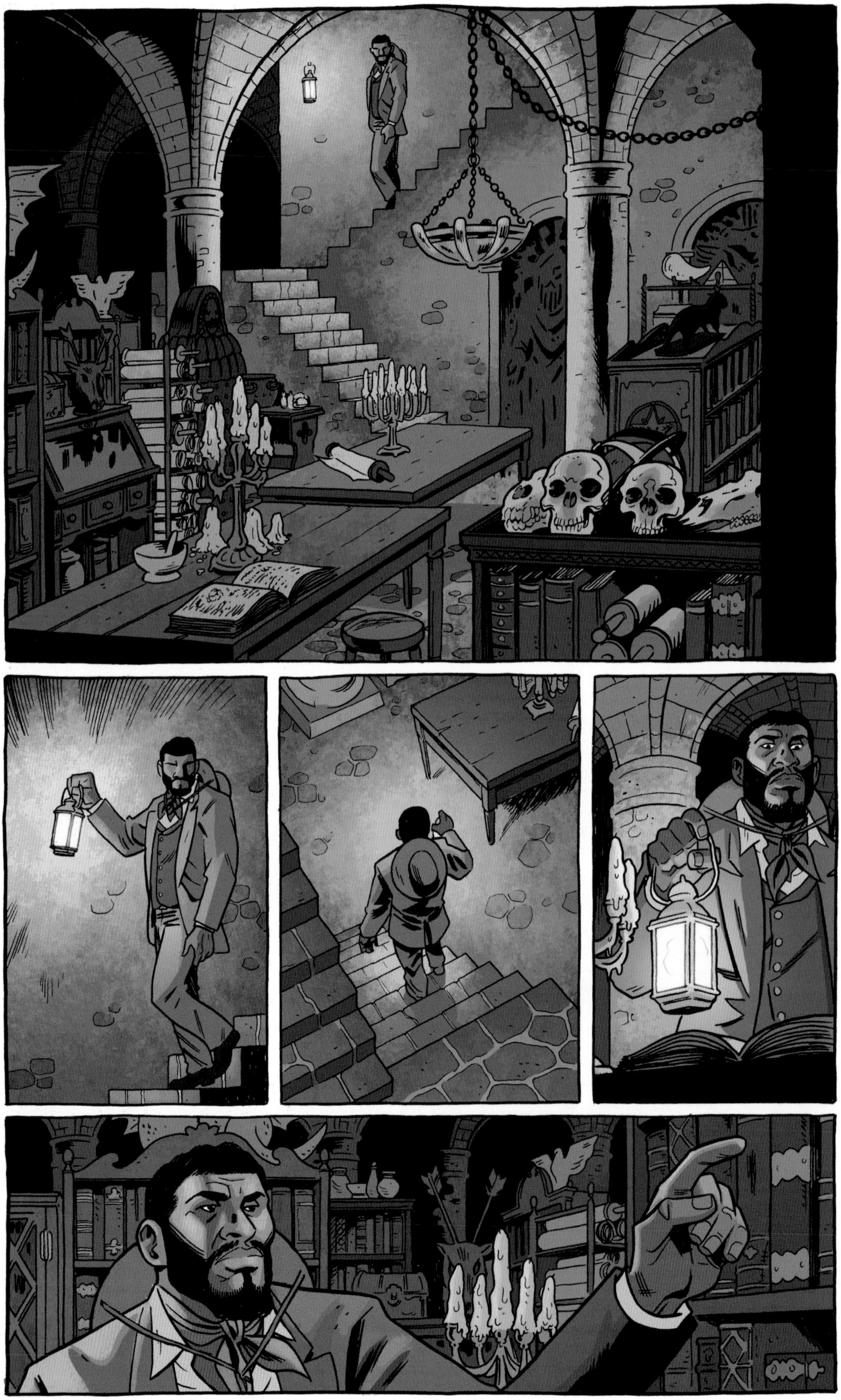

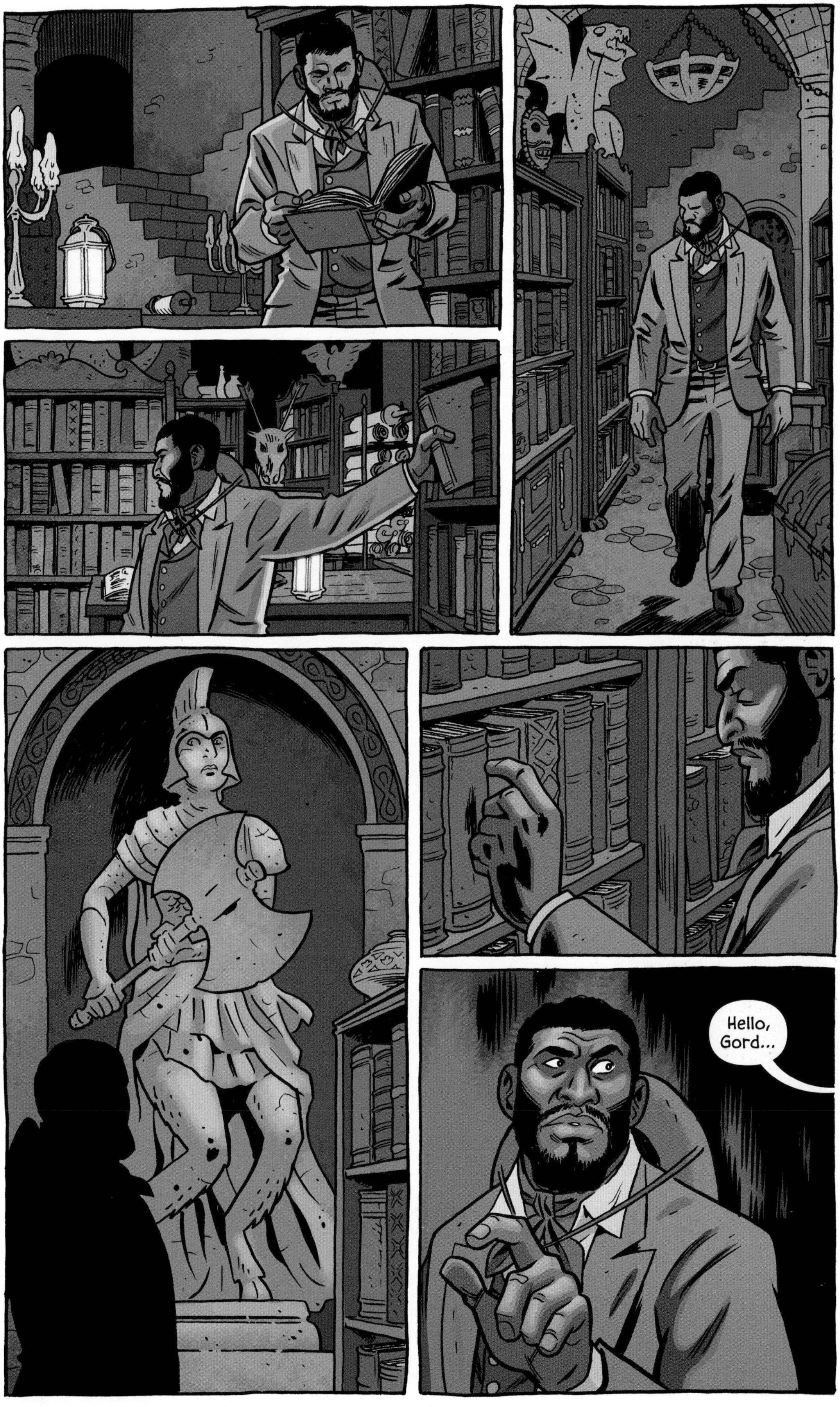
Hello, Gord...

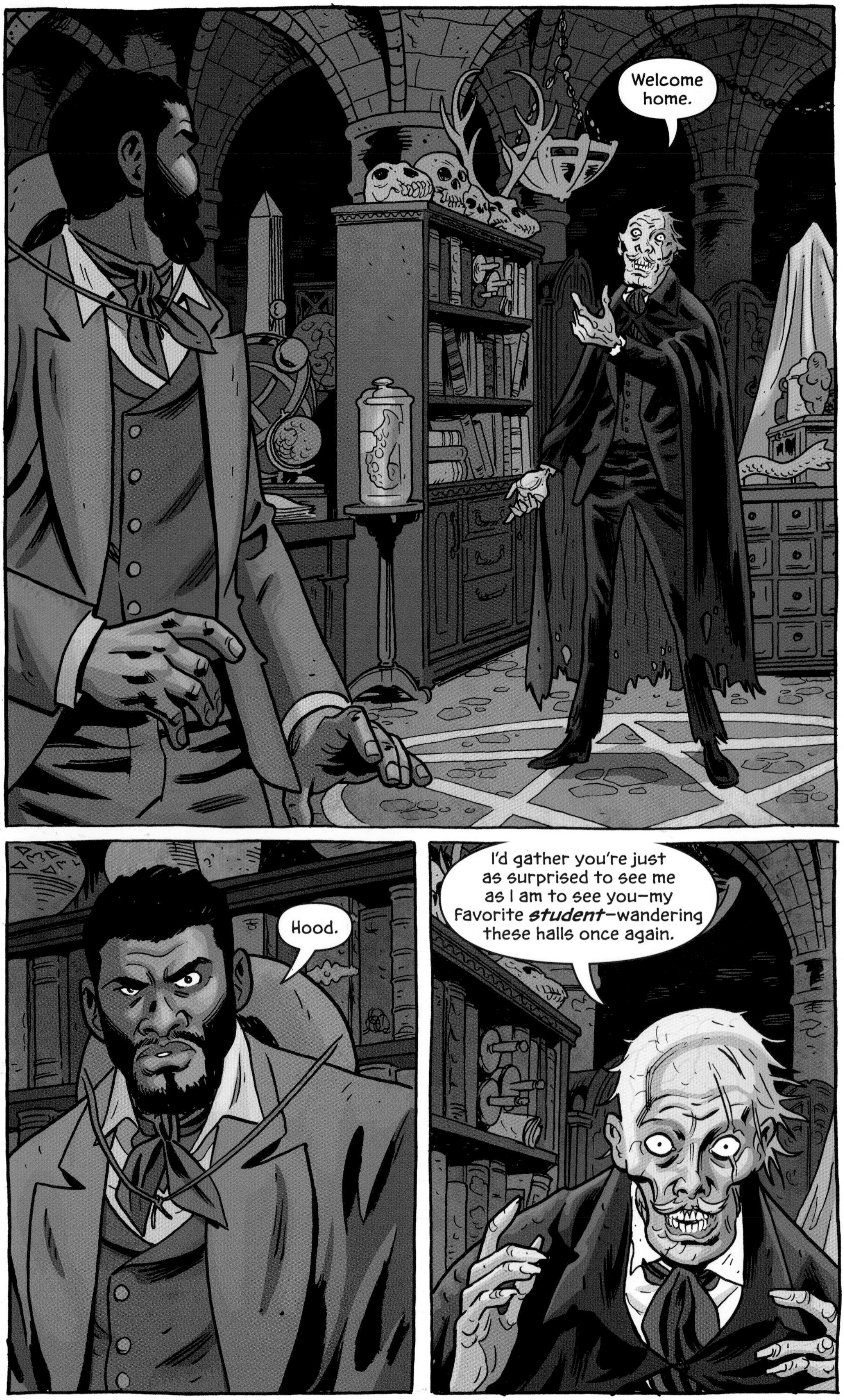
Welcome home.
Hood.
I'd gather you're just as surprised to see me as I am to see you—my favorite *student*—wandering these halls once again.

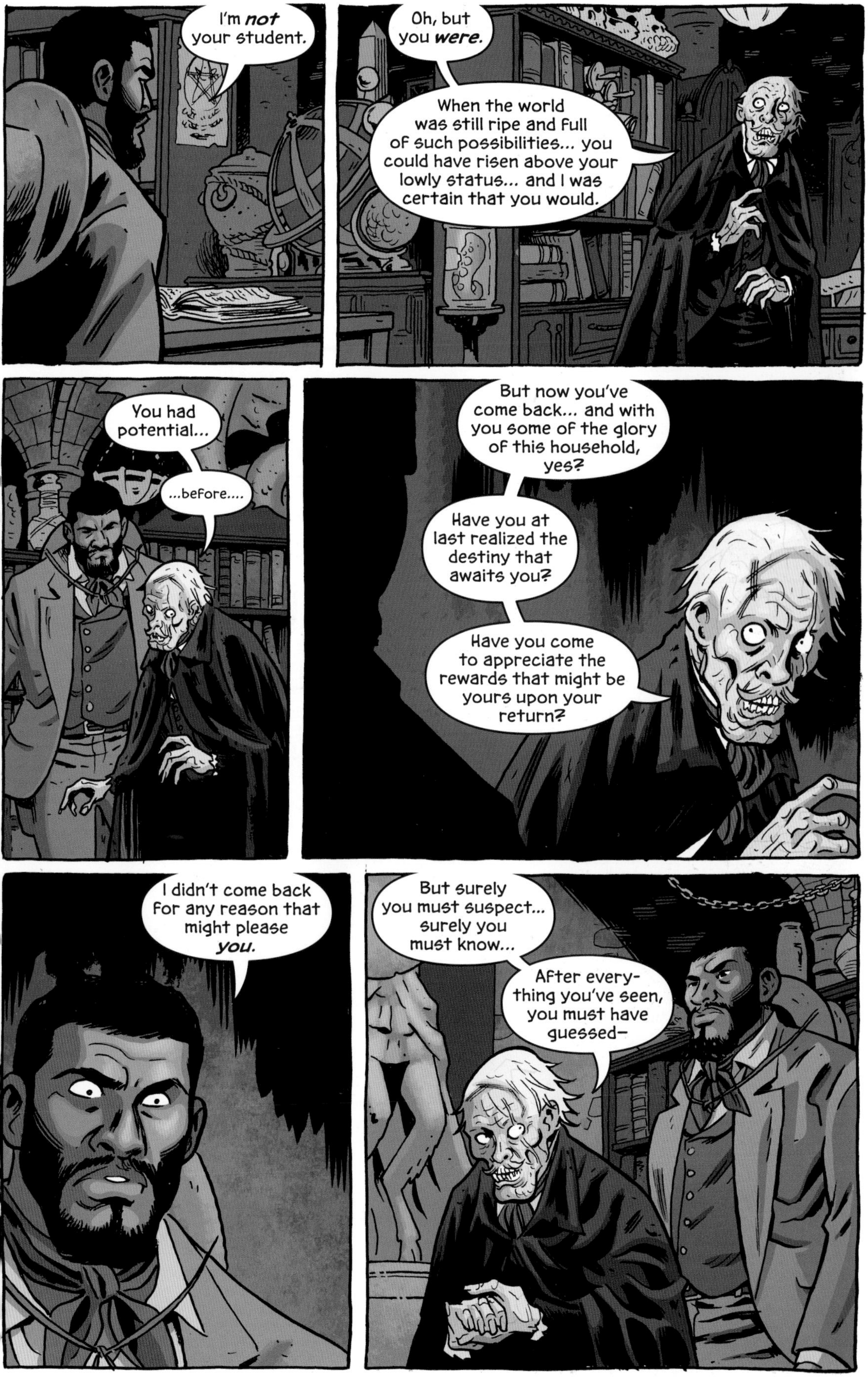
I'm *not* your student.
Oh, but you *were.*
When the world was still ripe and full of such possibilities... you could have risen above your lowly status... and I was certain that you would.
You had potential...
...before....
But now you've come back... and with you some of the glory of this household, yes?
Have you at last realized the destiny that awaits you?
Have you come to appreciate the rewards that might be yours upon your return?
I didn't come back for any reason that might please *you.*
But surely you must suspect... surely you must know...
After everything you've seen, you must have guessed—

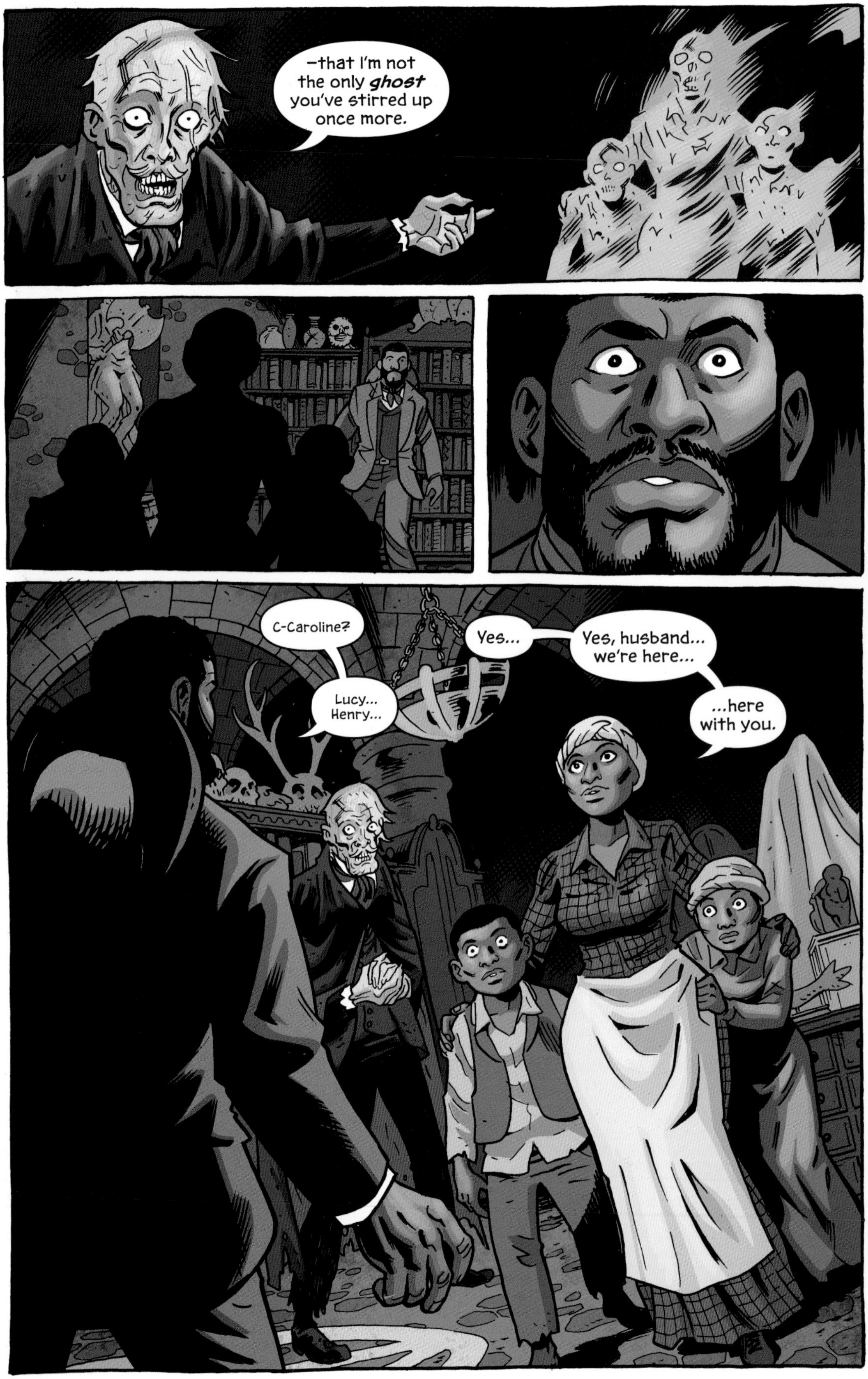
–that I'm not the only *ghost* you've stirred up once more.
C-Caroline?
Lucy... Henry...
Yes...
Yes, husband... we're here...
...here with you.

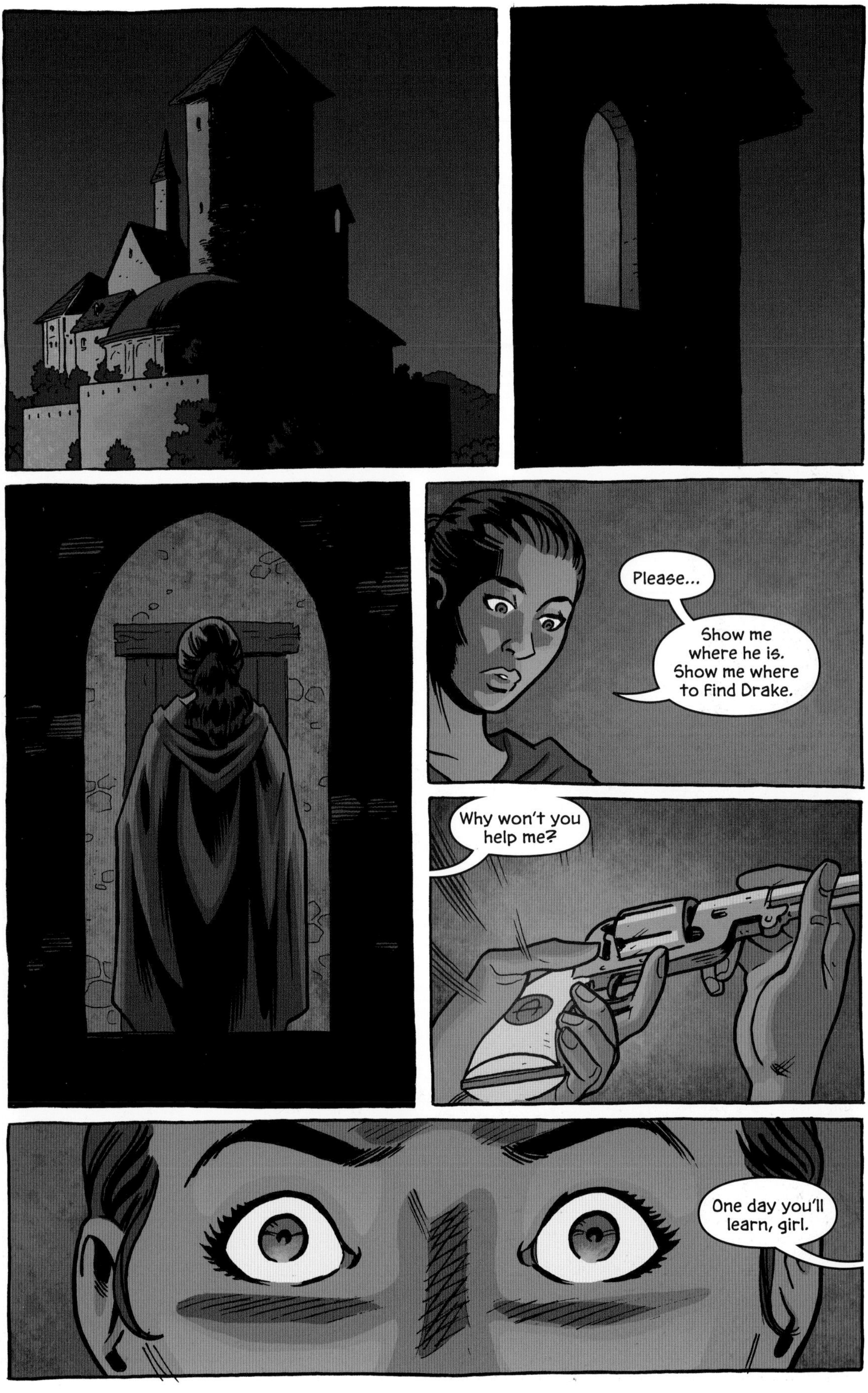
Please...
Show me where he is. Show me where to find Drake.
Why won't you help me?
One day you'll learn, girl.

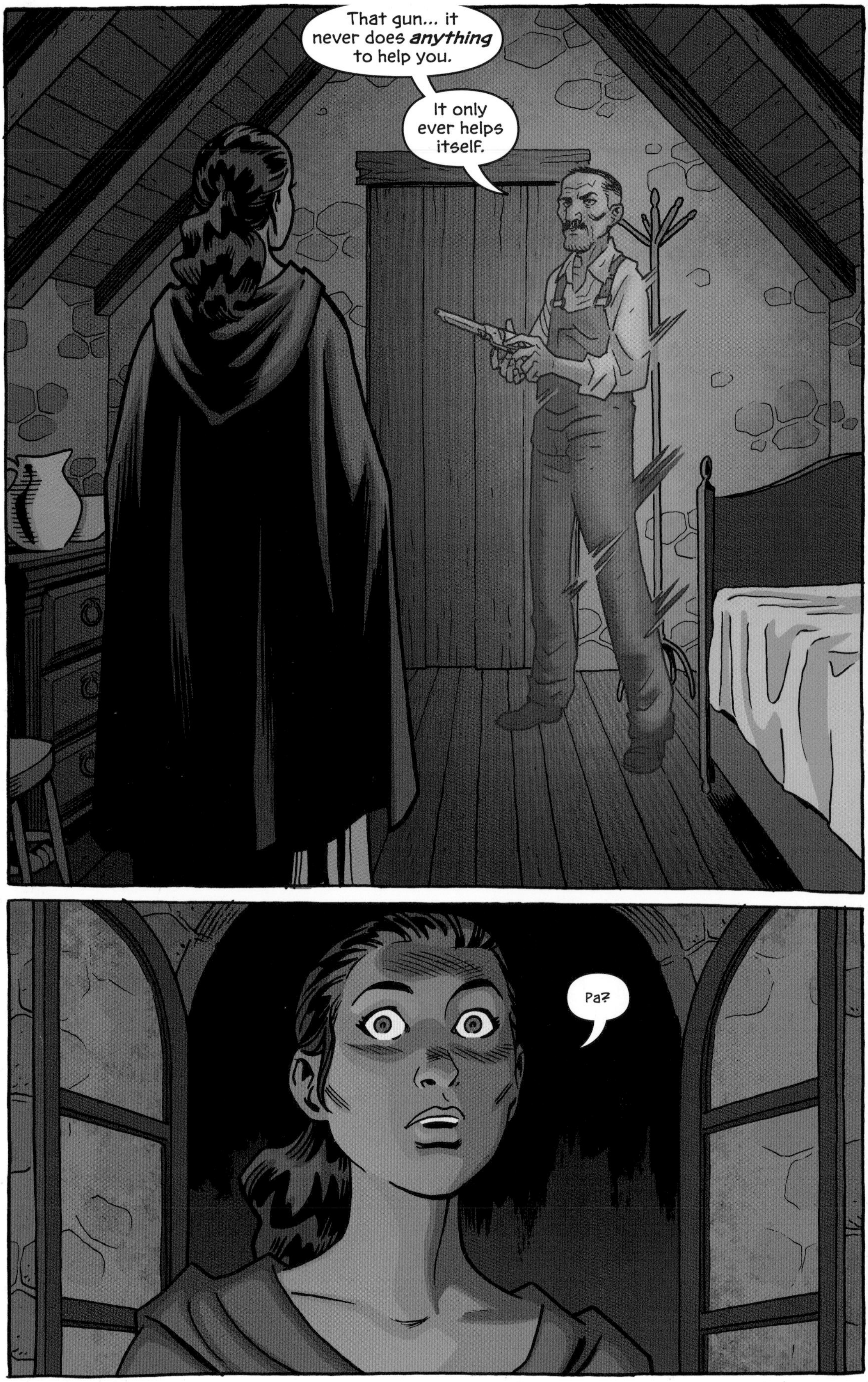

That gun... it never does *anything* to help you.
It only ever helps itself.
Pa?

CHAPTER
FIVE

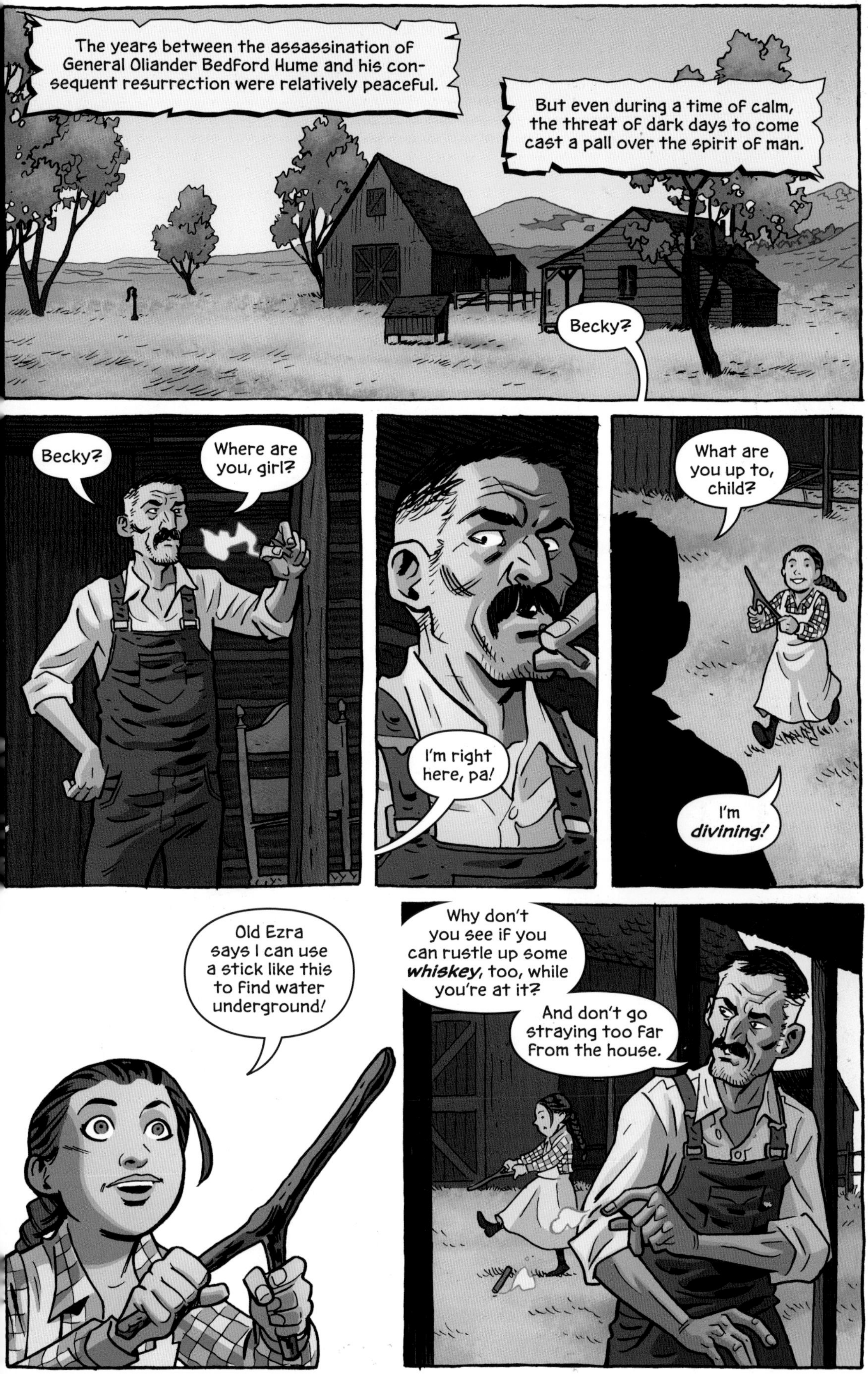

The years between the assassination of General Oliander Bedford Hume and his consequent resurrection were relatively peaceful.
But even during a time of calm, the threat of dark days to come cast a pall over the spirit of man.
Becky?
Becky?
Where are you, girl?
I'm right here, pa!
What are you up to, child?
I'm *divining!*
Old Ezra says I can use a stick like this to find water underground!
Why don't you see if you can rustle up some *whiskey*, too, while you're at it?
And don't go straying too far from the house.

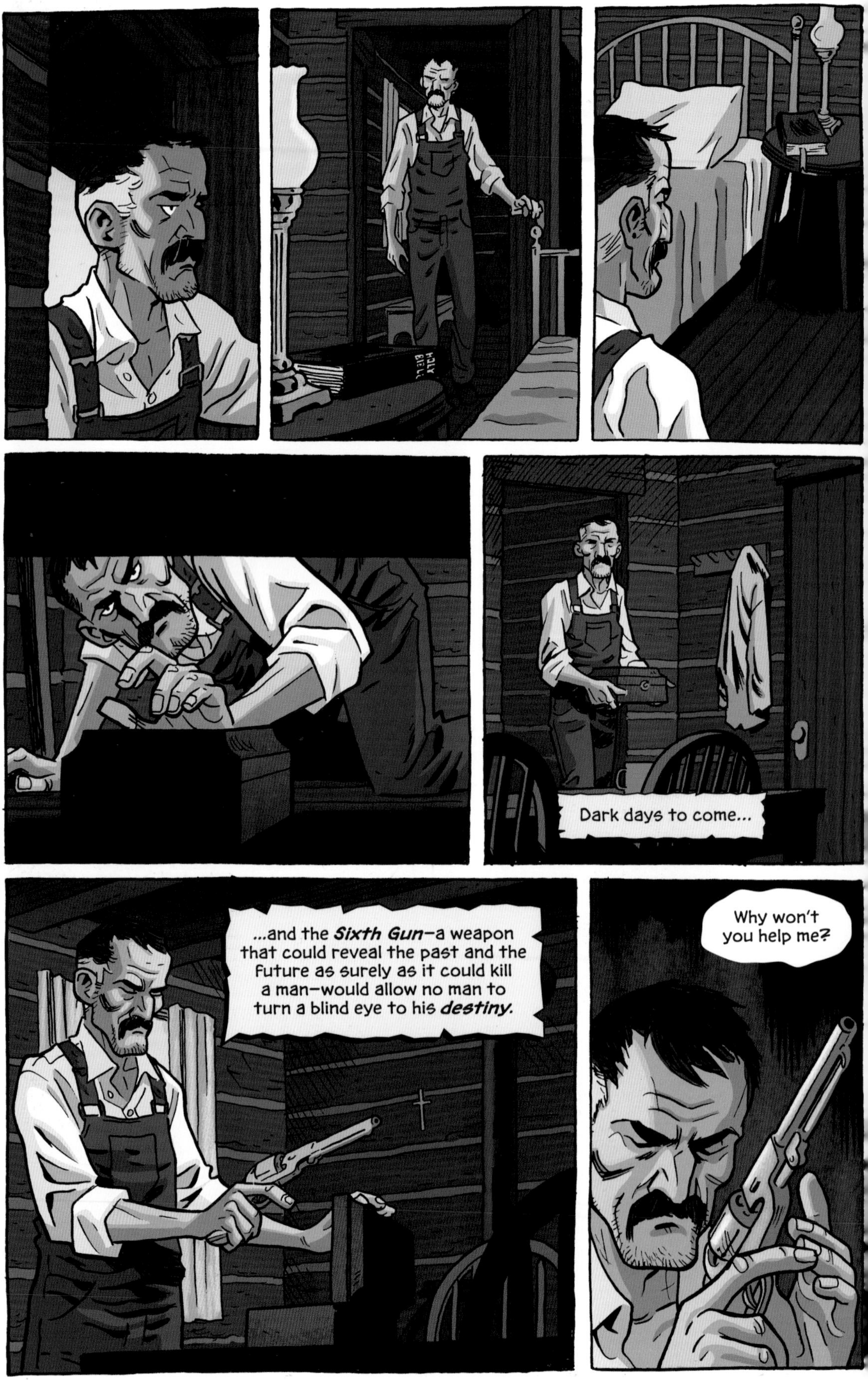
HOLY BIBLE
Dark days to come...
...and the Sixth Gun—a weapon that could reveal the past and the future as surely as it could kill a man—would allow no man to turn a blind eye to his destiny.
Why won't you help me?

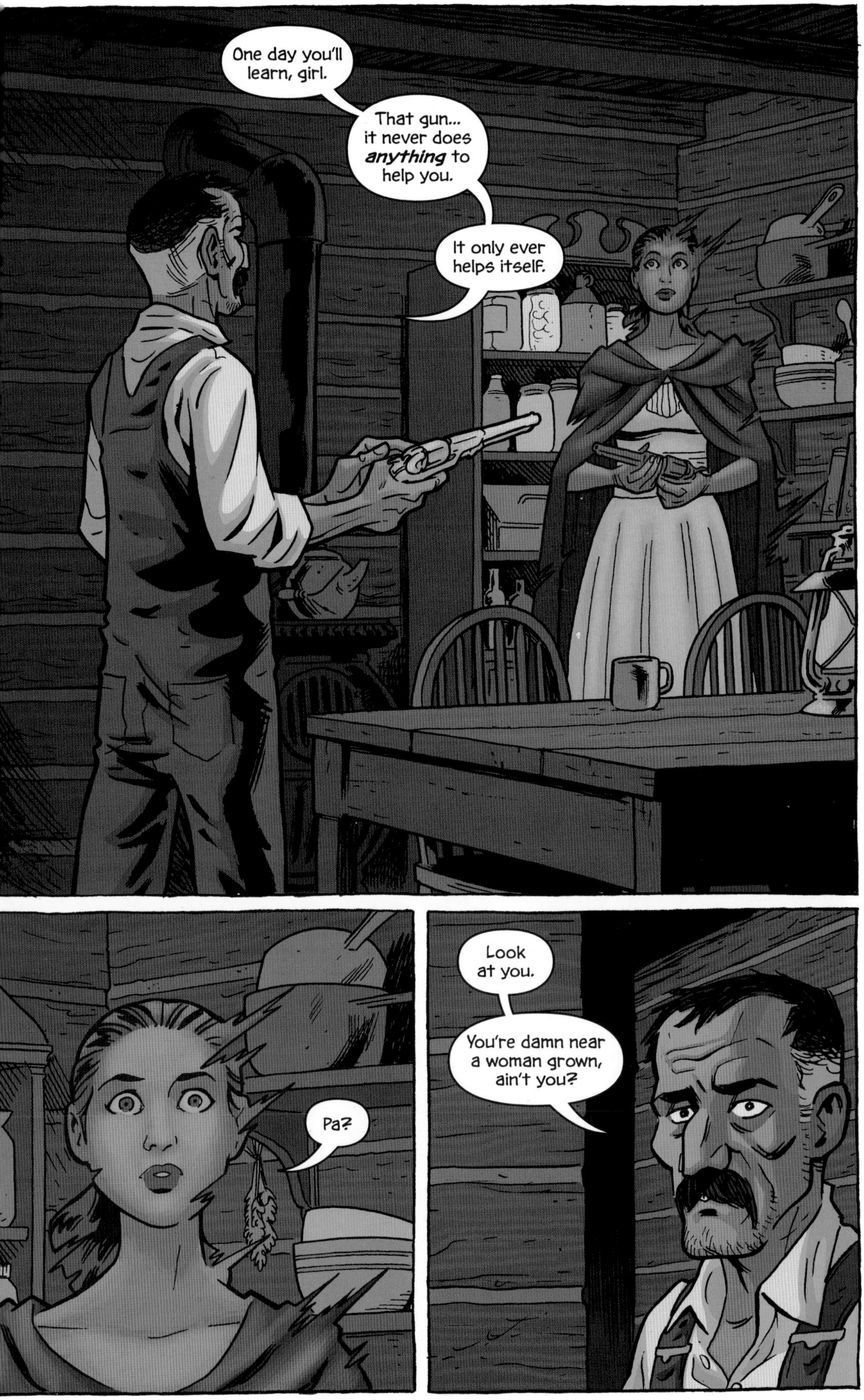
One day you'll learn, girl.
That gun... it never does *anything* to help you.
It only ever helps itself.
Pa?
Look at you.
You're damn near a woman grown, ain't you?

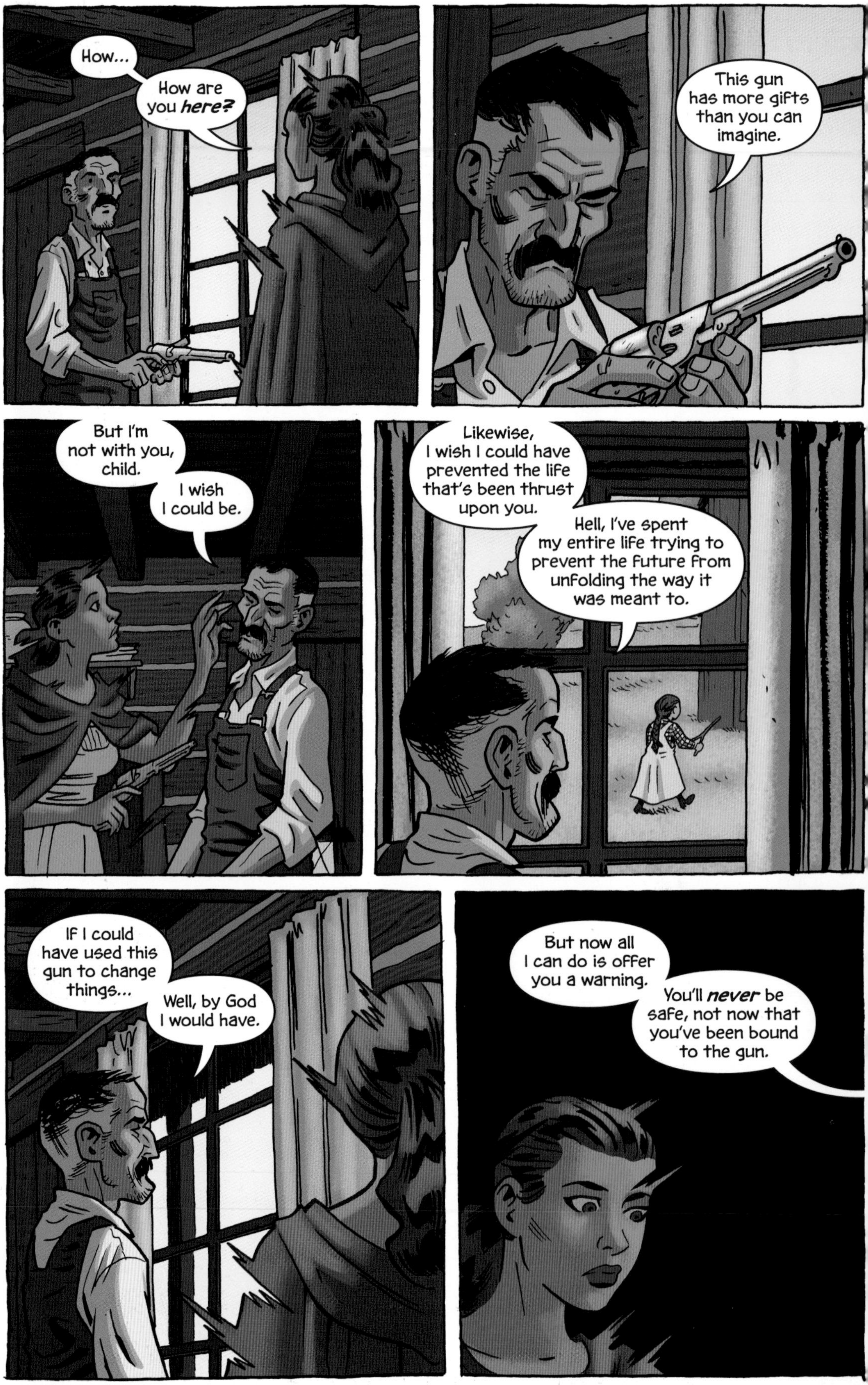
How...
How are you ***here?***
This gun has more gifts than you can imagine.
But I'm not with you, child.
I wish I could be.
Likewise, I wish I could have prevented the life that's been thrust upon you.
Hell, I've spent my entire life trying to prevent the future from unfolding the way it was meant to.
If I could have used this gun to change things...
Well, by God I would have.
But now all I can do is offer you a warning.
You'll ***never*** be safe, not now that you've been bound to the gun.

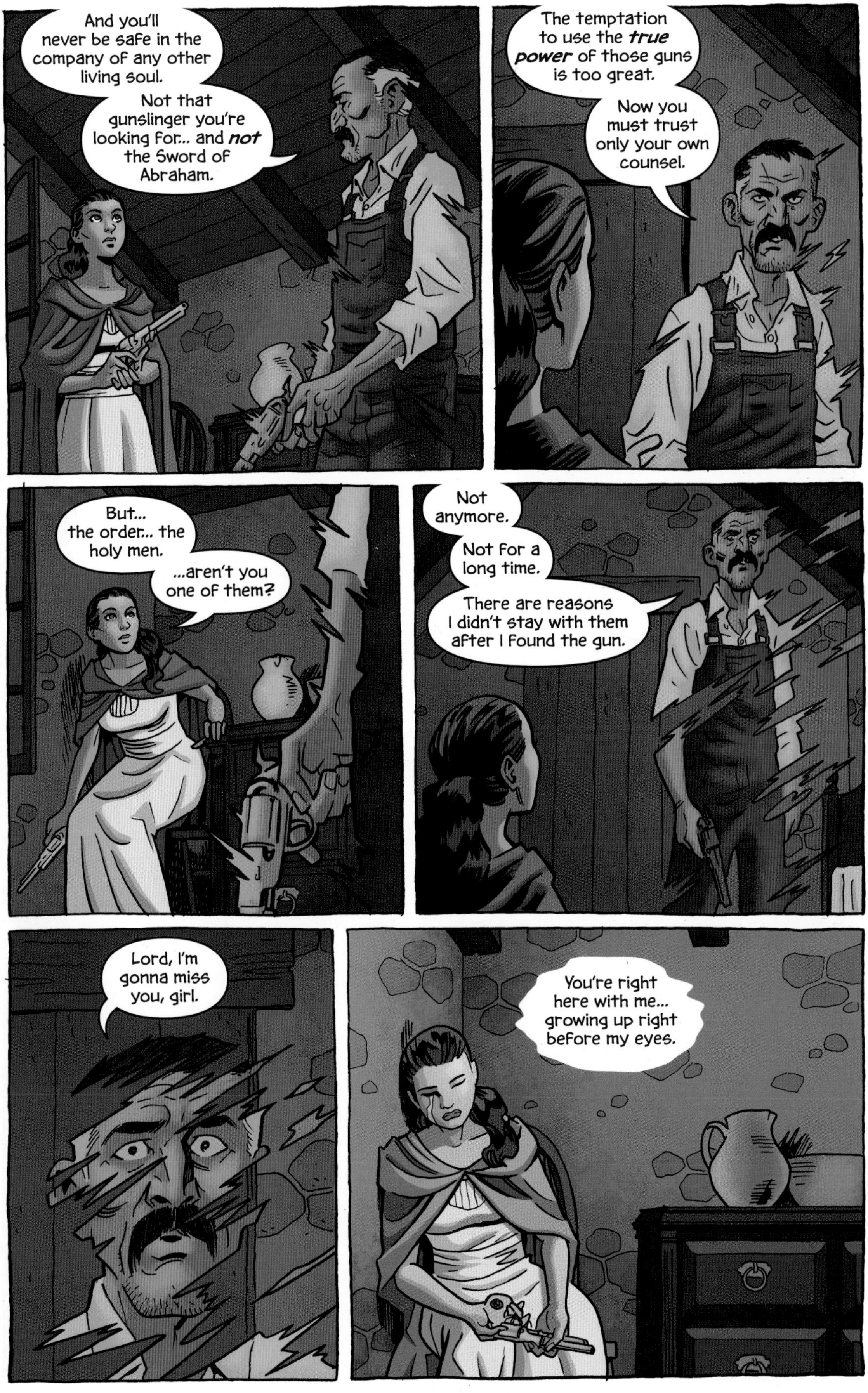
And you'll never be safe in the company of any other living soul.
Not that gunslinger you're looking for... and *not* the Sword of Abraham.
The temptation to use the *true power* of those guns is too great.
Now you must trust only your own counsel.
But... the order... the holy men.
...aren't you one of them?
Not anymore.
Not for a long time.
There are reasons I didn't stay with them after I found the gun.
Lord, I'm gonna miss you, girl.
You're right here with me... growing up right before my eyes.

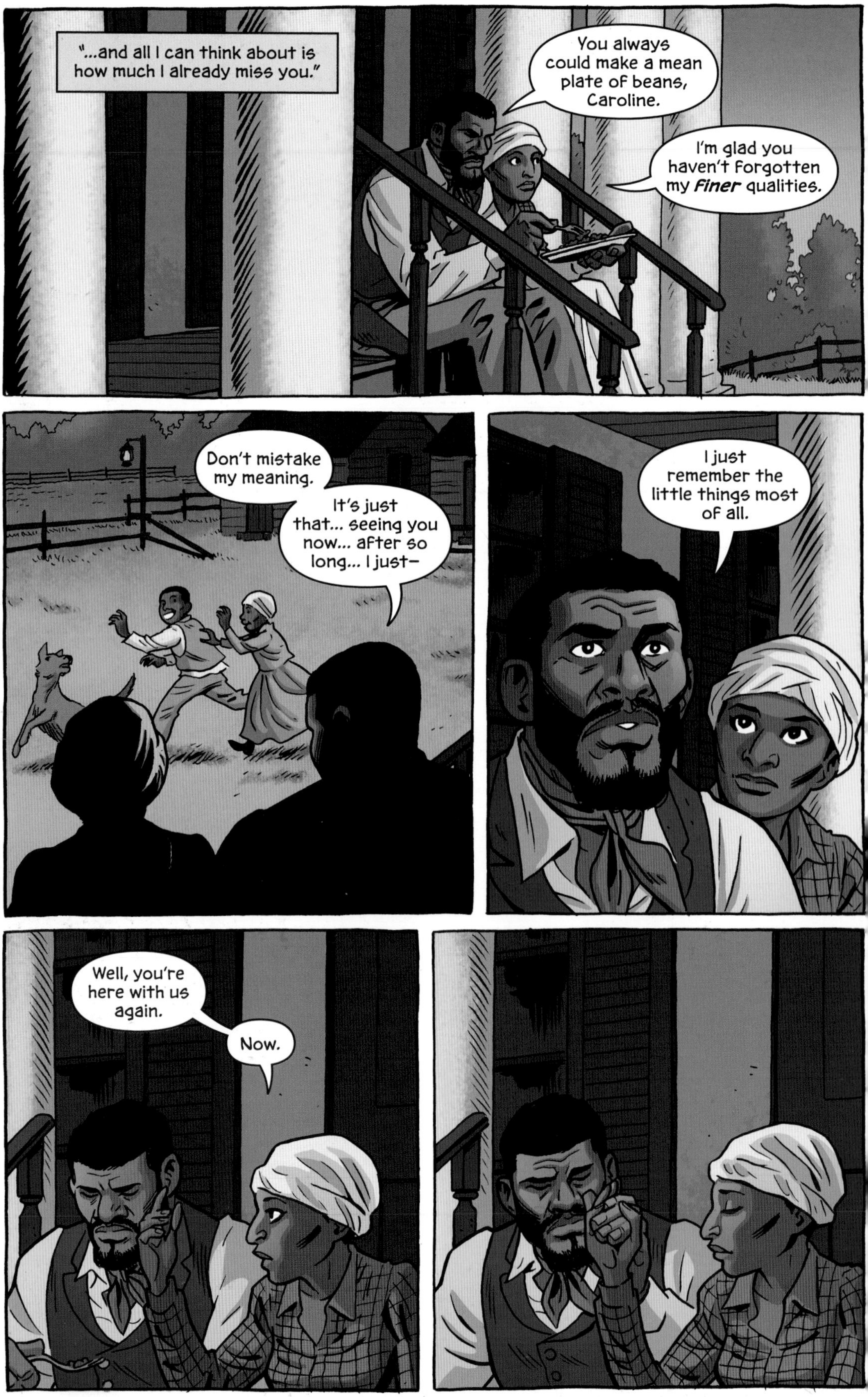
"...and all I can think about is how much I already miss you."
You always could make a mean plate of beans, Caroline.
I'm glad you haven't forgotten my *Finer* qualities.
Don't mistake my meaning.
It's just that... seeing you now... after so long... I just–
I just remember the little things most of all.
Well, you're here with us again.
Now.

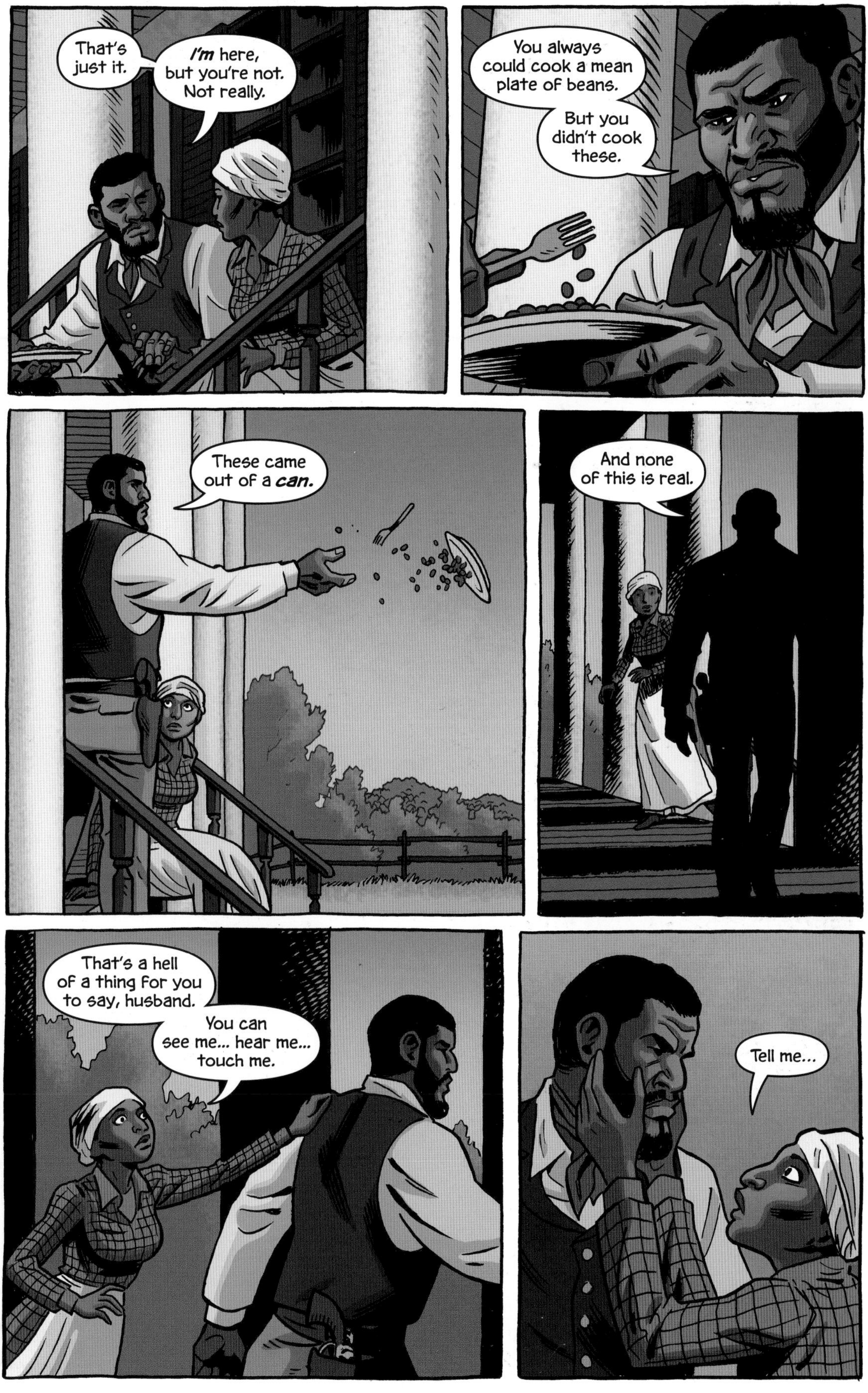
That's just it.
I'm here, but you're not. Not really.
You always could cook a mean plate of beans.
But you didn't cook these.
These came out of a *can.*
And none of this is real.
That's a hell of a thing for you to say, husband.
You can see me... hear me... touch me.
Tell me...

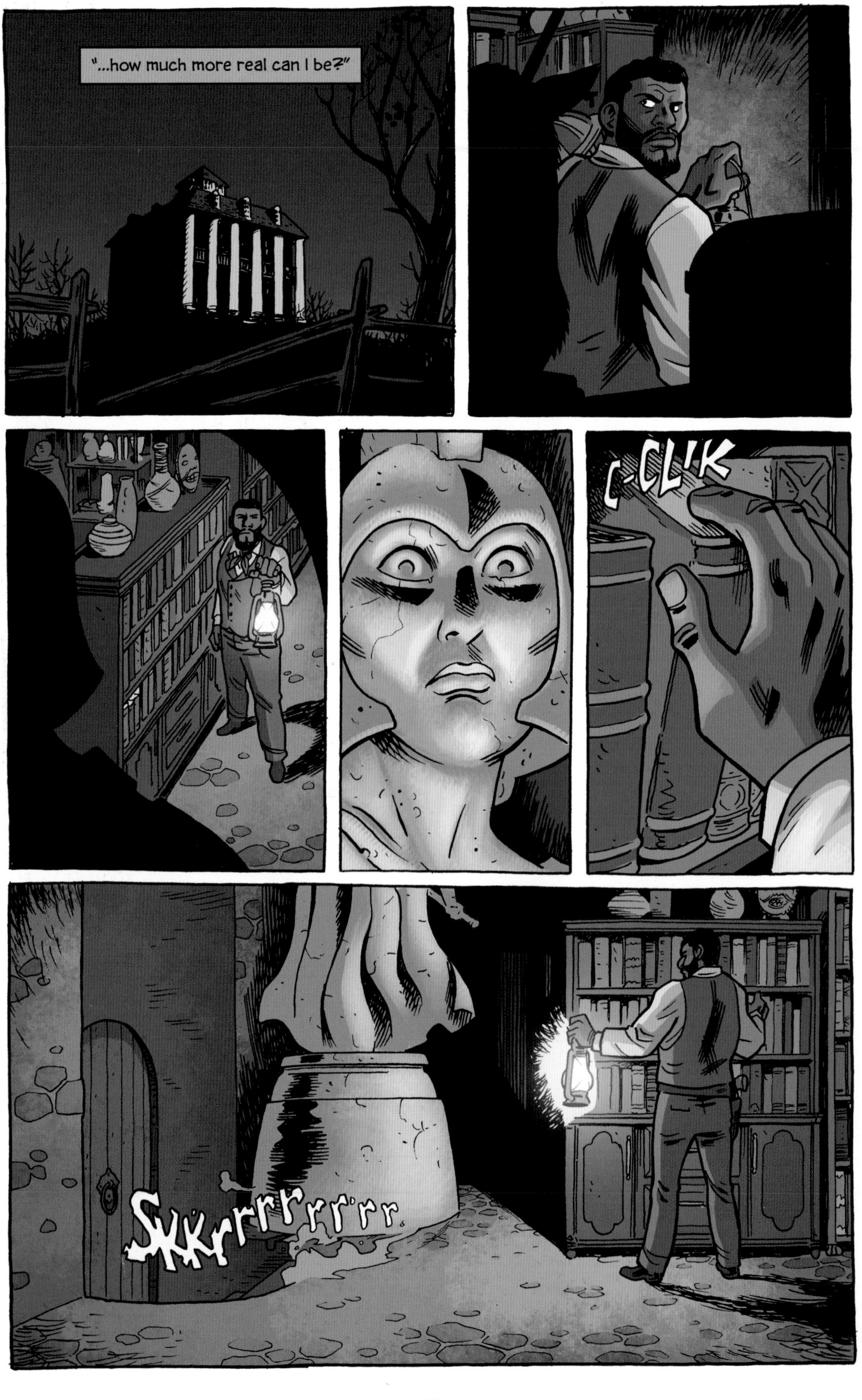
"...how much more real can I be?"
C-CLIK
SKKRrrrrrrr

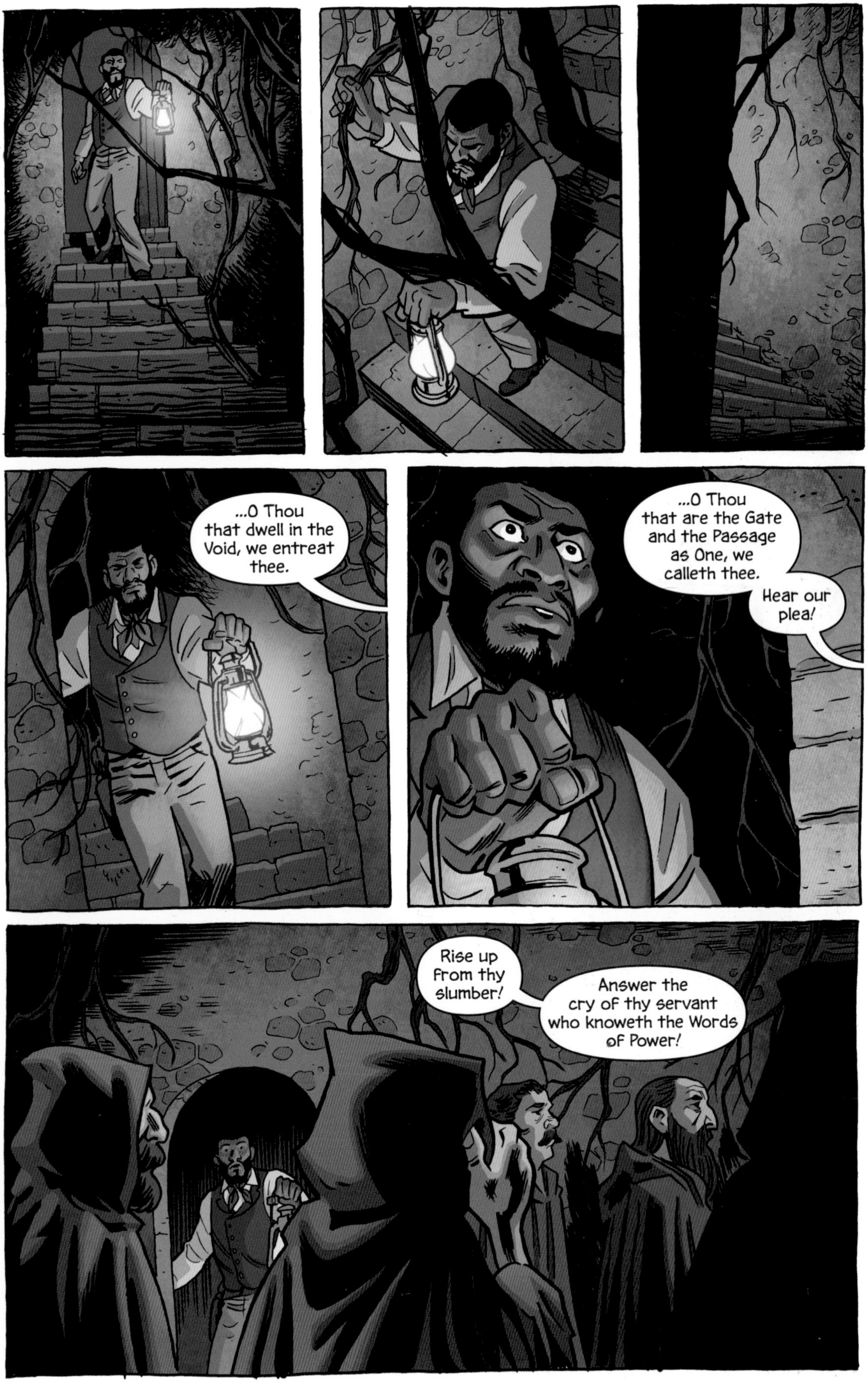
...O Thou that dwell in the Void, we entreat thee.
...O Thou that are the Gate and the Passage as One, we calleth thee.
Hear our plea!
Rise up from thy slumber!
Answer the cry of thy servant who knoweth the Words of Power!

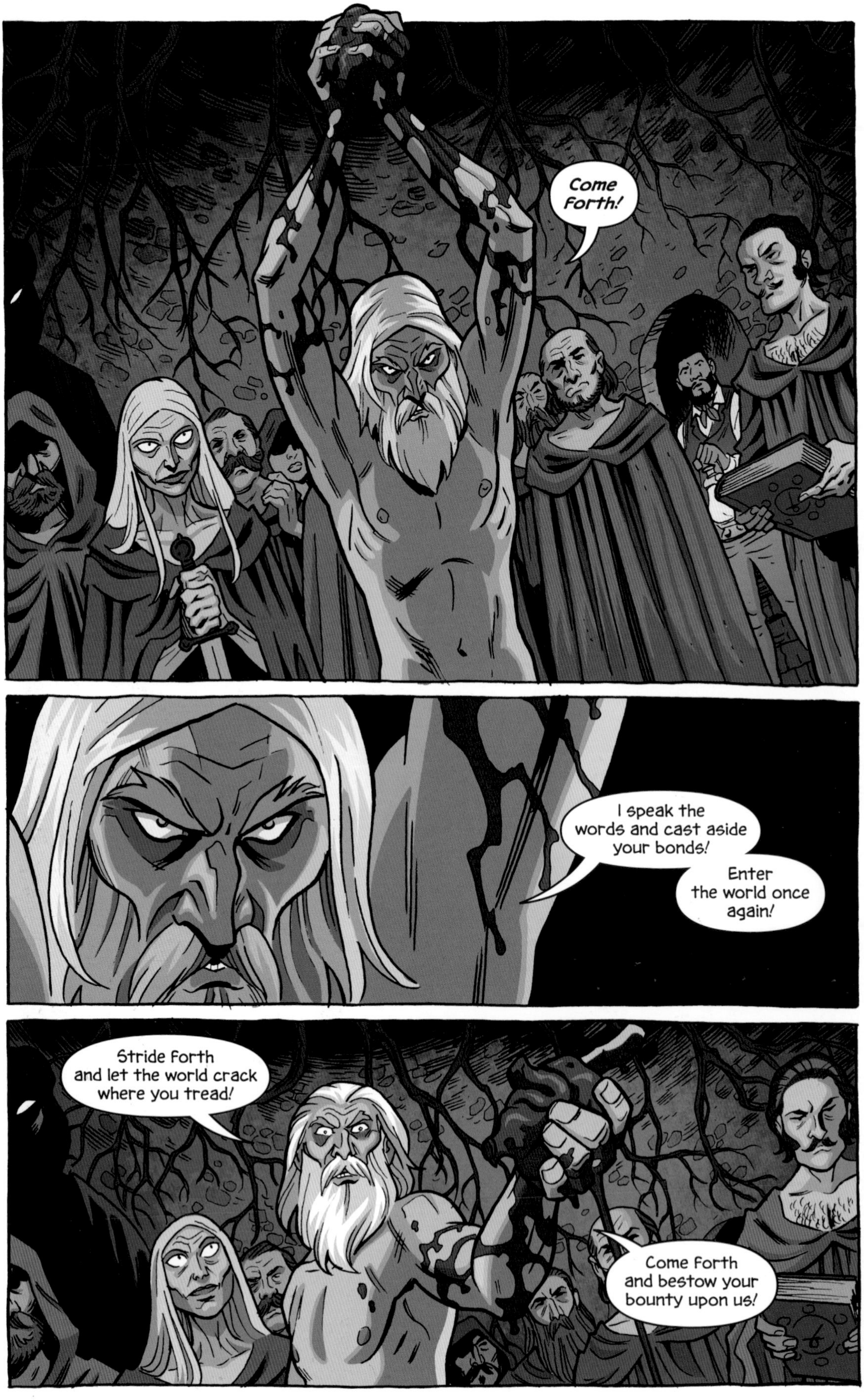
Come forth!
I speak the words and cast aside your bonds!
Enter the world once again!
Stride Forth and let the world crack where you tread!
Come Forth and bestow your bounty upon us!

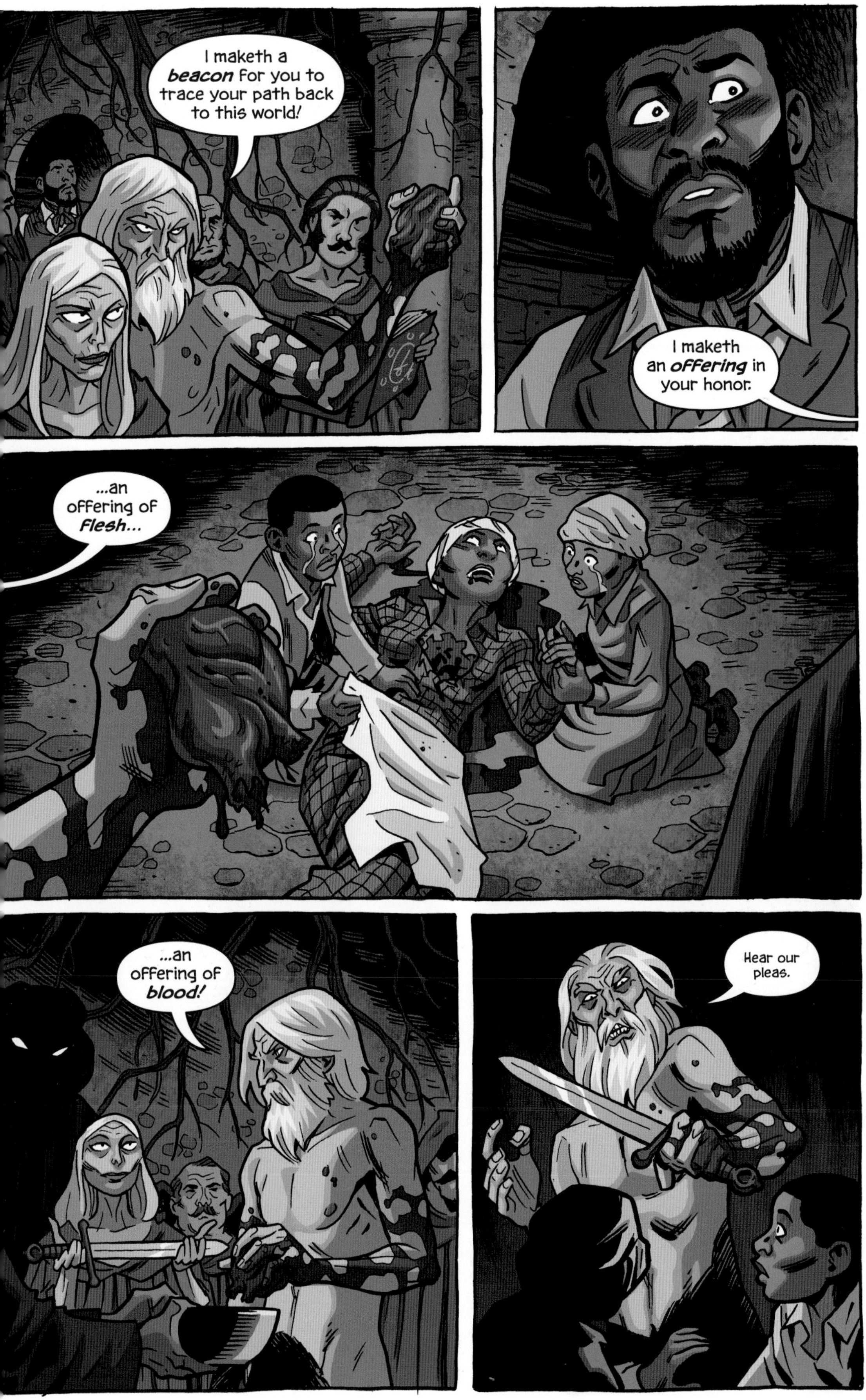
I maketh a beacon for you to trace your path back to this world!
I maketh an offering in your honor.
...an offering of flesh...
...an offering of blood!
Hear our pleas.

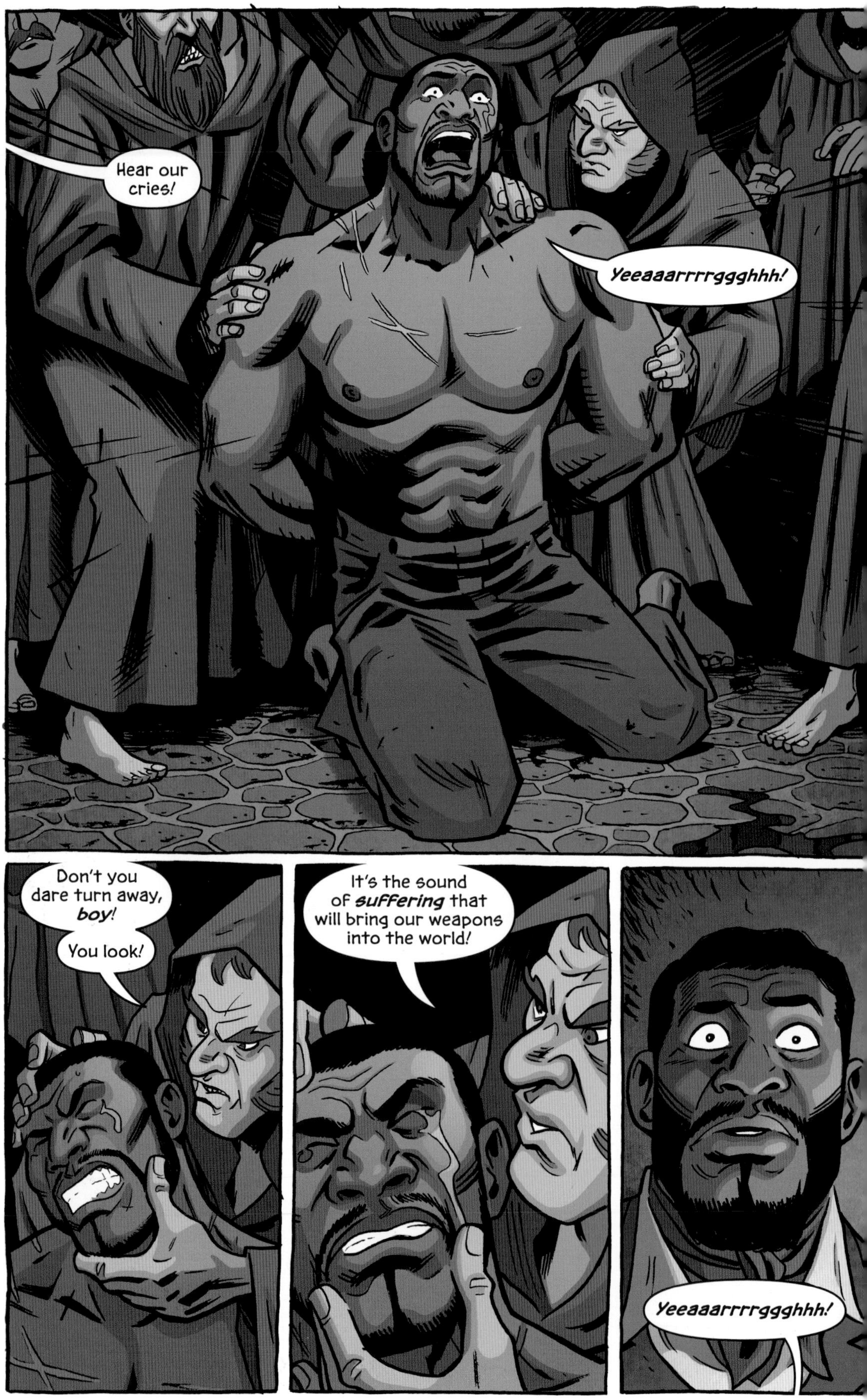

Hear our cries!
Yeeaaarrrrggghhh!
Don't you dare turn away, *boy*!
You look!
It's the sound of *suffering* that will bring our weapons into the world!
Yeeaaarrrrggghhh!

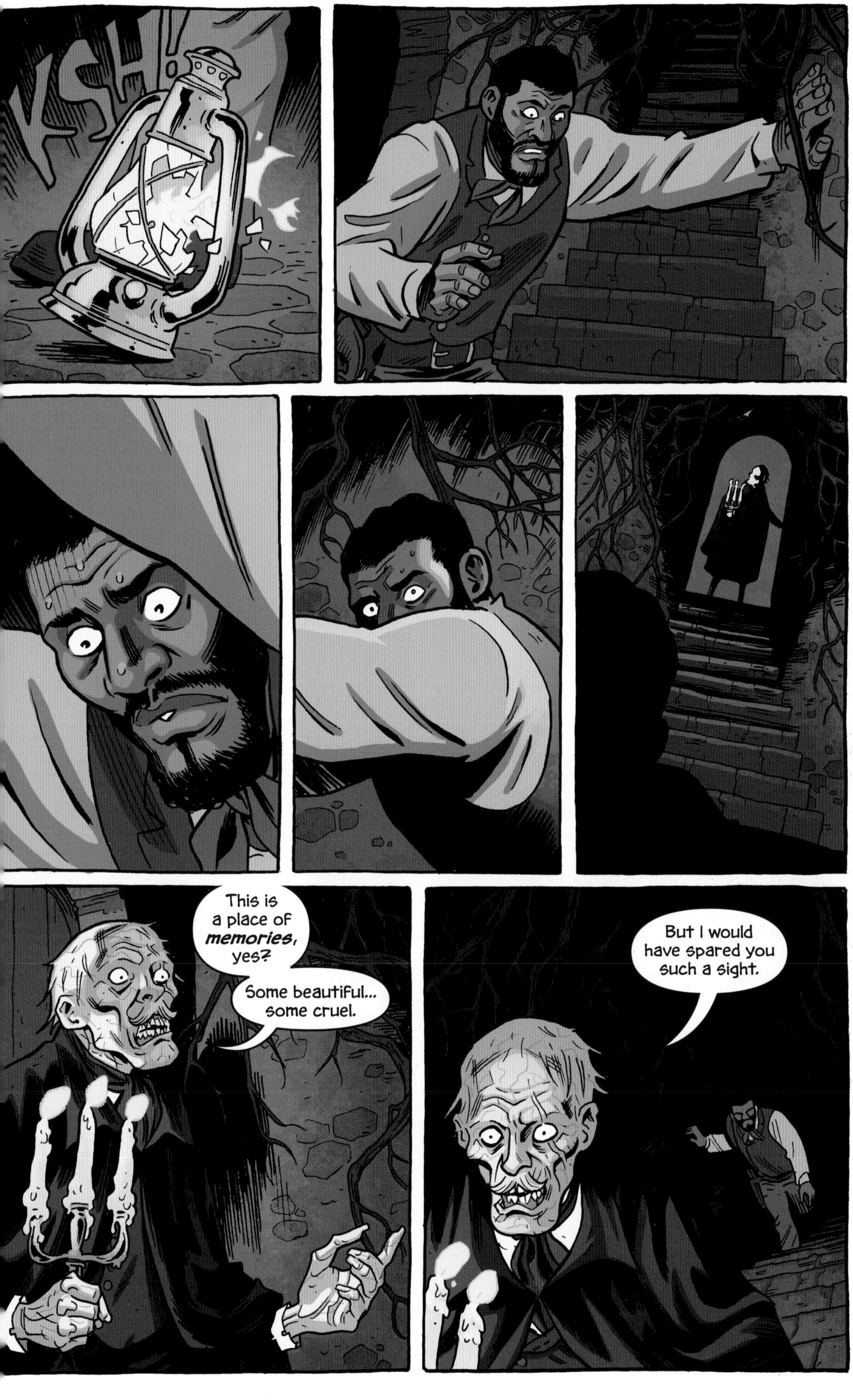
KSH!
This is a place of memories, yes?
Some beautiful... some cruel.
But I would have spared you such a sight.

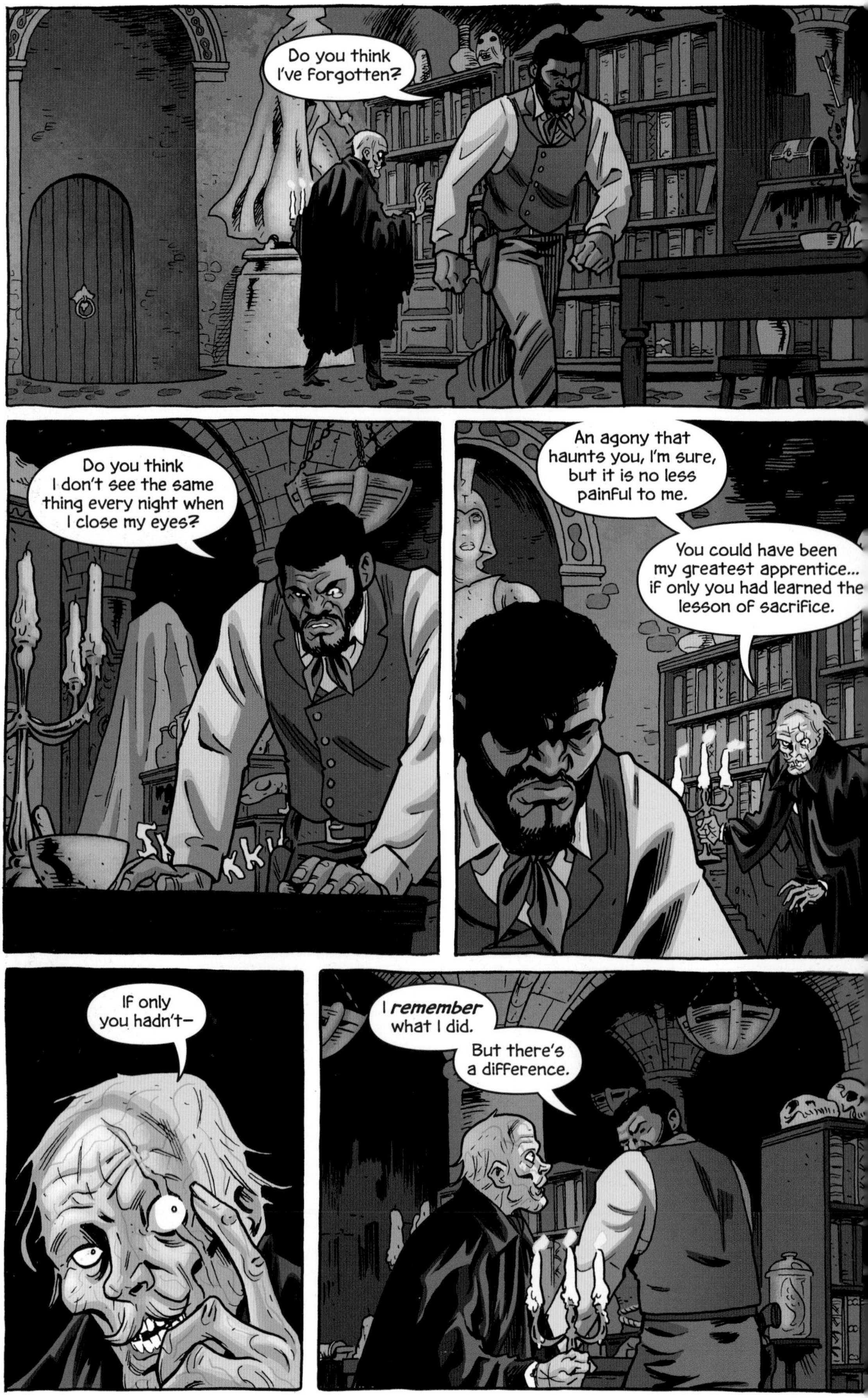
Do you think
I've forgotten?
Do you think
I don't see the same
thing every night when
I close my eyes?
An agony that
haunts you, I'm sure,
but it is no less
painful to me.
You could have been
my greatest apprentice...
if only you had learned the
lesson of sacrifice.
If only
you hadn't—
I **remember**
what I did.
But there's
a difference.

"...I want to see what happens next."

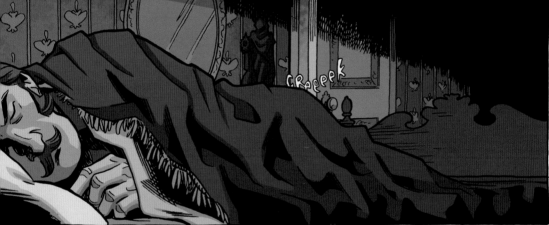

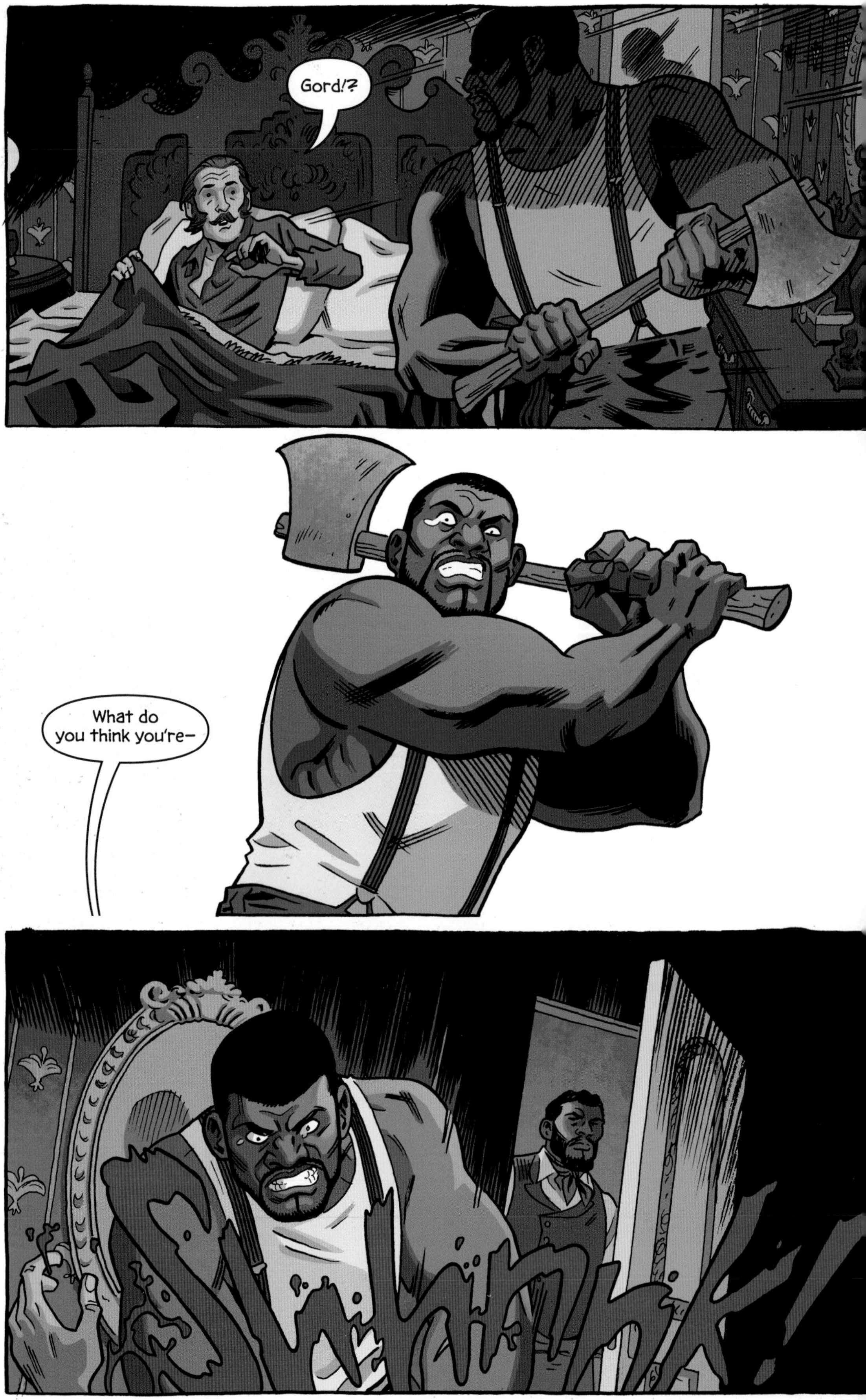
Gord!?
What do you think you're–

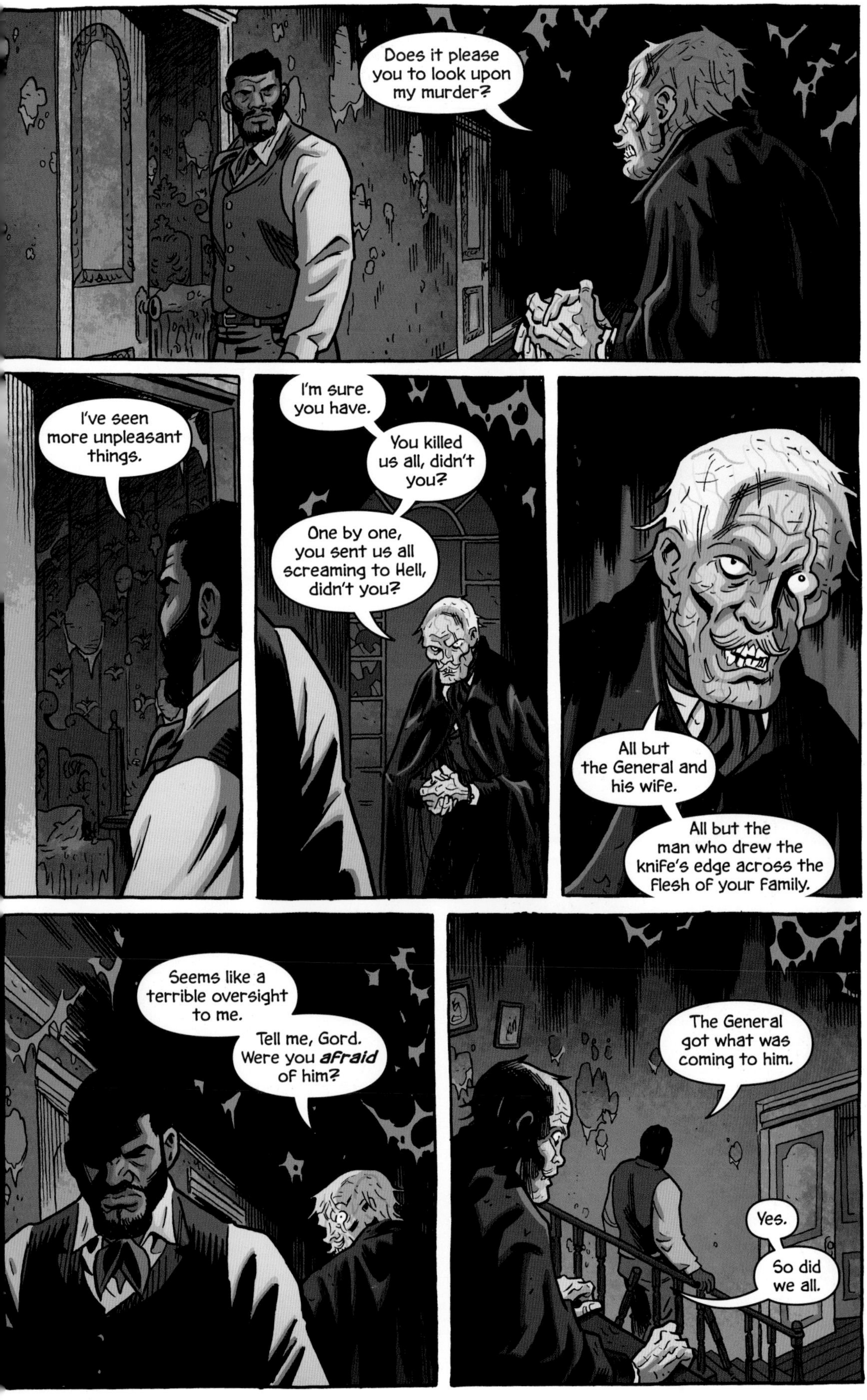
Does it please you to look upon my murder?
I've seen more unpleasant things.
I'm sure you have.
You killed us all, didn't you?
One by one, you sent us all screaming to Hell, didn't you?
All but the General and his wife.
All but the man who drew the knife's edge across the flesh of your family.
Seems like a terrible oversight to me.
Tell me, Gord. Were you *afraid* of him?
The General got what was coming to him.
Yes.
So did we all.

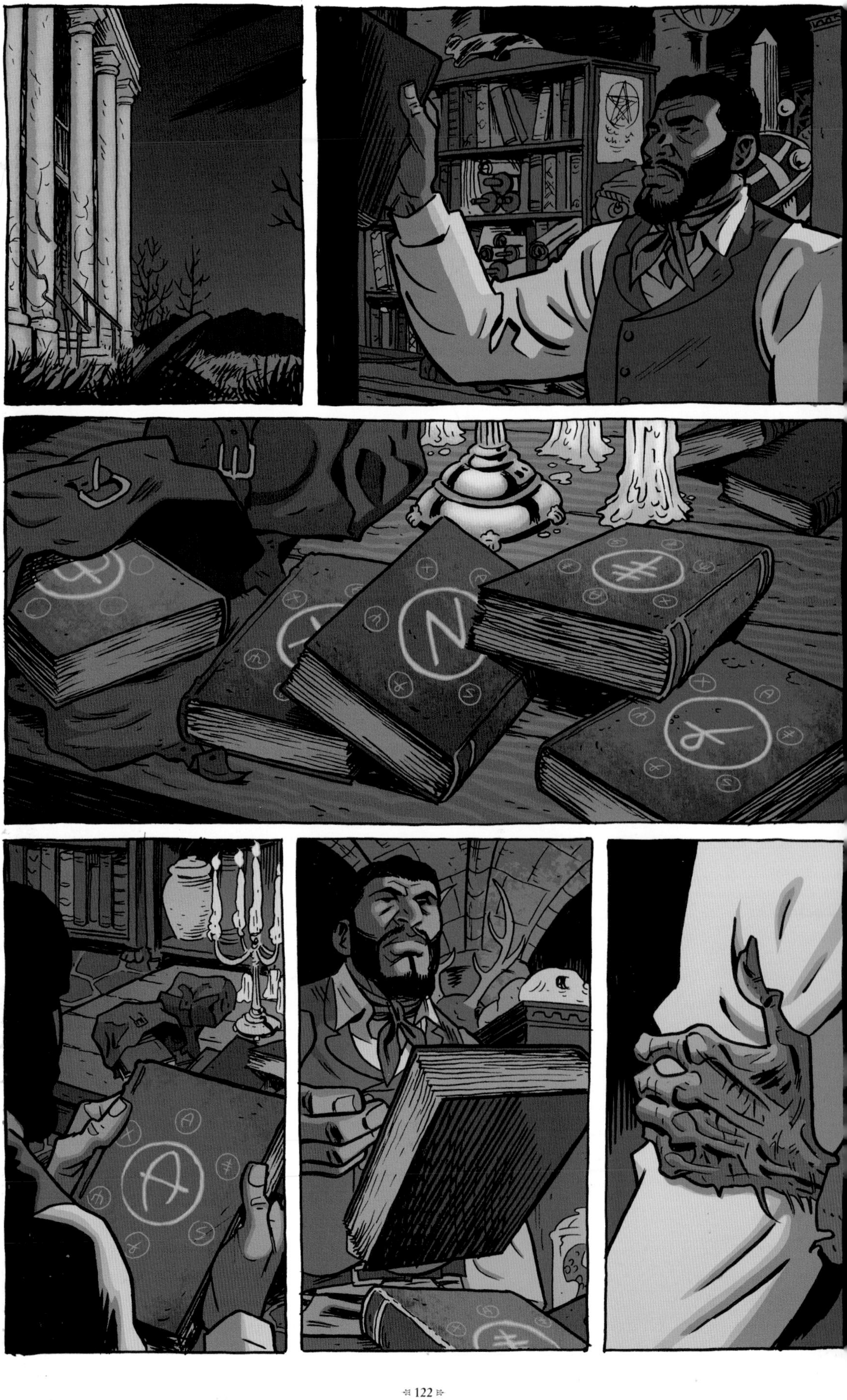

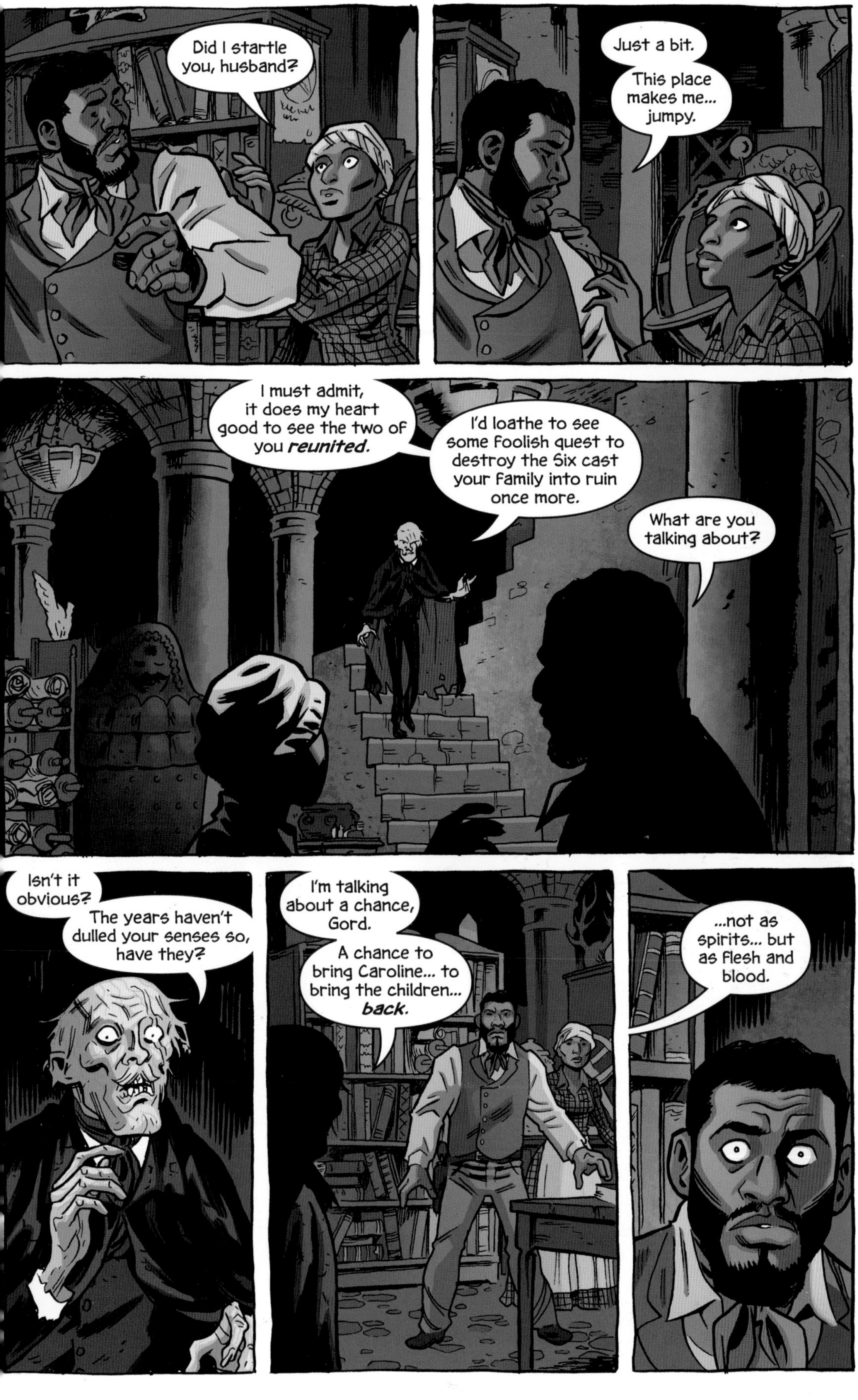
Did I startle you, husband?
Just a bit.
This place makes me... jumpy.
I must admit, it does my heart good to see the two of you *reunited.*
I'd loathe to see some foolish quest to destroy the Six cast your family into ruin once more.
What are you talking about?
Isn't it obvious?
The years haven't dulled your senses so, have they?
I'm talking about a chance, Gord.
A chance to bring Caroline... to bring the children... ***back.***
...not as spirits... but as flesh and blood.

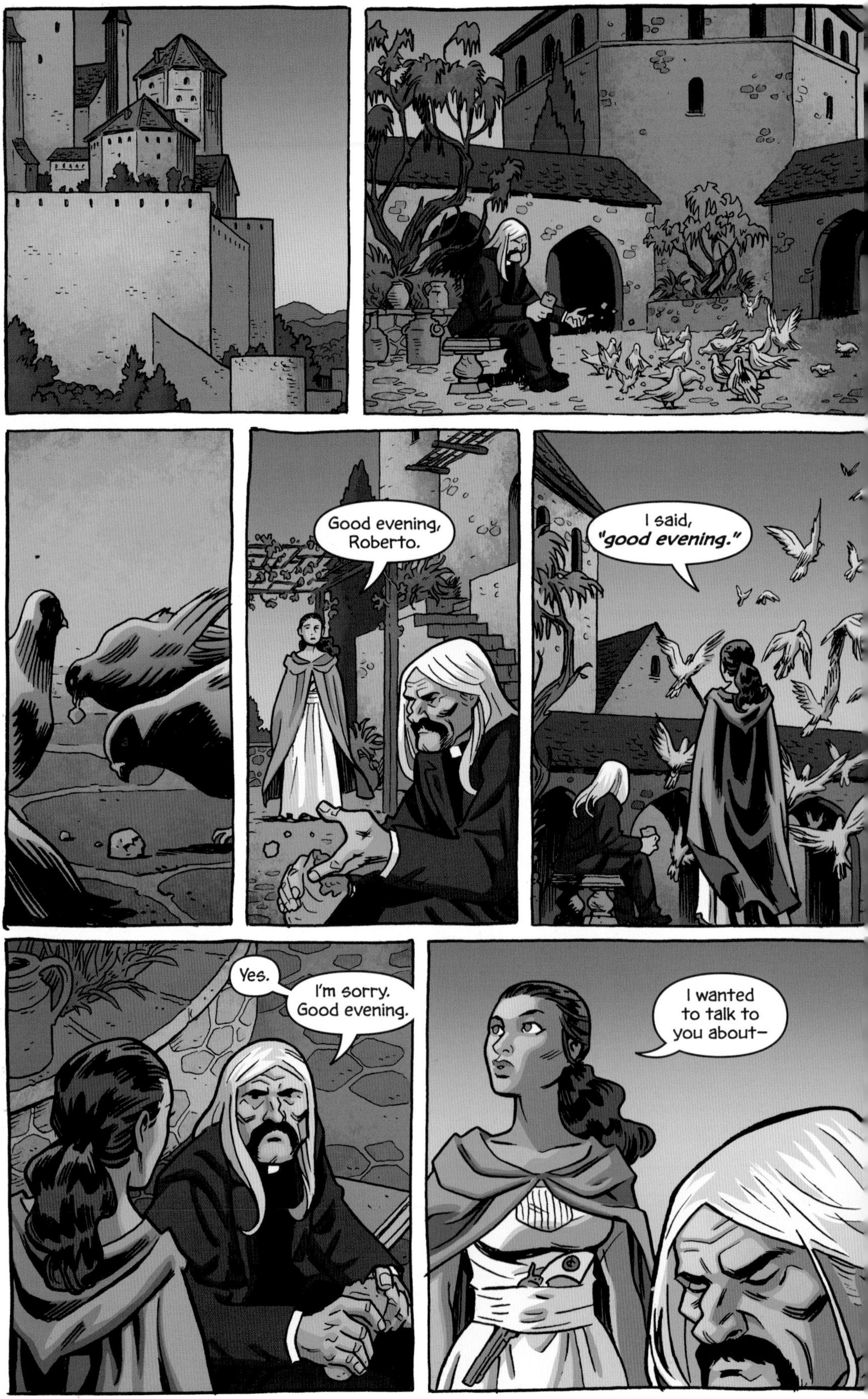
Good evening, Roberto.
I said, *"good evening."*
Yes.
I'm sorry. Good evening.
I wanted to talk to you about–

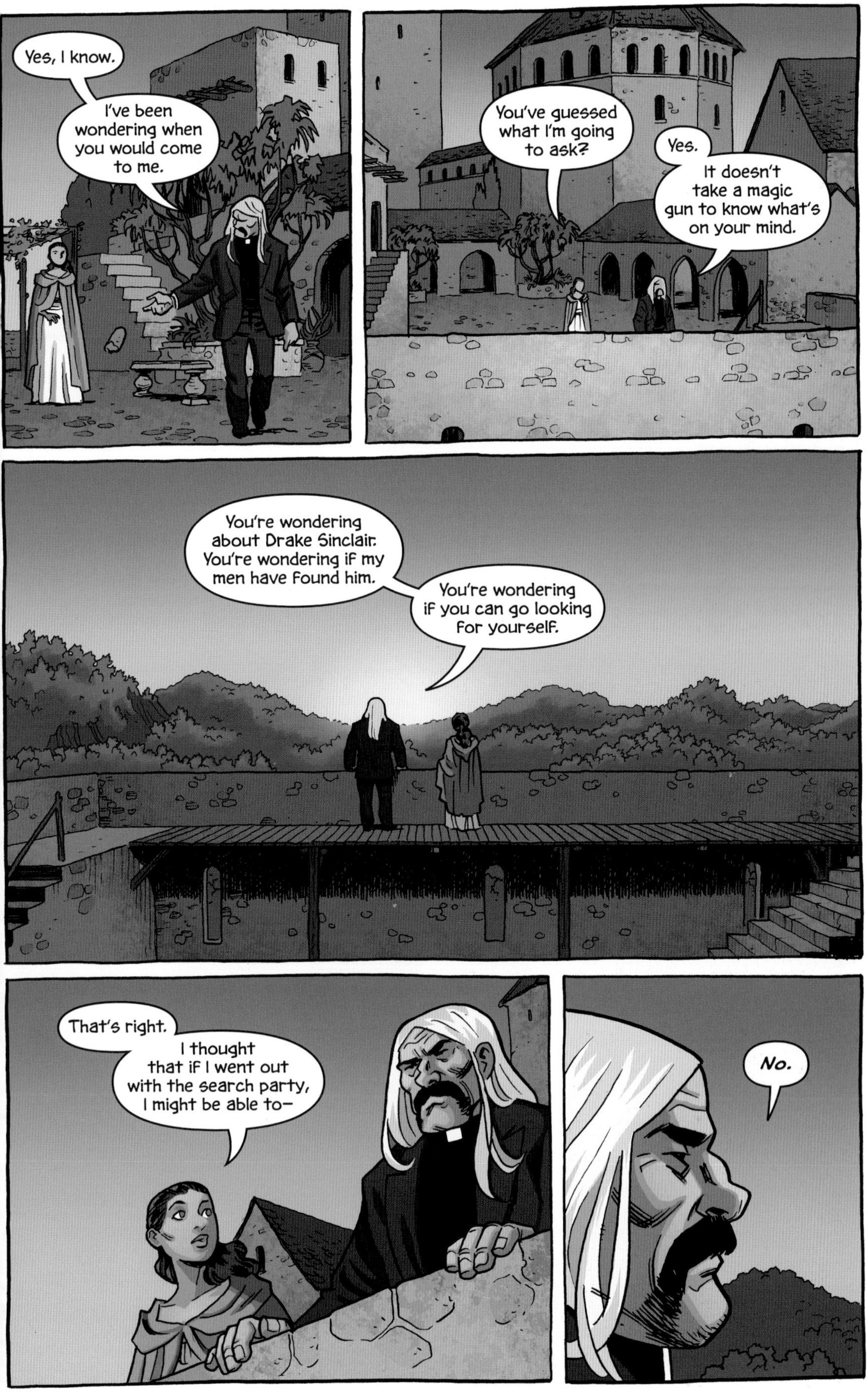
Yes, I know.
I've been wondering when you would come to me.
You've guessed what I'm going to ask?
Yes.
It doesn't take a magic gun to know what's on your mind.
You're wondering about Drake Sinclair. You're wondering if my men have found him.
You're wondering if you can go looking for yourself.
That's right.
I thought that if I went out with the search party, I might be able to—
No.

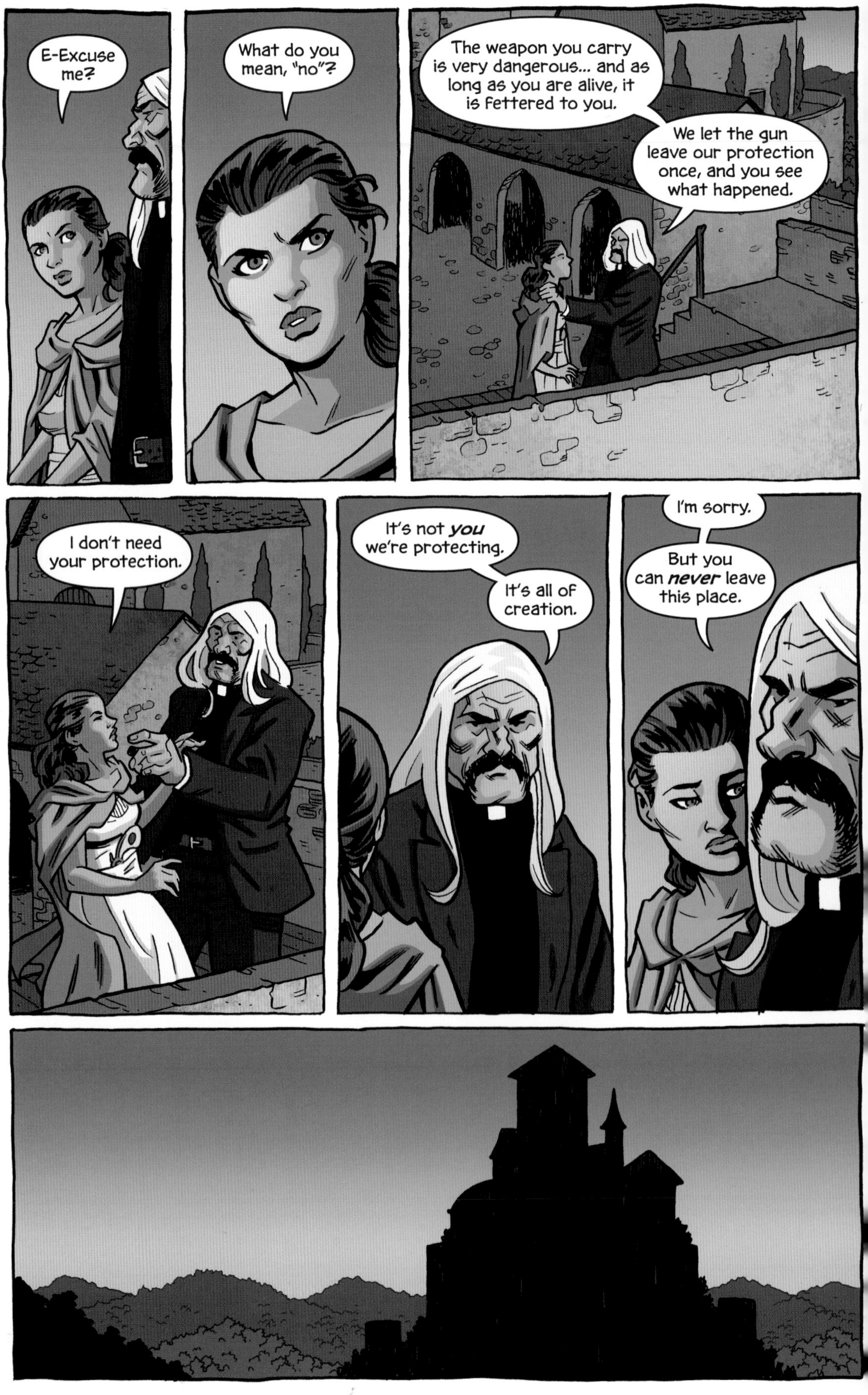
E-Excuse me?
What do you mean, "no"?
The weapon you carry is very dangerous... and as long as you are alive, it is fettered to you.
We let the gun leave our protection once, and you see what happened.
I don't need your protection.
It's not *you* we're protecting.
It's all of creation.
I'm sorry.
But you can *never* leave this place.

CHAPTER
SIX

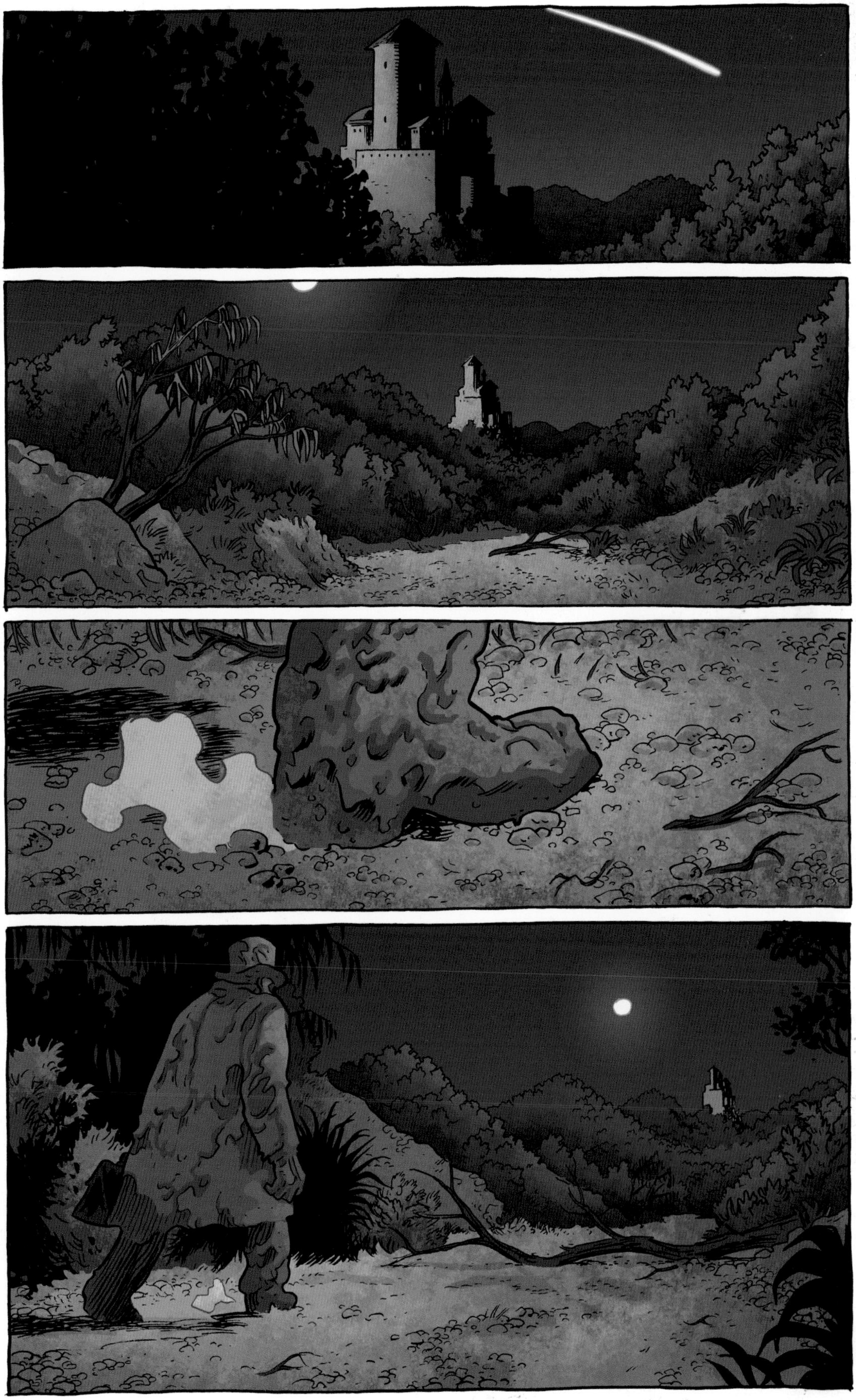

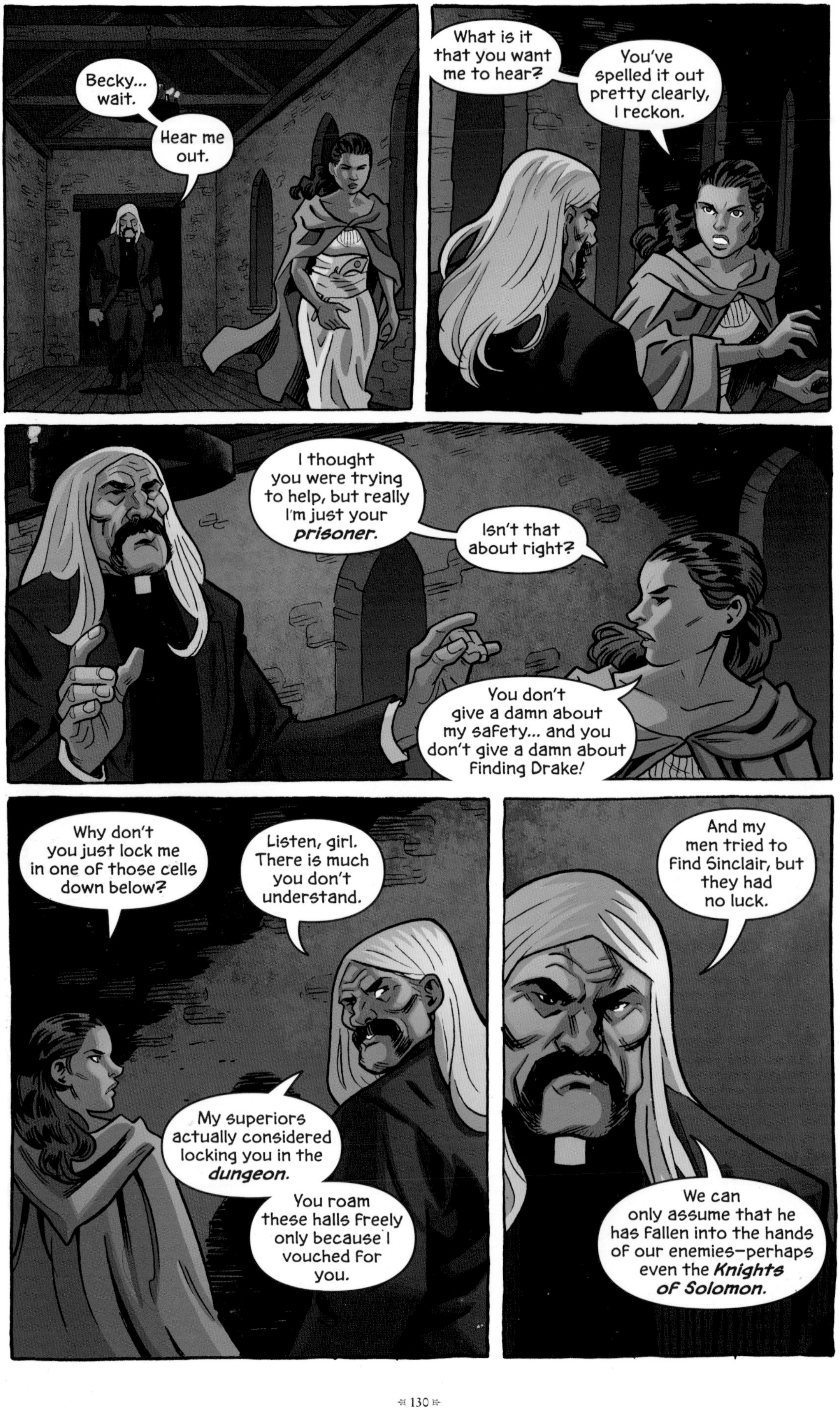

Becky... wait.
Hear me out.
What is it that you want me to hear?
You've spelled it out pretty clearly, I reckon.
I thought you were trying to help, but really I'm just your *prisoner.*
Isn't that about right?
You don't give a damn about my safety... and you don't give a damn about finding Drake!
Why don't you just lock me in one of those cells down below?
Listen, girl. There is much you don't understand.
My superiors actually considered locking you in the *dungeon.*
You roam these halls freely only because I vouched for you.
And my men tried to find Sinclair, but they had no luck.
We can only assume that he has fallen into the hands of our enemies—perhaps even the *Knights of Solomon.*

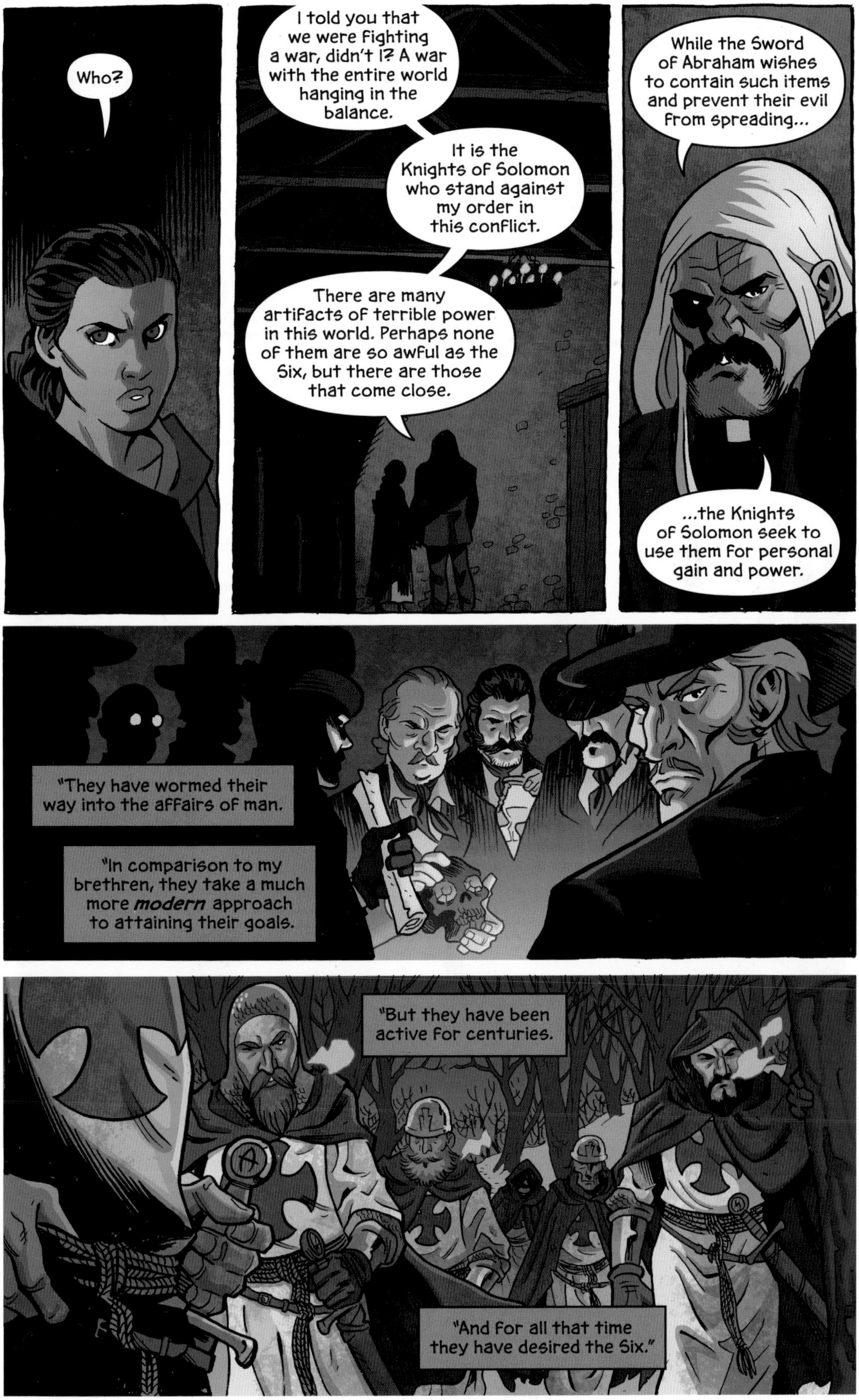
Who?
I told you that we were fighting a war, didn't I? A war with the entire world hanging in the balance.
It is the Knights of Solomon who stand against my order in this conflict.
There are many artifacts of terrible power in this world. Perhaps none of them are so awful as the Six, but there are those that come close.
While the Sword of Abraham wishes to contain such items and prevent their evil from spreading...
...the Knights of Solomon seek to use them for personal gain and power.
"They have wormed their way into the affairs of man.
"In comparison to my brethren, they take a much more *modern* approach to attaining their goals.
"But they have been active for centuries.
"And for all that time they have desired the Six."

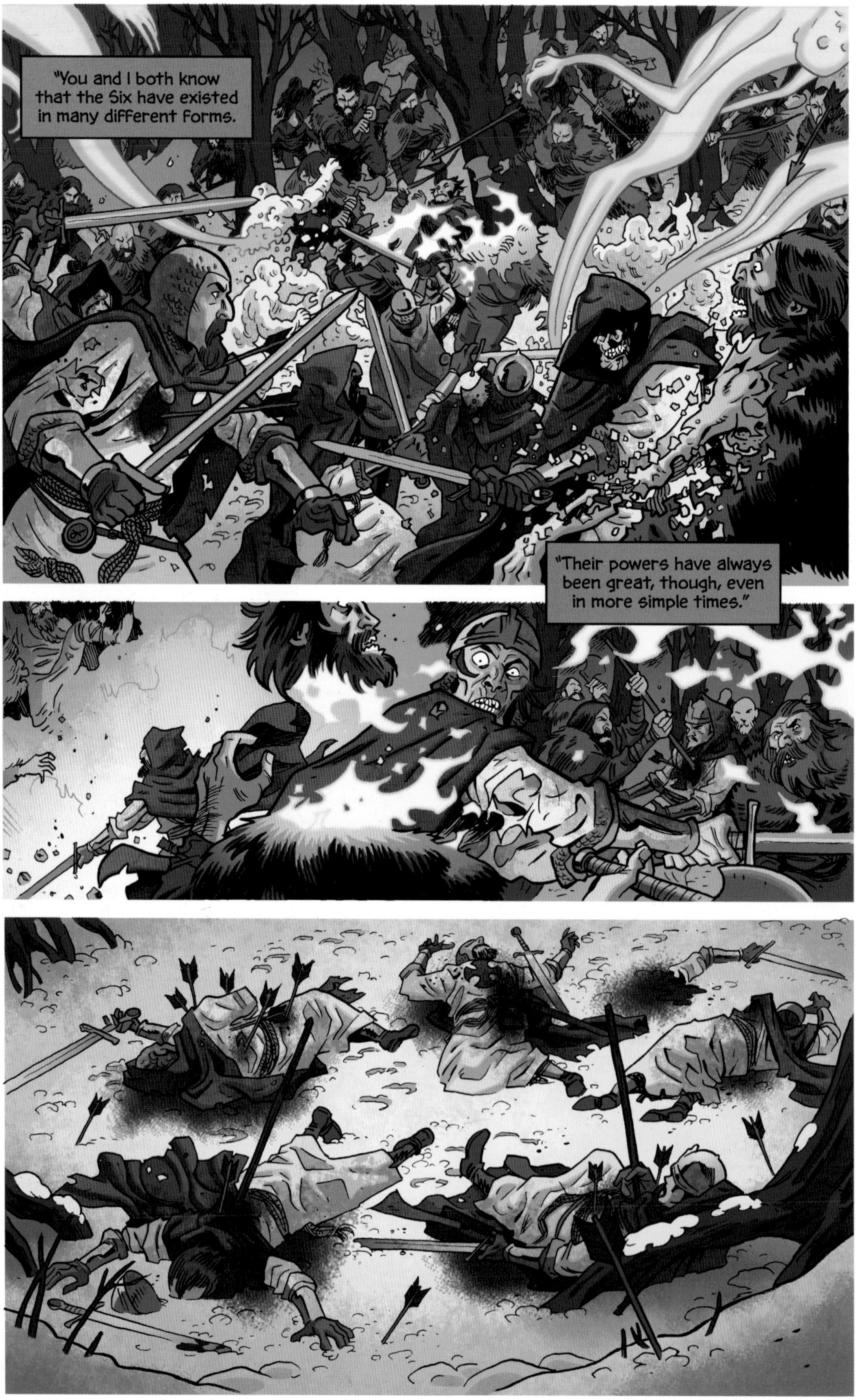

"You and I both know that the Six have existed in many different forms.
"Their powers have always been great, though, even in more simple times."

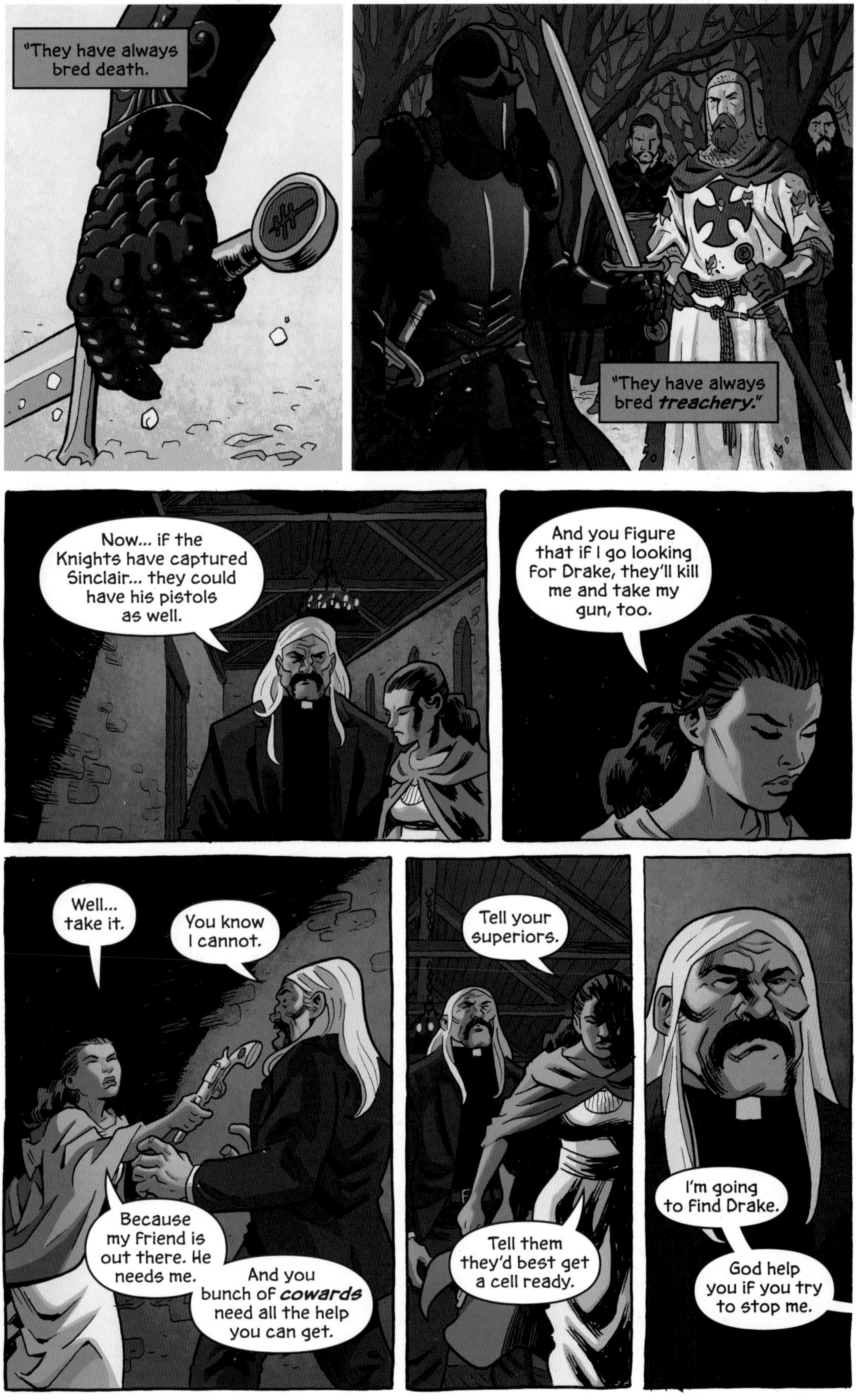
"They have always bred death.
"They have always bred *treachery*."
Now... if the Knights have captured Sinclair... they could have his pistols as well.
And you figure that if I go looking for Drake, they'll kill me and take my gun, too.
Well... take it.
You know I cannot.
Because my friend is out there. He needs me.
And you bunch of ***cowards*** need all the help you can get.
Tell your superiors.
Tell them they'd best get a cell ready.
I'm going to find Drake.
God help you if you try to stop me.

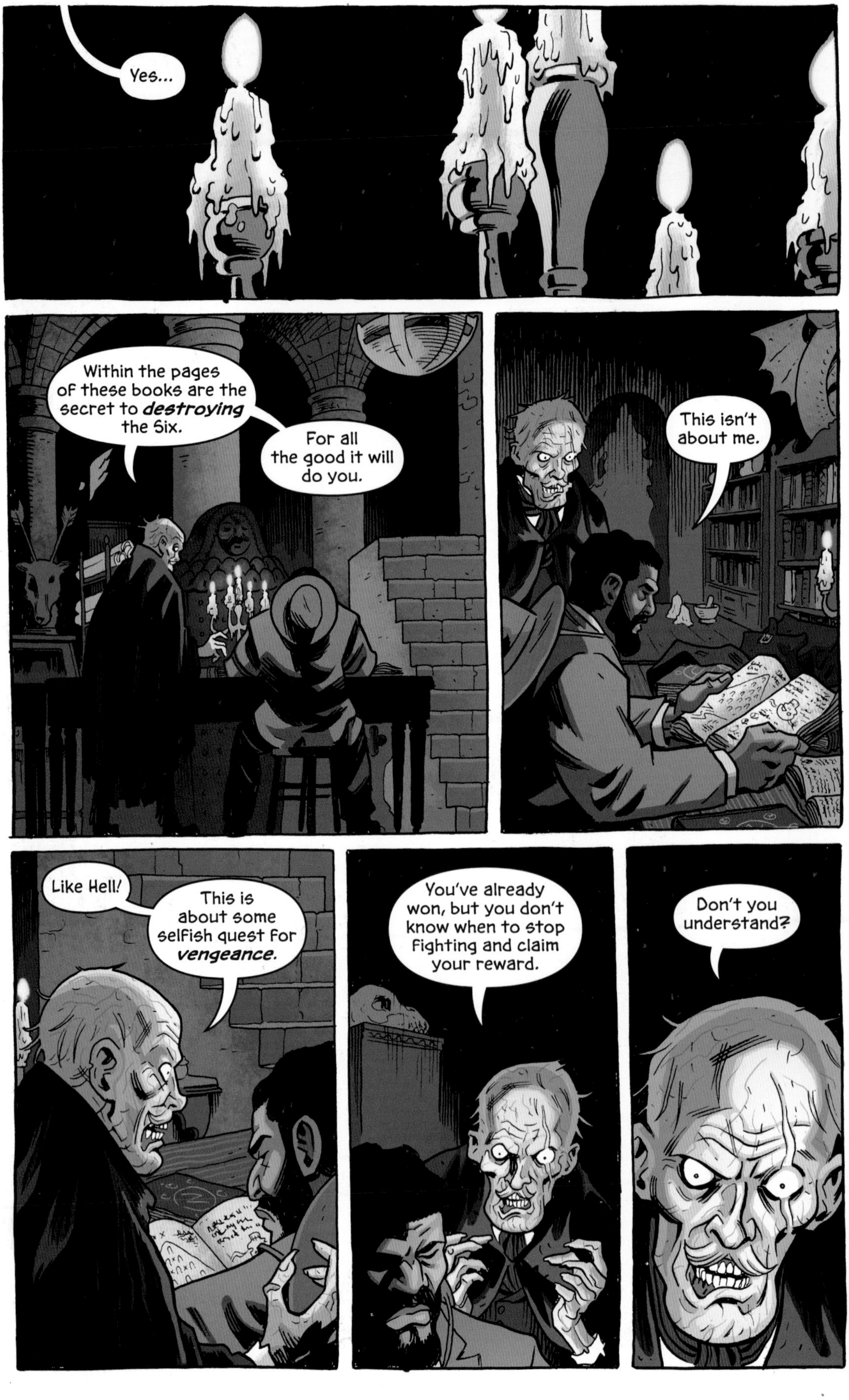
Yes...
Within the pages of these books are the secret to *destroying* the Six.
For all the good it will do you.
This isn't about me.
Like Hell!
This is about some selfish quest for *vengeance*.
You've already won, but you don't know when to stop fighting and claim your reward.
Don't you understand?

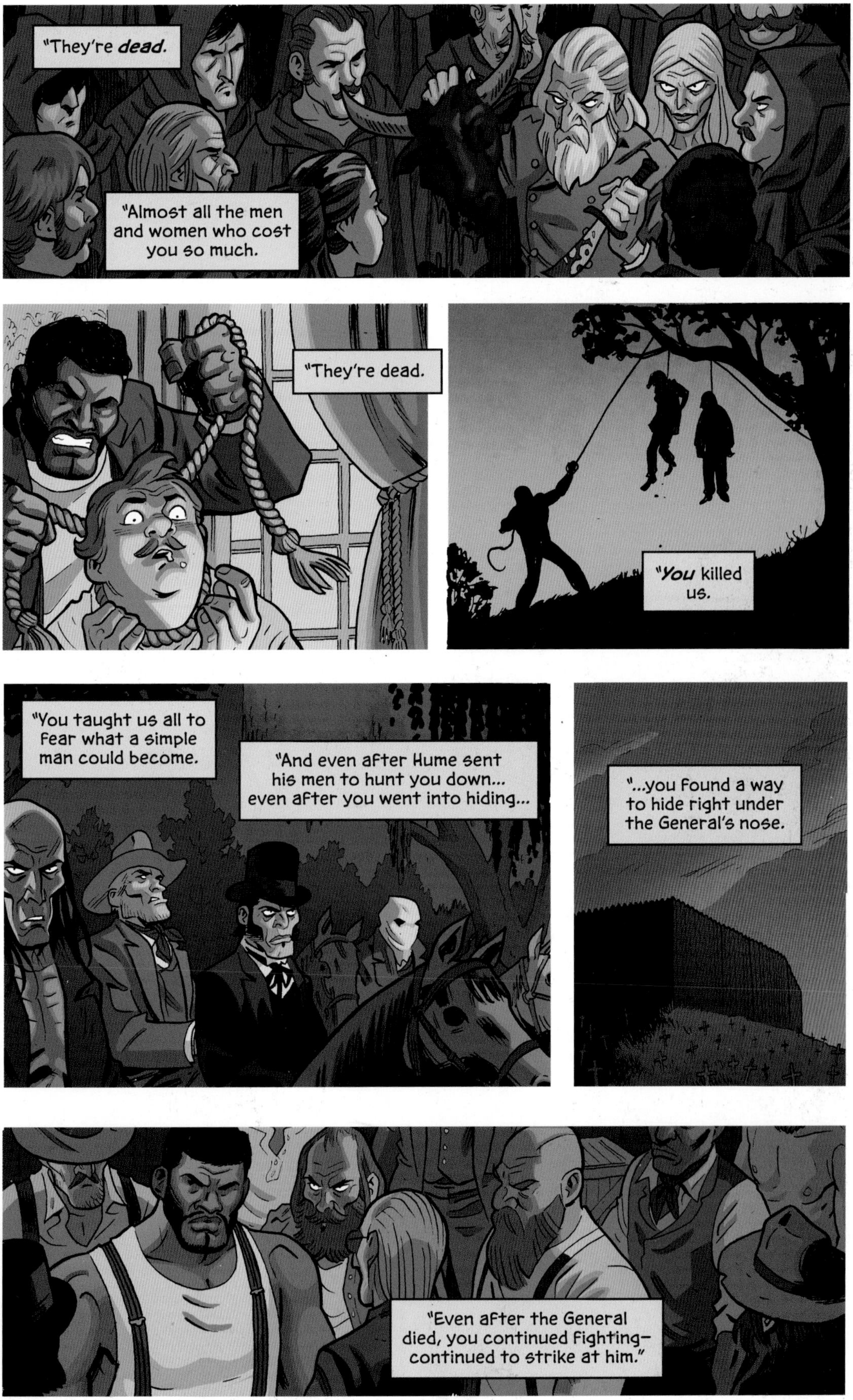
"They're *dead.*
"Almost all the men and women who cost you so much.
"They're dead.
"*You* killed us.
"You taught us all to fear what a simple man could become.
"And even after Hume sent his men to hunt you down... even after you went into hiding...
"...you found a way to hide right under the General's nose.
"Even after the General died, you continued fighting—continued to strike at him."

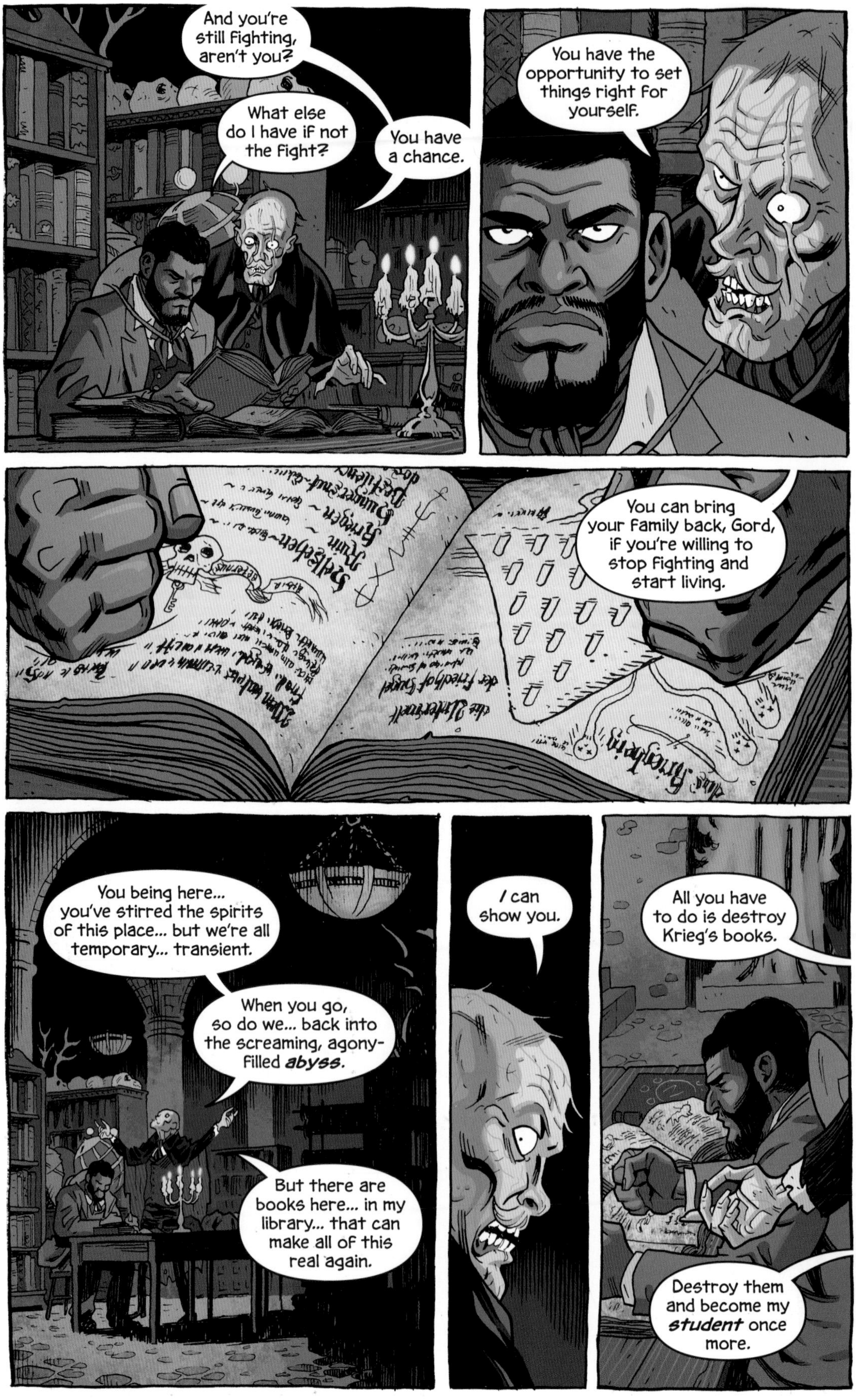
And you're still fighting, aren't you?
What else do I have if not the fight?
You have a chance.
You have the opportunity to set things right for yourself.
You can bring your family back, Gord, if you're willing to stop fighting and start living.
You being here... you've stirred the spirits of this place... but we're all temporary... transient.
When you go, so do we... back into the screaming, agony-filled *abyss.*
But there are books here... in my library... that can make all of this real again.
I can show you.
All you have to do is destroy Krieg's books.
Destroy them and become my *student* once more.

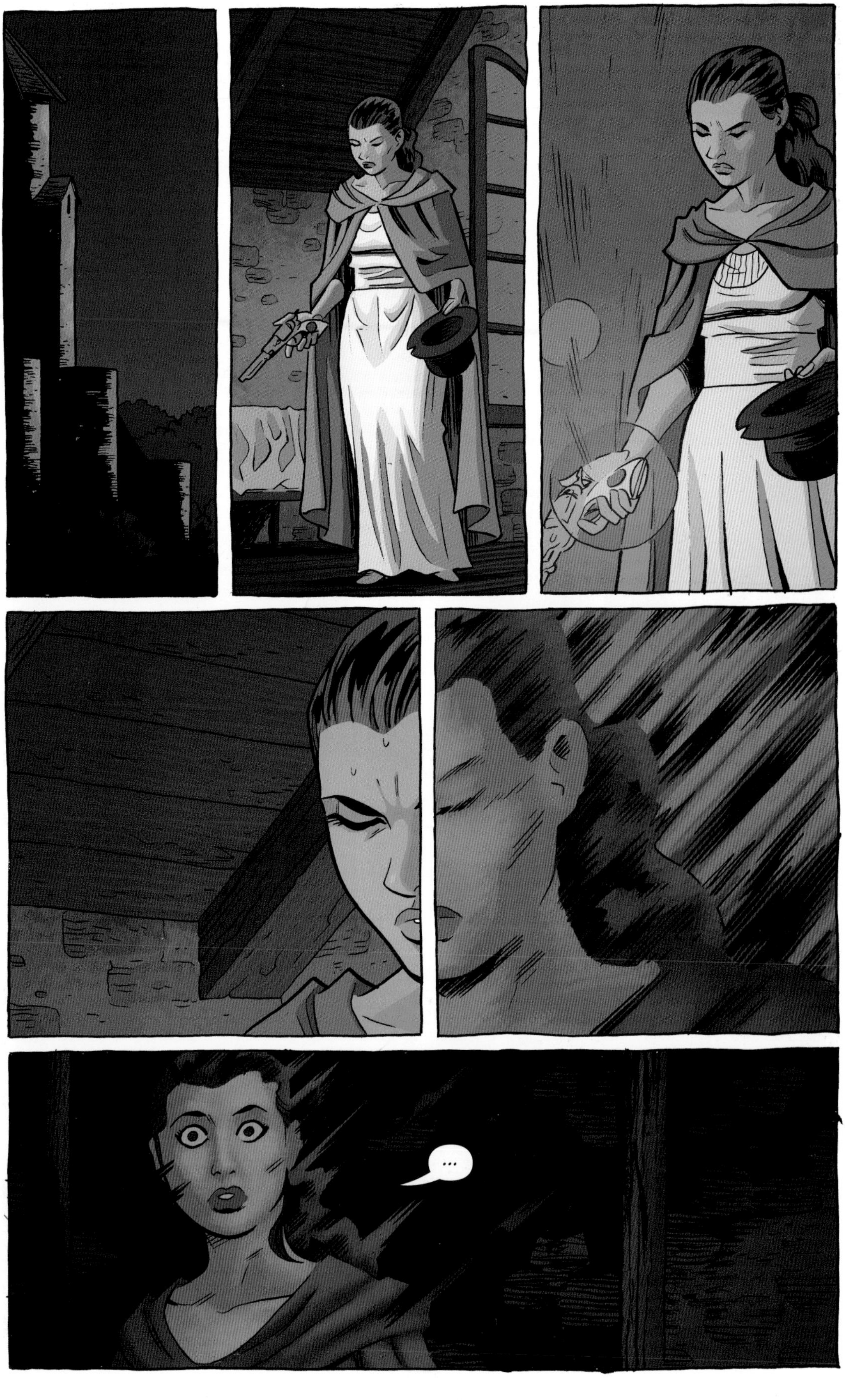
...

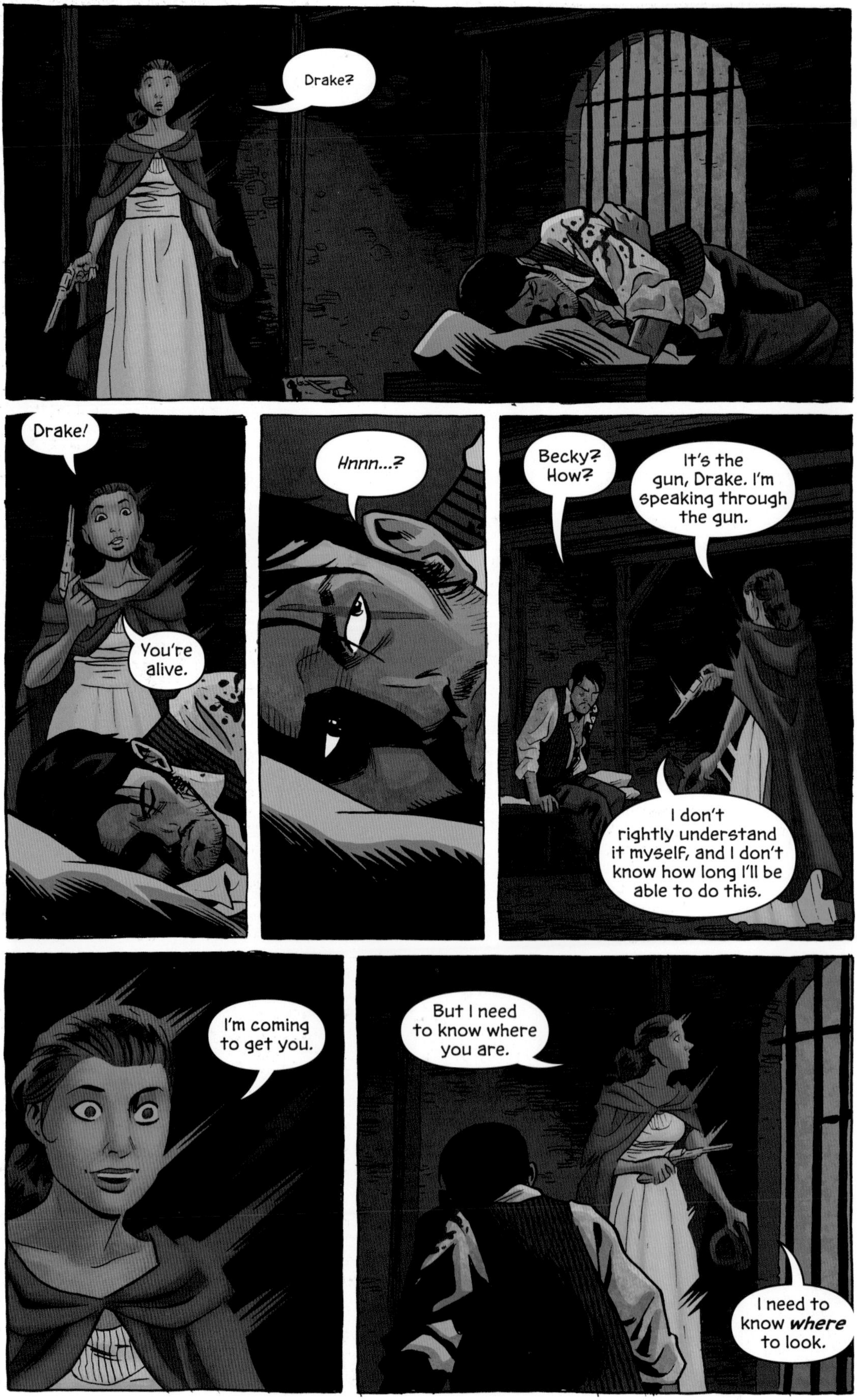
Drake?
Drake!
You're alive.
Hnnn...?
Becky? How?
It's the gun, Drake. I'm speaking through the gun.
I don't rightly understand it myself, and I don't know how long I'll be able to do this.
I'm coming to get you.
But I need to know where you are.
I need to know *where* to look.

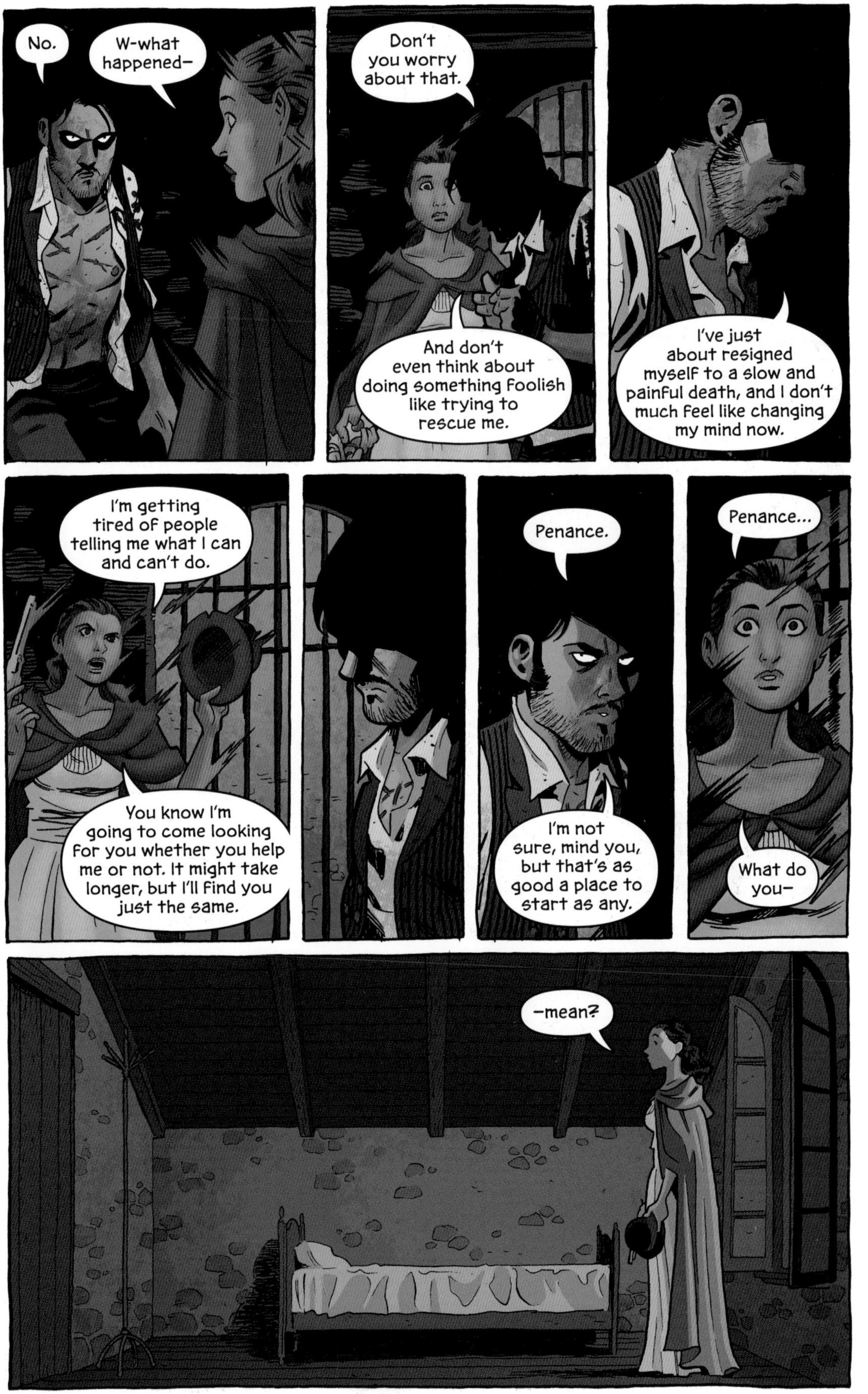
No.
W-what happened–
Don't you worry about that.
And don't even think about doing something foolish like trying to rescue me.
I've just about resigned myself to a slow and painful death, and I don't much feel like changing my mind now.
I'm getting tired of people telling me what I can and can't do.
You know I'm going to come looking for you whether you help me or not. It might take longer, but I'll find you just the same.
Penance.
I'm not sure, mind you, but that's as good a place to start as any.
Penance...
What do you–
–mean?

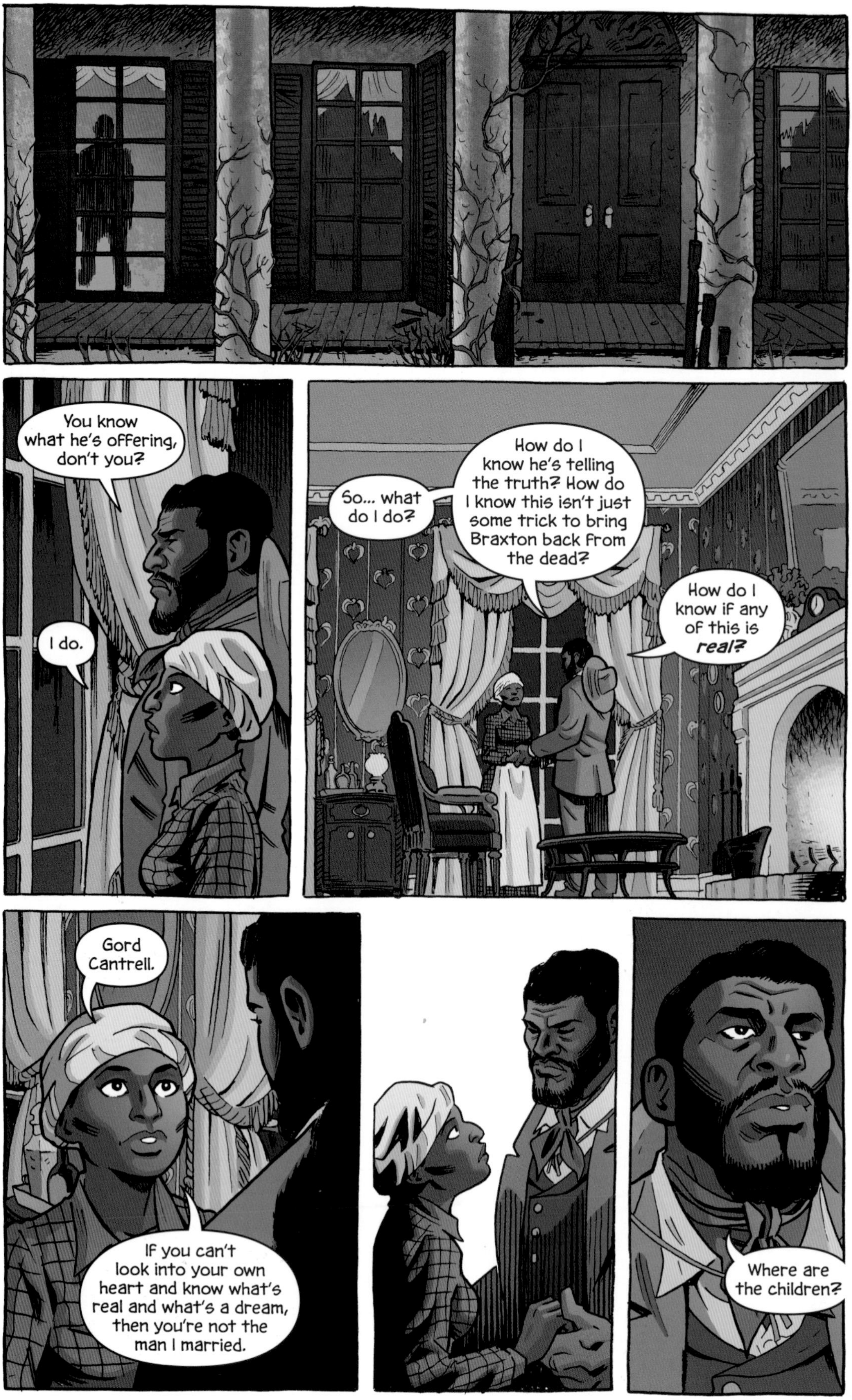
You know what he's offering, don't you?
I do.
So... what do I do?
How do I know he's telling the truth? How do I know this isn't just some trick to bring Braxton back from the dead?
How do I know if any of this is *real?*
Gord Cantrell.
If you can't look into your own heart and know what's real and what's a dream, then you're not the man I married.
Where are the children?

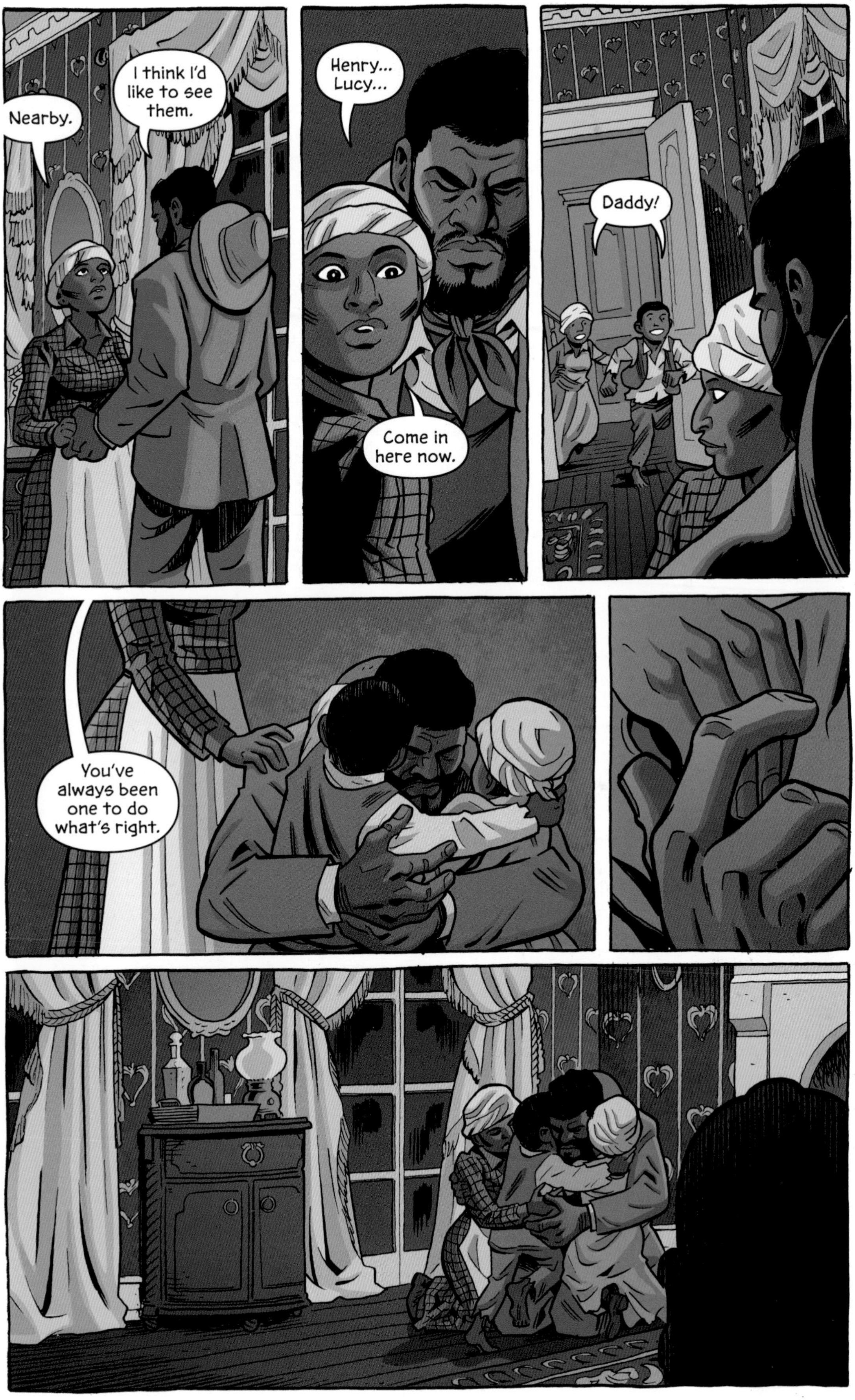
Nearby.
I think I'd like to see them.
Henry... Lucy...
Come in here now.
Daddy!
You've always been one to do what's right.

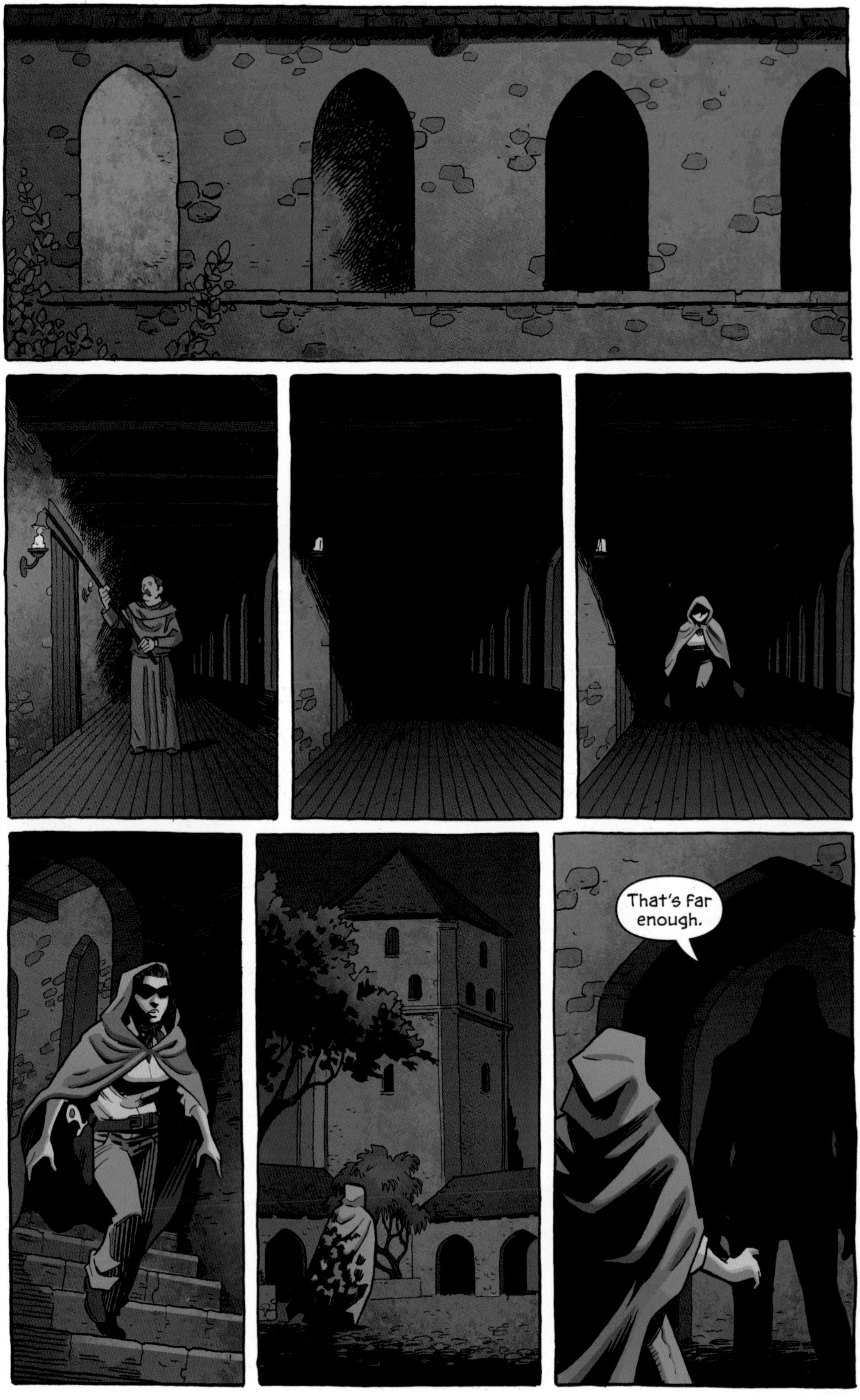
That's far enough.

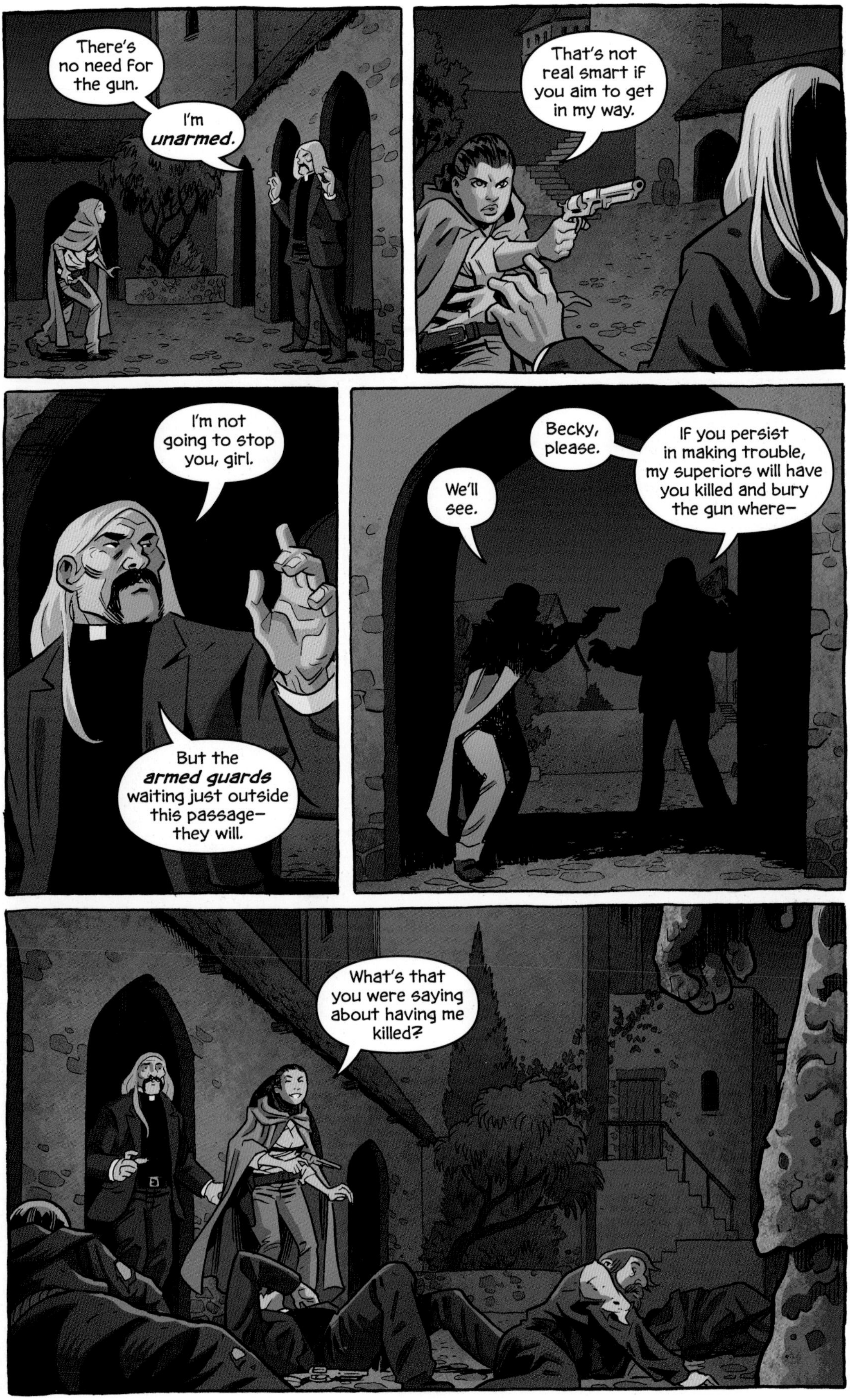

There's no need for the gun.
I'm *unarmed.*
That's not real smart if you aim to get in my way.
I'm not going to stop you, girl.
But the *armed guards* waiting just outside this passage— they will.
Becky, please.
If you persist in making trouble, my superiors will have you killed and bury the gun where—
We'll see.
What's that you were saying about having me killed?

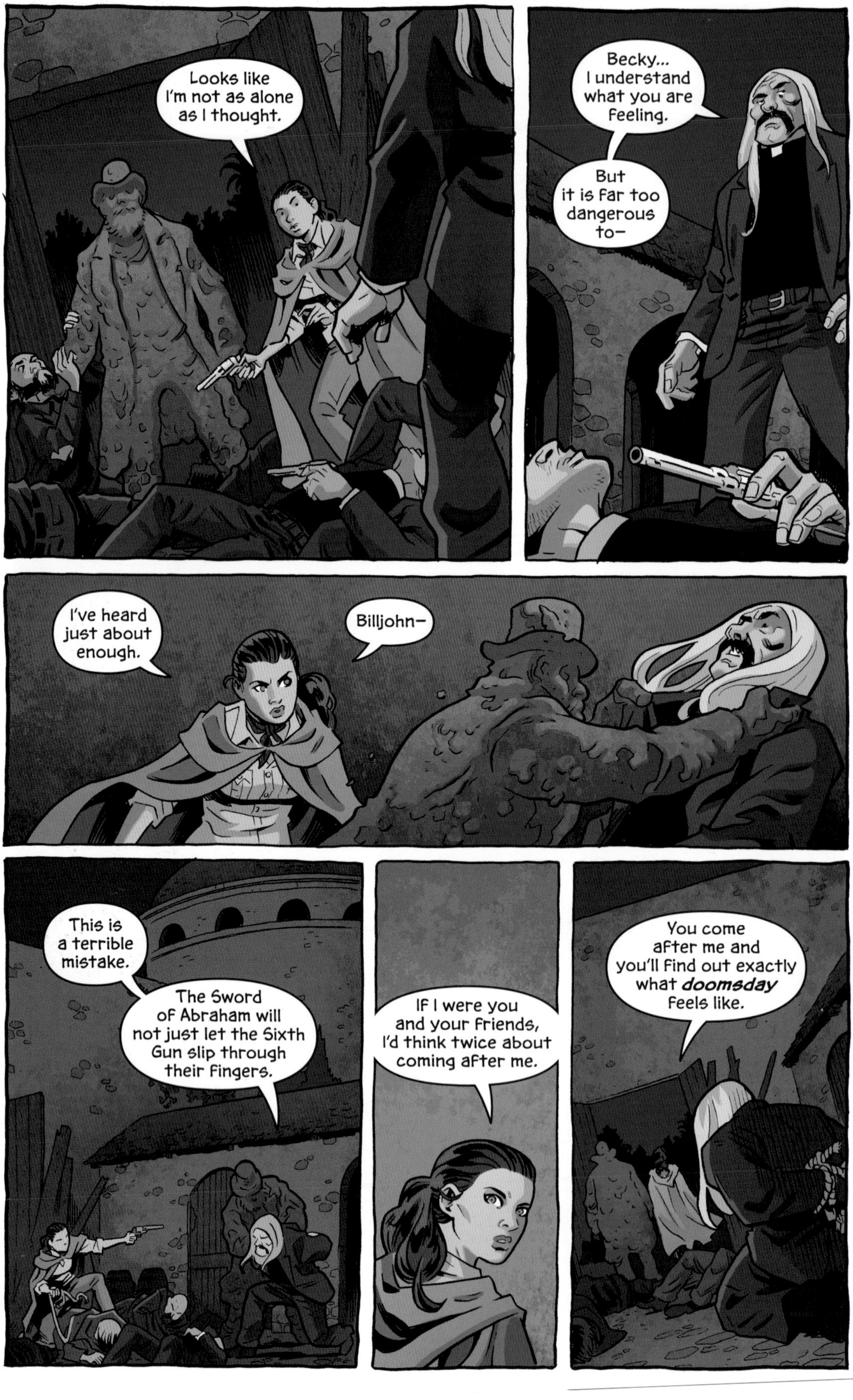
Looks like I'm not as alone as I thought.
Becky... I understand what you are feeling.
But it is far too dangerous to–
I've heard just about enough.
Billjohn–
This is a terrible mistake.
The Sword of Abraham will not just let the Sixth Gun slip through their fingers.
If I were you and your friends, I'd think twice about coming after me.
You come after me and you'll find out exactly what *doomsday* feels like.

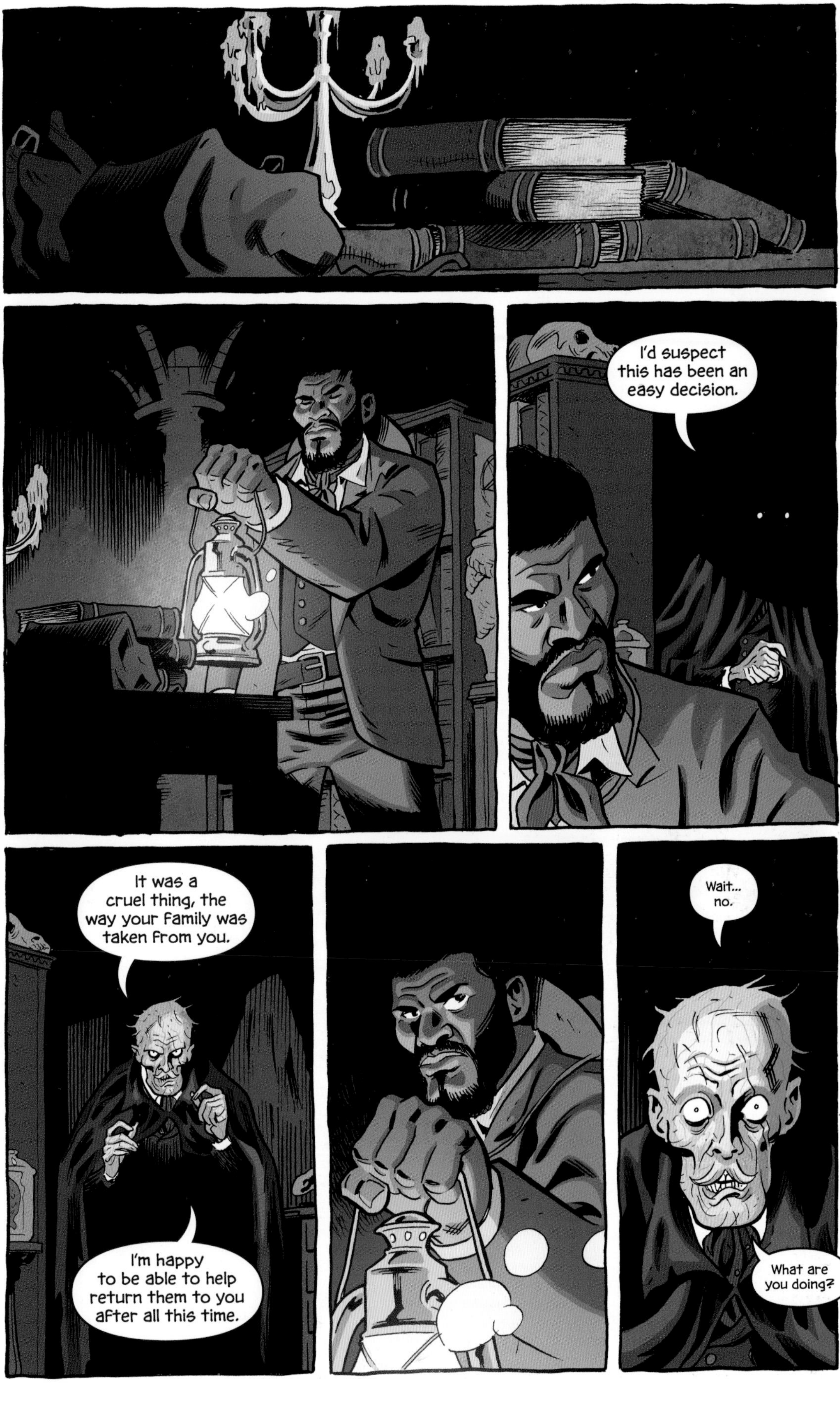
I'd suspect this has been an easy decision.
It was a cruel thing, the way your family was taken from you.
I'm happy to be able to help return them to you after all this time.
Wait... no.
What are you doing?

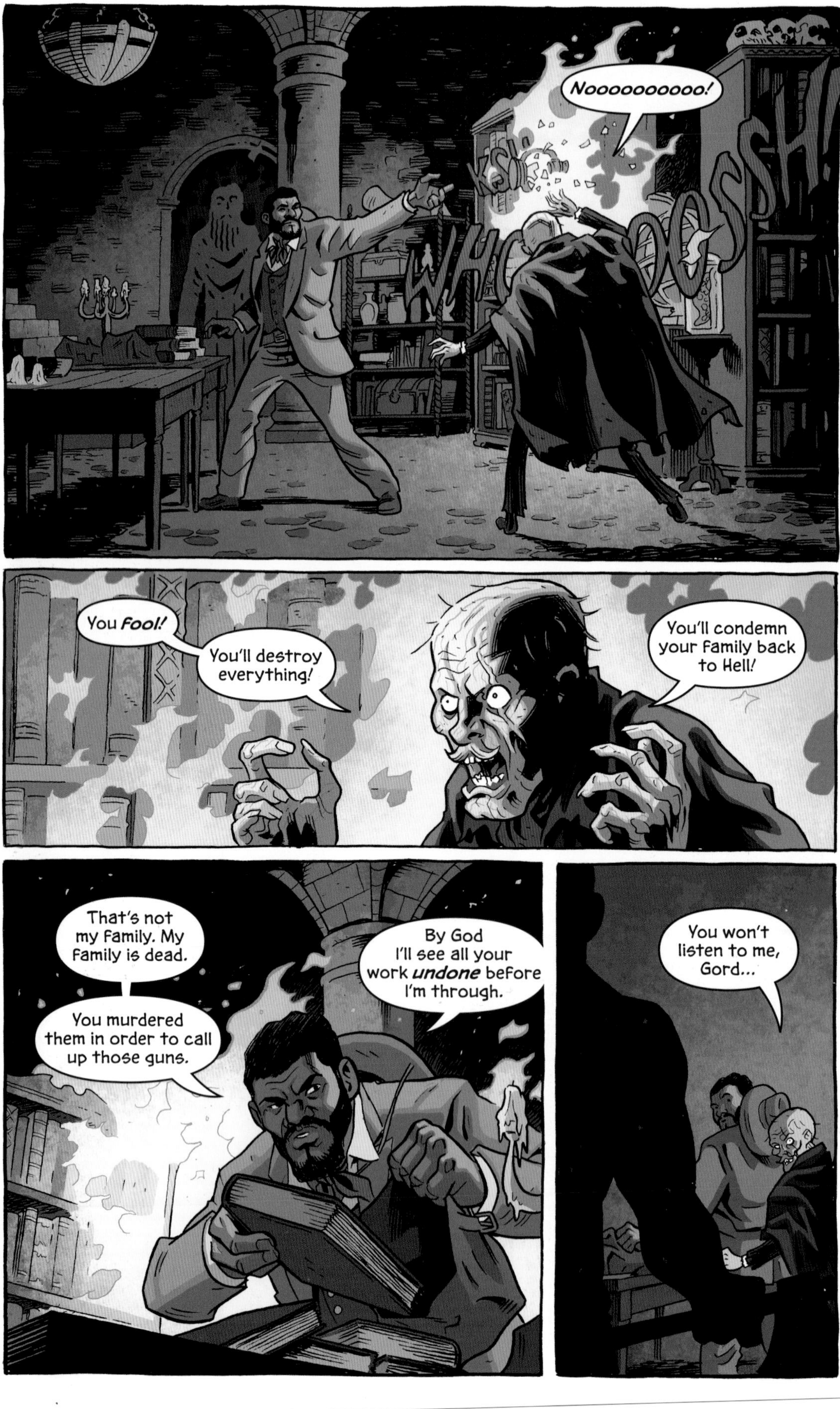
Noooooooooo!
KSH
WHOOOOSSH!
You *Fool!*
You'll destroy everything!
You'll condemn your family back to Hell!
That's not my family. My family is dead.
You murdered them in order to call up those guns.
By God I'll see all your work ***undone*** before I'm through.
You won't listen to me, Gord...

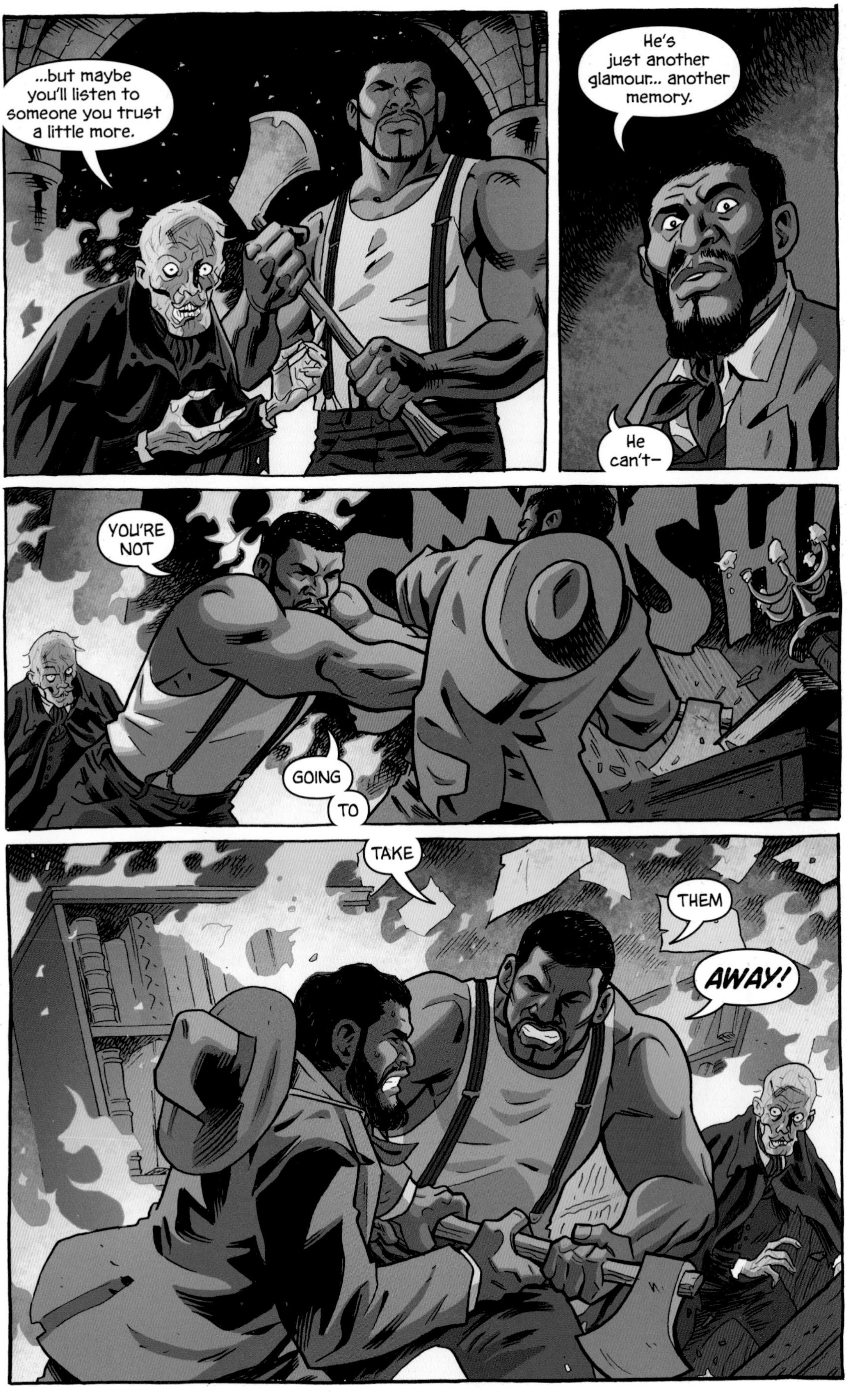

...but maybe you'll listen to someone you trust a little more.
He's just another glamour... another memory.
He can't–
YOU'RE NOT
GOING
TO
TAKE
THEM
AWAY!

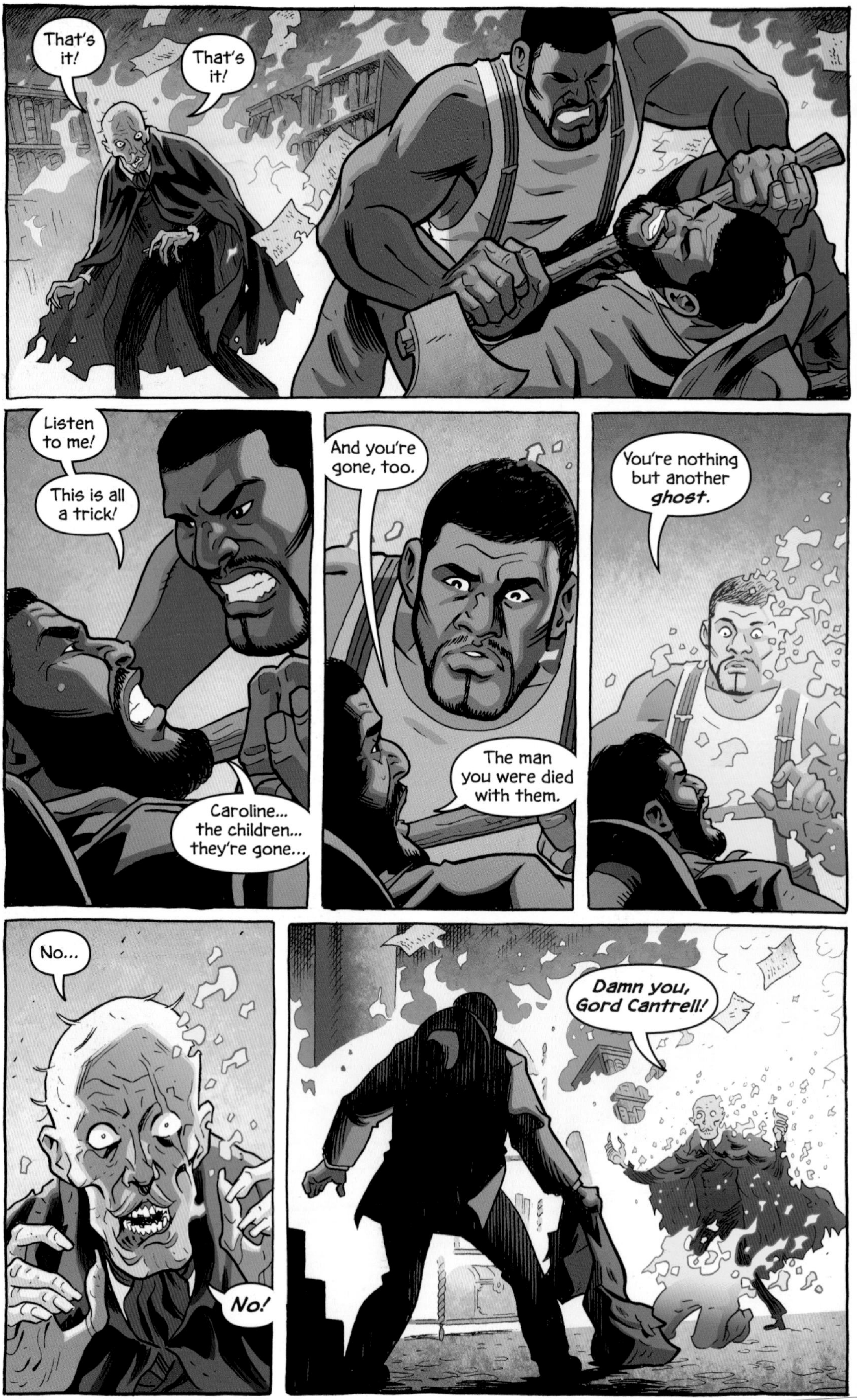
That's it!
That's it!
Listen to me!
This is all a trick!
Caroline... the children... they're gone...
And you're gone, too.
The man you were died with them.
You're nothing but another *ghost*.
No...
No!
Damn you, Gord Cantrell!

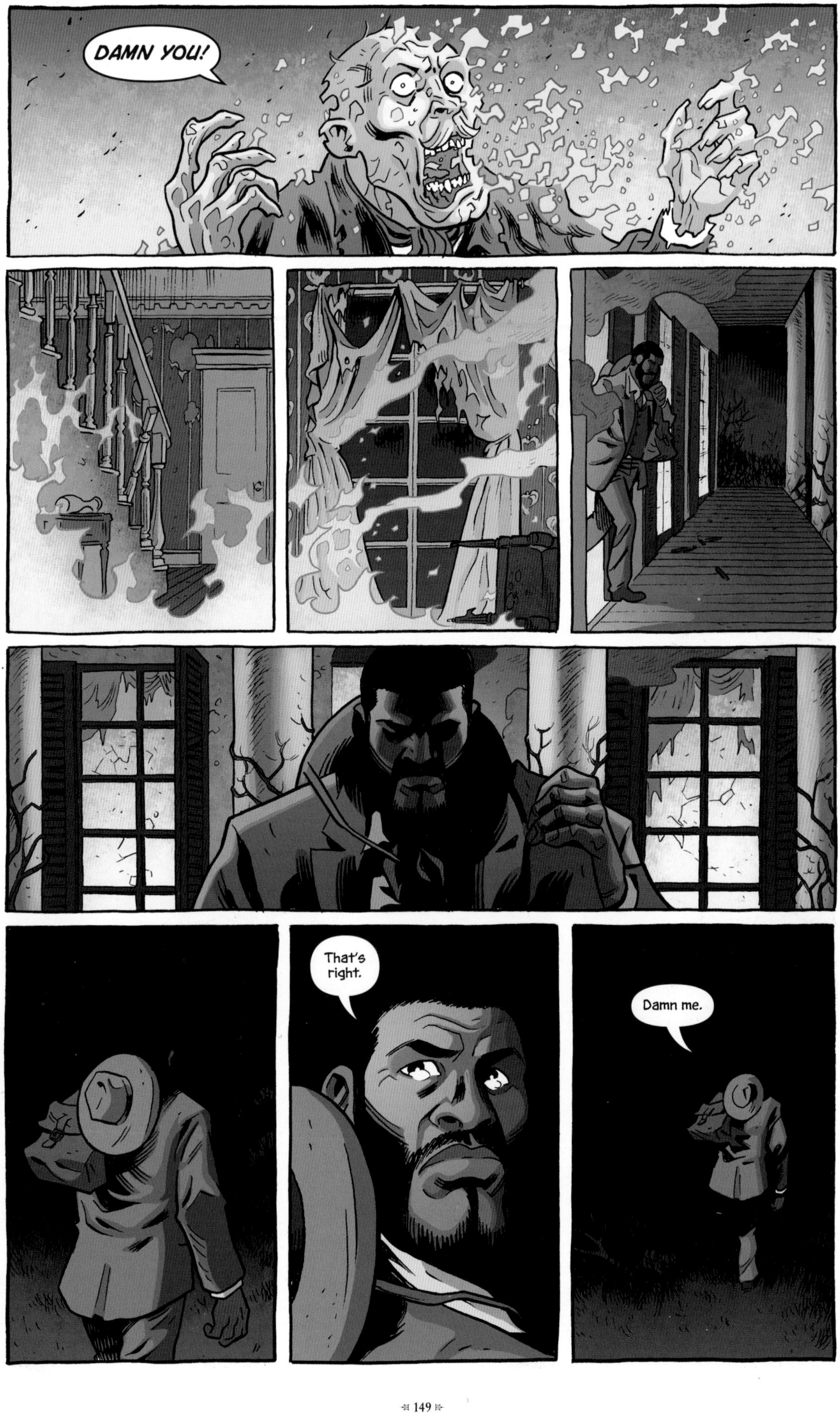
DAMN YOU!
That's right.
Damn me.

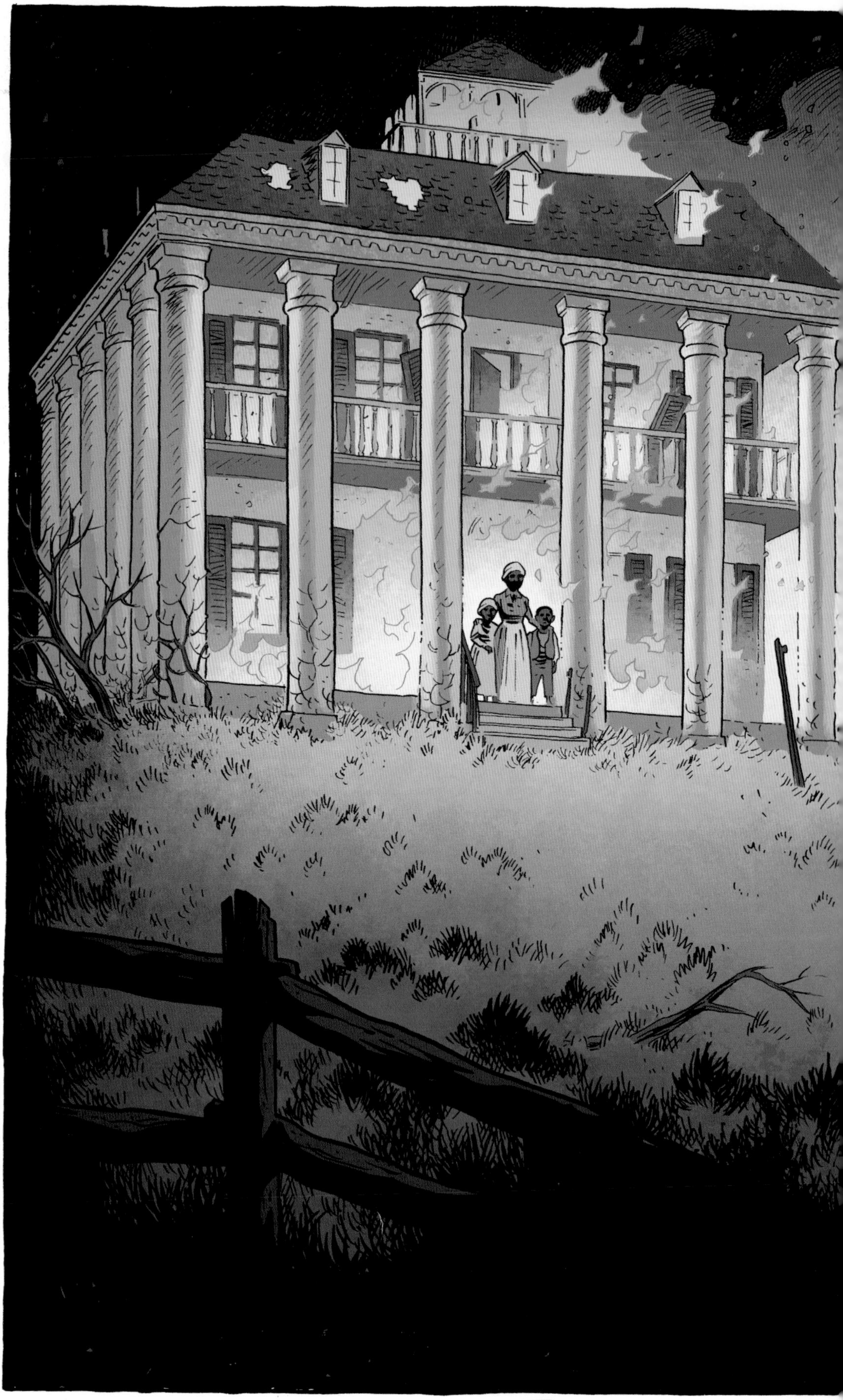

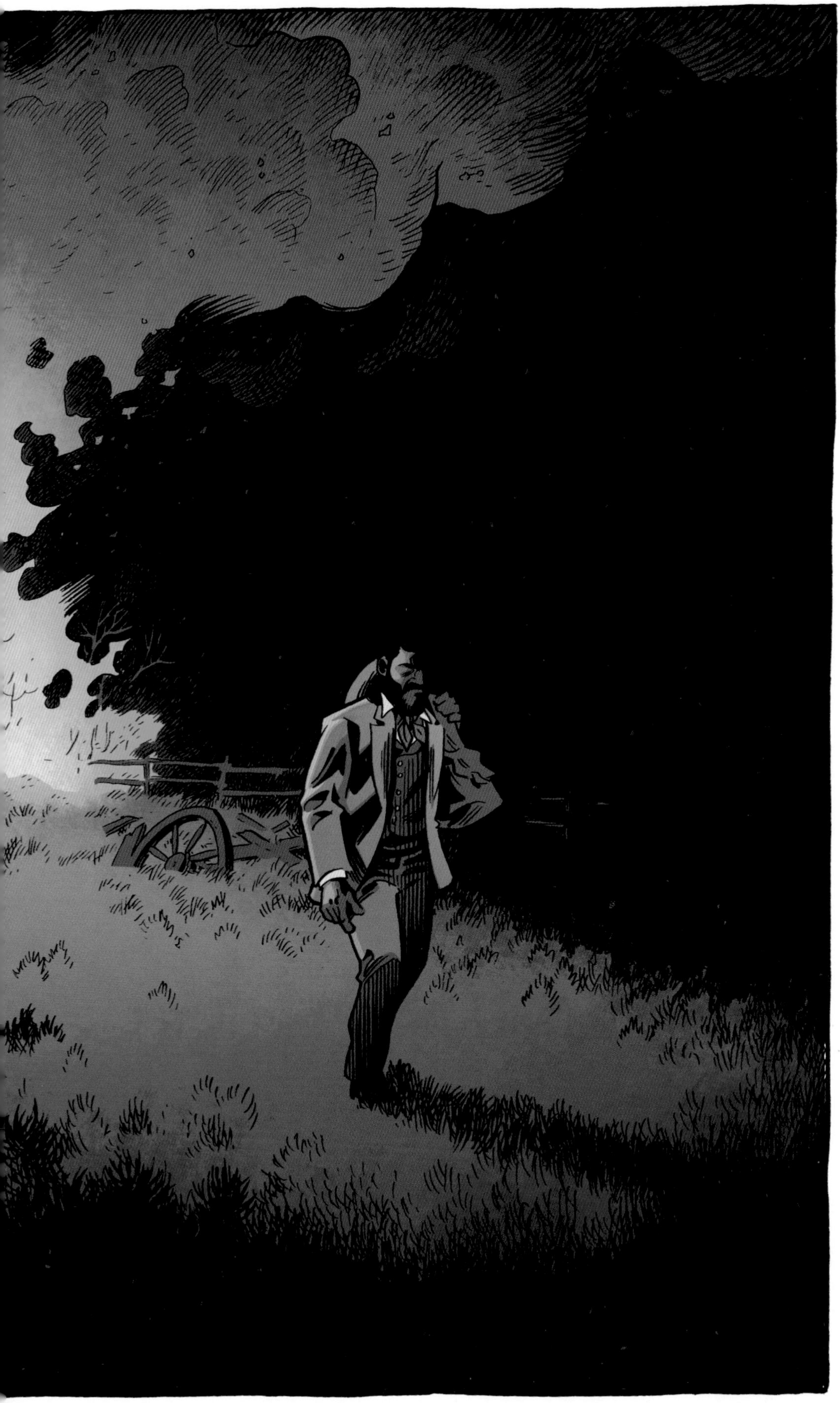

THE SIXTH GUN™

ADVENTURE CONTINUES...

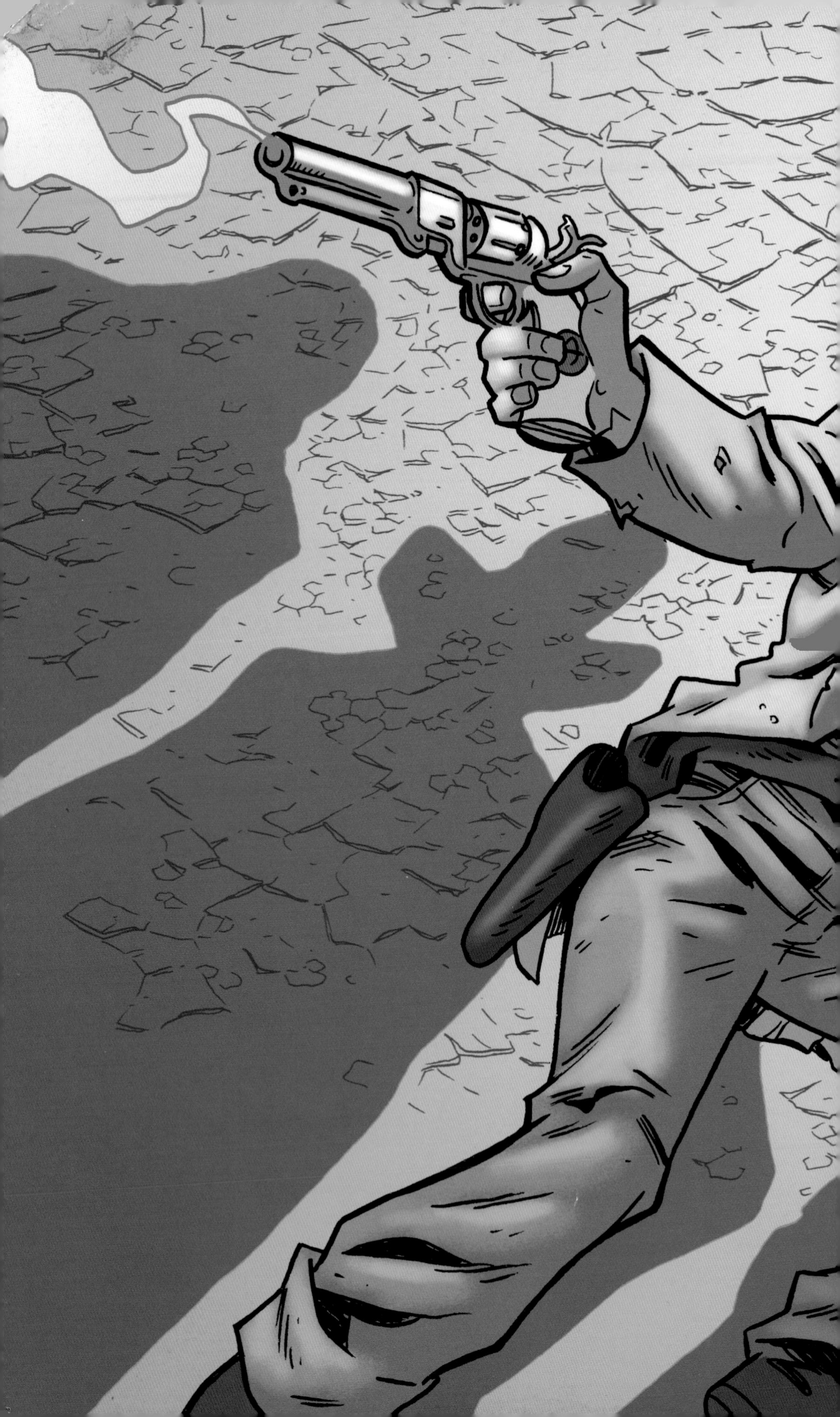

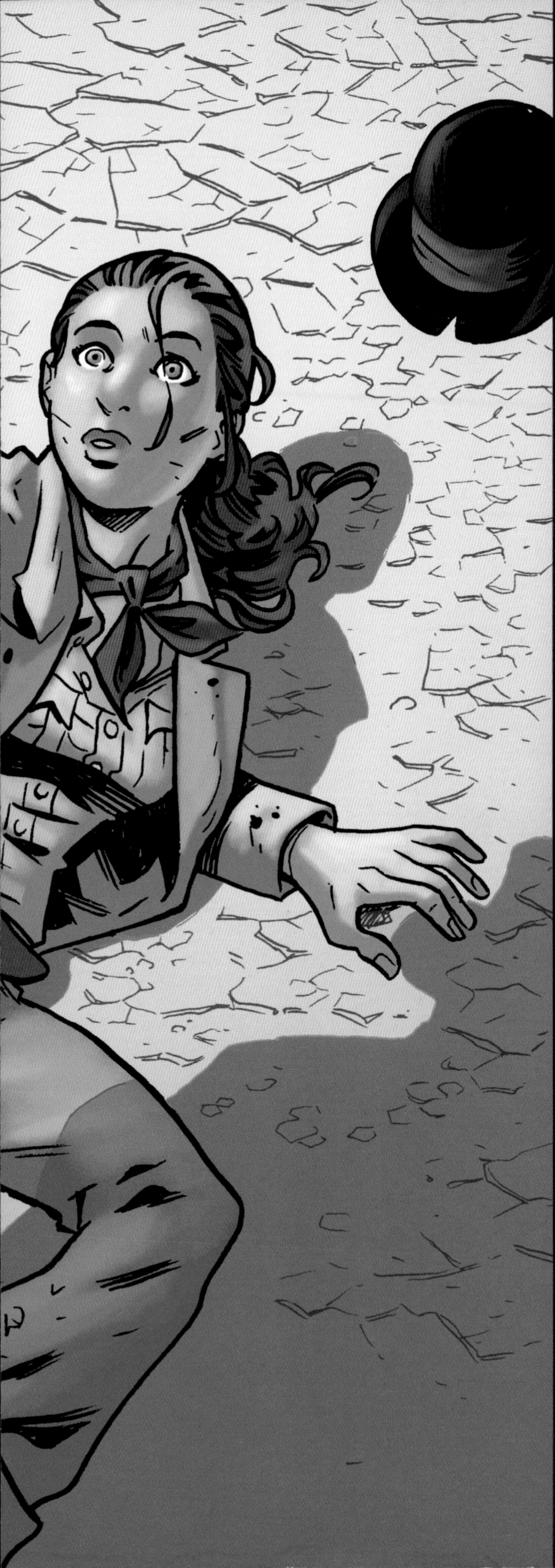

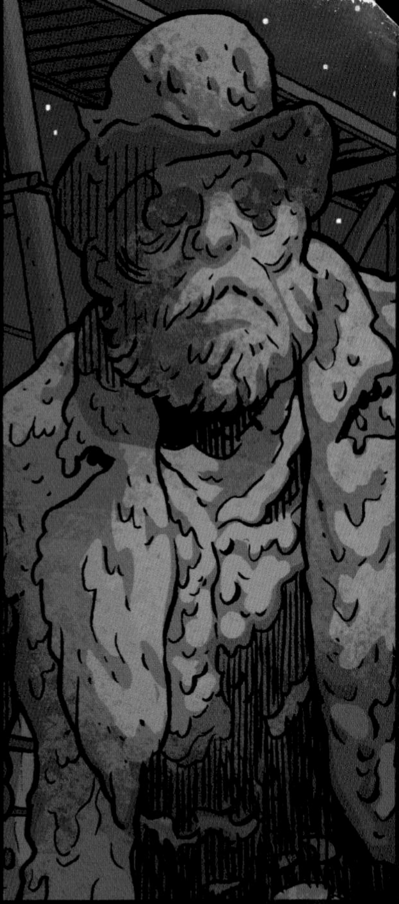

THE ADVENTURE CONTINUES EVERY MONTH!

On a night of blood and gunfire, Drake Sinclair vanished without a trace.

Setting out to find the missing gunslinger, Becky Montcrief journeys to the strange town of Penance—a place where every living soul is tainted by an otherworldly force. In order to find Drake, she must first survive the machinations of power-hungry and sinister men.

Meanwhile, the Knights of Solomon make Drake a final offer—join them and serve their cause... or suffer a painful death.

The secrets revealed will change everything Becky and Drake think they know and shake the foundations of reality!

Don't miss a single exciting issue of The Sixth Gun, *the critically acclaimed ongoing monthly series from Oni Press, available at finer comic book shops everywhere and also digitally on ComiXology!*

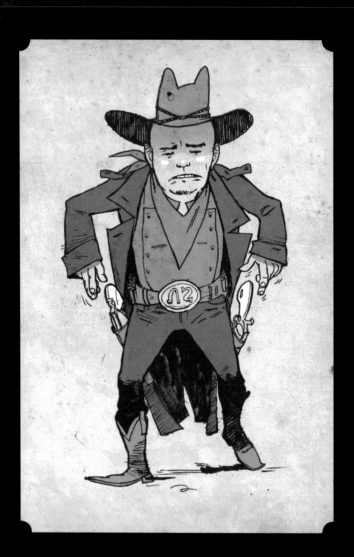

Cullen Bunn grew up in rural North Carolina, but now lives in the St. Louis area with his wife Cindy and Jackson, his son. His noir/horror comic (and first collaboration with Brian Hurtt), *The Damned*, was published in 2007 by Oni Press. The follow-up, *The Damned: Prodigal Sons*, was released in 2008. In addition to *The Sixth Gun*, his current projects include *The Tooth*, an original graphic novel from Oni Press; *Crooked Hills*, a middle reader horror prose series from Evileye Books; and various work for Marvel and DC. Somewhere along the way, Cullen founded Undaunted Press and edited the critically acclaimed small press horror magazine, *Whispers from the Shattered Forum*.

All writers must pay their dues, and Cullen has worked various odd jobs, including Alien Autopsy Specialist, Rodeo Clown, Professional Wrestler Manager, and Sasquatch Wrangler.

And, yes, he has fought for his life against mountain lions and he did perform on stage as the World's Youngest Hypnotist. Buy him a drink sometime, and he'll tell you all about it.

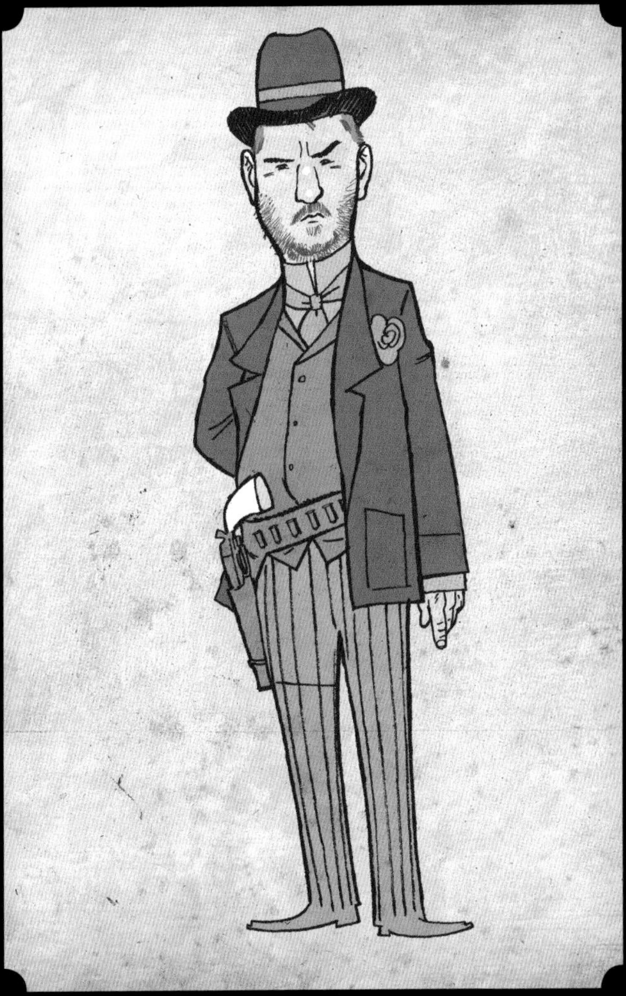

Author portrait illustrated by

Brian Hurtt got his start in comics pencilling the second arc of Greg Rucka's *Queen & Country*. This was followed by art duties on several projects including *Queen & Country: Declassified*, *Three Strikes*, and Steve Gerber's critically acclaimed series *Hard Time*.

In 2006, Brian teamed with Cullen Bunn to create the Prohibition-era monster-noir sensation *The Damned*. The two found that their unique tastes and storytelling sensibilities were well-suited to one another and were eager to continue that relationship.

The Sixth Gun is their sophomore endeavor together and the next in what looks to be many years of creative collaboration.

Brian lives in St. Louis where the summers are too hot, the winters too cold, but the rent is just right.

He can be found online at thehurttlocker.blogspot.com.

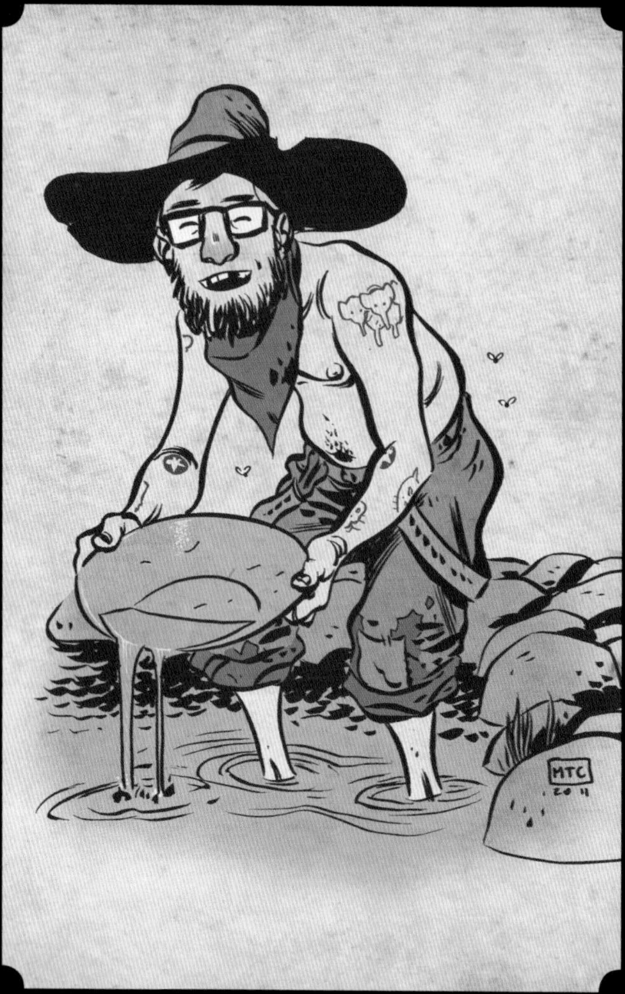
MTC
2011

Illustration by Tyler Crook.

Mr. Tyler Crook is an American artist living in the 21st century. For twelve years he lived in an unlit cubicle making art for sports video games. This left him bearded and almost completely translucent. Then in 2011, he struck gold, *comic book gold*, with the release of *Petrograd*, an original graphic novel he illustrated and which was written by Philip Gelatt and published by Oni Press. He is survived by his wife and many pets, but he's not dead... yet. In fact, he is currently very busy working on *B.P.R.D. Hell on Earth* for Dark Horse Comics.

Visit him on the Universal Hive Brain at www.mrcrook.com

Illustration by Bill Crabtree

Bill Crabtree's career as a colorist began in 2003 with the launch of Image Comic's *Invincible* and *Firebreather*. He would go on to color the first 50 issues of *Invincible*, which would become a flagship Image Comics title, along with garnering Bill a Harvey Awards nomination.

He continues to color *Firebreather*, which was recently made into a feature film on Cartoon Network, as well as *Godland* and *Jack Staff*.

Perhaps the highlight of his comics career, his role as colorist on *The Sixth Gun* began with issue 6, and has since been described as "like Christmas morning, but with guns."

FROM CULLEN BUNN, BRIAN HURTT & ONI PRESS...

THE SIXTH GUN, VOLUME 1:
COLD DEAD FINGERS
By Cullen Bunn & Brian Hurtt
176 pages • Trade Paperback
Color • $19.99
ISBN 978-1-934964-60-6

THE SIXTH GUN, VOLUME 2:
CROSSROADS
By Cullen Bunn & Brian Hurtt
136 pages • Trade Paperback
Color • $19.99
ISBN 978-1-934964-67-5

DAMNED, VOLUME 1:
THREE DAYS DEAD
By Cullen Bunn & Brian Hurtt
160 pages • 6"x9" Trade Paperback
B&W • $14.99 US
ISBN 978-1-932664-6-38

THE TOOTH
By Cullen Bunn, Shawn Lee, and Matt Kindt
184 pages • Hardcover
Color • $24.99
ISBN 978-1-934964-52-1

GHOST PROJEKT
By Joe Harris & Steve Rolston
152 pages • Hardcover
Color • $19.99
ISBN 978-1-934964-42-2

GUERILLAS, VOLUME 1
By Brahm Revel
168 pages, 6"x9" Trade Paperback
B&W • $14.99
ISBN 978-1-934964-43-9

QUEEN & COUNTRY
DEFINITIVE EDITION, VOLUME 1
By Greg Rucka with Steve Rolston,
Brian Hurtt, and Leandro Fernandez
366 pages • 6"x9" Trade Paperback
B&W • $19.99
ISBN 978-1-932664-87-4

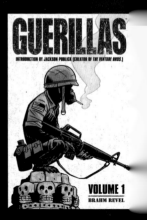

STUMPTOWN, VOLUME 1
By Greg Rucka & Matthew Southworth
144 pages • Hardcover
Color • $29.99
ISBN 978-1-934964-37-8

ONI PRESS
ONI COMICS
www.onipress.com

For more information on these and other fine Oni Press comic book and graphic novels visit www.onipress.com. To find a comic specialty store in your area visit www.comicshops.us.